Making Sense of Television

THE PSYCHOLOGY
OF AUDIENCE INTERPRETATION

SONIA M. LIVINGSTONE

Butterworth-Heinemann
Linacre House, Jordan Hill, Oxford OX2 8DP
A division of Reed Educational and Professional Publishing Ltd

 A member of the Reed Elsevier plc group

OXFORD   BOSTON   JOHANNESBURG
NEW DELHI   SINGAPORE   MELBOURNE

First published 1990
Paperback edition 1995
Reprinted 1996

British Library Cataloguing in Publication Data
Livingstone, Sonia M.
  Making sense of television: the psychology of audience
  interpretation – (International series in experimental social psychology)
  Includes bibliographical references
  1. Television – psychosocial aspects
  I. Title   II. Series
  302.2'345

Library of Congress Cataloguing in Publication Data
Livingstone, Sonia M.
  Making sense of television: the psychology of audience
  interpretation – (International series in experimental social
  psychology; v.18)
  Includes bibliographical references
  1. Television audiences – psychological aspects
  2. Television – social aspects   3. Social psychology
  I. Title   II. Series: International series in experimental
  social psychology; v.18
  PN1992.6.L56 1989   302.23'45–dc20   89-38071

ISBN 0 7506 2744 1

Printed and bound in Great Britain by Athenæum Press Ltd, Gateshead, Tyne & Wear

Making Sense of Television

International Series in Social Psychology

Series Editor: Professor W. Peter Robinson, University of Bristol, UK

Adolescence: From Crisis to Coping (Gibson-Cline)

Assertion and its Social Context: (Wilson and Gallois)

Children's Social Competence in Context: The Contributions of Family, School and Culture: (Schneider)

Emotion and Social Judgements: (Forgas)

Game Theory and its Applications in the Social and Biological Sciences: (Colman)

Genius and Eminence, 2nd edition: (Albert)

Making Sense of Television: The Psychology of Audience Interpretation: (Livingstone)

The Psychology of Gambling: (Walker)

Social Dilemmas: Theoretical Issues and Research Findings: (Liebrand)

The Theory of Reasoned Action: Its Application to AIDS Preventive Behaviour: (Terry, Gallois and McCamish)

To obtain copies of any of the above books approach your bookseller or, in case of difficulty, contact the Sales Department, Butterworth-Heinemann, Linacre House, Jordan Hill, Oxford OX2 8DP, UK. If you wish to contribute to the series please send a synopsis to Matthew Deans, Commissioning Editor, at the same address.

For order or further details you may also contact Butterworth-Heinemann on e-mail: matthew.deans.@bhein.rel.co.uk.

Preface

Television has made enormous changes in people's everyday lives over the last few decades. Developments in new technologies and increased leisure time ensure that the mass media will continue to structure and influence people's experiences and understanding of their social world. The media thus pose important questions for social science. While much research has been conducted, many—if not more—problems remain.

Making Sense of Television addresses an issue central to the social psychological perspective on the mass media—how viewers interpret the programmes that they see. This raises a further set of questions concerned with social perception and representation: how do people use their everyday knowledge to guide their interpretations; how sensitive are they to structural features of a text; how far do viewers agree with the text and each other in making sense of television; do different ways of interacting with programmes lead to different interpretations; and so forth.

These questions are addressed theoretically and empirically in *Making Sense of Television*. Following a critical review of several relevant literatures—psychology, communications and literary criticism—an analysis is offered which seeks to integrate these research literatures to provide a new perspective on the audience's everyday interpretations of television An integration of cognitive social psychology with reception theories from literary criticism is proposed as a way of analysing the processes of interpretation which mediate between television content and effects.

A body of empirical studies on viewers' interpretations of the characters and narratives of popular soap operas is presented which addresses the social perception questions outlined above and demonstrates the value of the proposed perspective. As one might expect, new questions are raised in the process, and the implications of the present analysis and findings for social psychology and mass communications are explored.

Acknowledgements

The empirical research reported in this book was conducted with the financial support of an Economic and Social Research Council award linked with the Independent Broadcasting Authority, held at Wolfson College and the Department of Experimental Psychology at the University of Oxford. The writing of the book was made possible by an award from the Leverhulme Trust and by a research fellowship from Nuffield College, Oxford. I took the Leverhulme award to the Communications Institute at the Hebrew University of Jerusalem, where I was made very welcome and to whom I am grateful for the intellectual home I was offered in the spring and summer of 1988.

I would particularly like to thank Michael Argyle, Jay Blumler, Elihu Katz, Tamar Liebes and Mallory Wober for their generous help, constructive criticism and encouragement during the research and writing stages of this book. Others who have read parts of this work or have kept me going during the often laborious process of writing include Rodney Livingstone, Robert McHenry, Roger Silverstone and Naomi Tadmor; I am grateful to all of them. Most of all, I thank Peter Lunt, for more reasons than I can say: to him, I dedicate this book.

The extract from *EastEnders* in Chapter 1 is quoted with permission of the BBC and the author, Tony McHale; the extracts from *Coronation Street* in Chapter 3 are quoted with permission of Granada Television. The figures for Table 1 in Chapter 2 were obtained from BARB/AGB, UK, and are reproduced with permission.

Some of the research reported in this book has also been published in Livingstone (1987b, 1987c, 1988a, 1988b, 1989a, and 1989b).

Contents

1

The Social Psychology of the Television Viewer

The Role of Television in Everyday Life

The research for this book began with my interest in the structures of social knowledge. Many social psychologists ask how people make sense of social phenomena and how they integrate new perceptions with prior knowledge and experience. My particular interest was in the ways people made sense of ordinary, everyday phenomena—people and events which are complex, structured and which they experience naturally—rather than the idealised, simplified and controlled materials of experimental research. I began to think about television when searching for a domain which was both complex and yet commonplace and which was available equally to everybody without my artificially exposing people to it. For television uniquely constitutes a domain in which, especially for popular programmes, people ordinarily share experiences of the same complex, social 'stimuli'.

The research question then became, how do people make sense of television programmes, programmes which they have watched and interpreted under natural circumstances and which they have presumably integrated with their prior knowledge of the events portrayed? Thus I arrived at the study of the media, and specifically of the soap opera audience. Again, soap opera fitted my concerns with complex and gradually constructed knowledge representations, because it is a genre containing many familiar characters whose personalities, for example, could be contrasted and compared by the audience. Incidentally, soap opera also appealed as the underdog of television programming (and of television research) and, moreover, because of its unusually sympathetic portrayal of dominant women which women viewers often consider more realistic and engaging. I wondered if these points were related.

At the same time, I had been reading Goffman for his attack in *Forms of Talk* on the speaker–hearer metaphor which dominates the psychology of communication, for his attempt to recognise the complexity of the relation between communicator and audience (for example, by including the bystander, the colluder and the eavesdropper). His was also an attack on the communication as stimulus, on the recipient of communication as

1

unengaged, neutral. And it was an attack on cognition as asocial. But to continue my story, how was I to bring these two interests together?

Then it dawned on me. There was a 'soap opera boom' going on around me: in research, in public discussion, in audience ratings. Soap opera was the 'in thing'. And as I listened to the debates (though I had to seek them out, they were not to be found in Oxford!), I realised that soap opera was the connection I had sought—between the problems of studying the role of complex, everyday, social knowledge and the problems of assuming a simple speaker–hearer model of communication in both social psychology and media studies. In soap opera, there is no simple speaker–hearer relationship: viewers are engaged in 'parasocial interaction' (as if engaging with real people), they participate without passive identification, they blur boundaries between viewing and living by endless 'what happened then' discussions and by bringing their everyday experience to judge the drama. And the genre invited all this. Further, within the programmes, there was no simple message to be passively received, but a cacophony of voices, of colluders and eavesdroppers, of bystanders and involved protagonists with their own histories and perspectives. The 'message' was a product of all this. Moreover, 'the message' is inevitably made plural, open to interpretation.

People were arguing that this is because soap opera is a 'feminine' genre: there is no dominant, linear, closed message; no orderly, authoritative meaning. The matriarchal content and the multifaceted and nonlinear form are related. And they both posed a fascinating challenge to social psychology, for whom people are traditionally gender stereotyped, seekers after simplicity and order, linear information-processors of unitary messages. How could social psychology rise to the challenge of 'filling in' a much needed conceptualisation of the newly active viewer of television, thereby not only benefiting from the application of social psychology to the media but also benefiting the media literature in turn? Could the social psychology of implicit representation and social knowledge provide the theoretical repertoire and resource for conceptualising the active viewers' own interpretative repertoires and resources? And, to return to my original problem, what could all this tell us about the role of everyday social knowledge as applied to common yet complex, ordinary experiences of the world?

As the soap opera debate matured, it became more focused. It centred on the text-reader metaphor—analysing television and its audience by analogy to the semiotic approach to literature (whose audience is the literary critics themselves). This involved a reconceptualisation of both programmes and viewers, and it challenged traditional methodologies. I recognised that this specific focus was pertinent to social psychology more generally: that we needed to replace the stimulus with the text, the information processor with the interpreter, and psychological reductionism with a sociocultural context. What are the implications of this metaphor, as it has been applied to media studies, within the field of social psychology and the problems of social knowledge and everyday sense-making? Let us first consider the significance of sense-making, the role of television, and some problems of social psychological and media research, thus mapping out the scope and aims of this book.

The centrality of interpretation

All day, every day, people create and recreate meanings in their everyday lives. Whether they are working, talking to their children, watching television, judging the weather, planning a meal or playing a record, people routinely and apparently unproblematically make sense of their circumstances. Yet as we think through this activity of making sense, we see that it is far from unproblematic. Even the simplest utterance requires considerable work to perceive the utterance as meaningful, to understand its relation to its context and to judge the appropriate response. And everyday life is far from simple. Perhaps one should say, everyday life is often simple to carry out, but never simple to analyse.

Just as with everyday interactions, watching television has often been seen as a routine, unproblematic, passive process: the meanings of programmes are seen as given and obvious; the viewer is seen as passively receptive and mindless. Again, this simplicity is illusory. In recent years, both interpersonal and mediated communication have been increasingly recognised as complex, rule-governed, constructive set of processes. People's role in such communications must be correspondingly understood as knowledgeable, skilled, motivated, and diverse.

Social psychologists have devoted much attention to revealing the complexities of everyday, apparently transparent, social situations. They have examined the patterns of social interaction and the rules of social situations which give meaning to everyday interactions. They have focused on the social knowledge needed by participants in interactions, the narrative patternings which order everyday events, the subtleties of conversations, and the power of different types of groups. While many areas of everyday life have come under scrutiny, the central place of the mass media has been largely neglected. Yet television has come to dominate the hours in our day, the organisation of our living rooms, the topics of our conversations, our conceptions of pleasure, the things to which we look forward, the way we amuse and occupy our children, and the way we discover the world we live in. Many also argue that television has come to dominate what we think, how we think, and what we think about.

The ever increasing amounts of time spent watching television should not be underestimated. In 1987, children spent some 19 hours each week watching television: those between 16 and 34 spent around 20 hours, those between 35 and 64 spent over 27 hours, and the elderly spent over 37 hours each week watching television (Social Trends, 1989). This does not include the amount of time in which the television is switched on but only partially or sporadically attended to in a household.

How are we to think about the relationship between television and everyday social life? A powerful common-sense assumption, which has influenced psychologists as well as popular thinking, has been that the two are quite separate: everyday life is real, important, and factual while television is unreal, trivial, and fantastic. Yet television has become inextricably part of, and often indistinguishable from everyday life. We often do not remember whether we learnt of a certain fact from a friend or television, we fail to notice that our images of the elderly, for example, derive more from television than everyday interactions, and when we recount an anecdote or interesting observation, does it matter if it came from watching television or from a personal experience? Can we argue, then, that despite the physical difference between television images and 'real-life' perceptions, symbolically they are the same? Each is perceived through our interpretative frameworks—here we are all readers, each provides a structured cluster of meanings—here both are texts, being both loaded with messages about, for example, the family as well as being simply images or the presence of a family. I do not mean here to refer to the study of those who confuse television and everyday life. There has been much discussion of those who send wreaths to soap opera funerals or apply for jobs in the *Crossroads* motel, debating whether such people are in fact deluded or instead whether their actions have been interpreted too literally rather than seen as gestures of participation and pleasure. The issue is not whether television is indistinguishable from everyday life but whether the symbolic role of each can be better understood in a similar rather than an oppositional fashion.

The interpretative process

Let us think about the interpretative or sense making process. Many of the conventional frames by which television is structured differ according to programme genre: for example, recency signifies importance, a close-up shot signifies intimacy, fast cutting signifies high drama. Similarly one may see life too as having certain interpretative frames or genres dependent on different situations (Argyle *et al.*, 1981; Goffman, 1974). Research on the rules-roles approach to social situations or the script theory approach to event sequences (Schank and Abelson, 1977) are analogous to work on media genres (Fiske, 1987) in that here social psychologists are similarly engaged in defining the conventional structures and hence interpretive frames for different everyday social situations. Many of these conventions overlap between media and interpersonal situations (such as, height signifies importance, proximity signifies intimacy or threat, the ritualised openings and resolutions to sequences, the use of gender-stereotyped connotations).

One might protest that people use different interpretative frames for television and everyday life, that they can maintain a distance from the former, bracketing it off from the latter as unreal. This is doubtful as a general claim on several grounds, although clearly it occurs sometimes. Careful analysis of people's reception of television programmes—to be discussed later—reveals the complex intertwining which takes place between television and everyday meanings. Conversations around the set tend not to discriminate among these meanings, and viewers frequently interpret the television referentially, as if it referred to outside events or ideas. Conversely, they also bring to their interpretation ideas and recalled events which they have encountered, to provide a context for the television meanings (Katz and Liebes, 1986).

Psychologically it does not seem plausible that our assumptions, images and knowledge of the world portrayed by television can be strictly separated from our assumptions, images and knowledge of everyday life. Further, while people may on some occasions distance themselves from television meanings, so too may they distance themselves from everyday meanings, withholding judgement, withdrawing trust, rejecting assumptions: television is not thereby inherently different from other social meanings. A parallel argument can be made for the claim that people do not attend to television as they do to interpersonal events. True, people often sleep in front of the television set, talk over it, forget it after five minutes, and treat it as 'moving wallpaper'. But the same could be said for interpersonal events, where people are often inattentive or 'mindless' (Langer *et al.*, 1978). If we avoid this polarised comparison, we can begin to focus on the more productive questions of when, where and why people attend or ignore—under what conditions are viewers active or passive or are people mindful or mindless? In sum, although in some ways people may frame television as different and thus draw upon different interpretive conventions, the very activity of framing, or applying conventions to the act of interpretation, is a common activity across media and interpersonal interactions and thus the analysis of each may reveal much about the other.

In many ways, the very tangibility of television makes it easier to study these issues than otherwise. Its programmes are more accessible, hard as they are to decode, than are the texts of everyday conversations; its images are a clearer source of social representations than the representations and repertoires shared by social groups; and its programmes provide more complex and naturalistic texts for social perception, attribution and stereotyping research than the artificial scenarios often used by social psychology. The fact–fiction distinction has been a hindrance to theorising. Not only is it increasingly meaningful to see life as fiction, as games or as ritual, but also psychologically both television and 'life' are to the participating individual equally a source of meanings. Thus each must be interpreted according to the same wealth of social knowledge derived from, in a cyclic fashion, his or her previous experiences with both everyday life and television-in-life.

Television as text

Of what value is the recent argument in media studies that we should conceptualise television programmes as texts? This argument focuses attention on their structure or the complex interrelationships among units of meaning, on their construction or the cultural practices on which they depend, and their implied reader or the requirements placed on the person who makes sense of them. To use the metaphor of the text in relation to television is to emphasise that programmes are structured, culturally-located, symbolic products to be understood only in relation to readers and which, together with readers, generate meanings. Can we also see life as text? This metaphor of the text, with its associated concept of the reader, is intended to counter the prevailing notions of life as external stimulus, person as respondent, with their associated notions of clear, unique and given meanings and the passive, powerless image of the person. As I will argue, such notions have served to delimit and impede developments in social psychology and media studies. How far then can the concepts of text and reader offer a way forward in thinking about the relation between television and life and in thinking about the interpretative role of the person in each? This book will explore the value of these concepts.

General orientation of this book

Media studies should, it is argued, be more to social psychology than a subsection of an undergraduate course or an optional chapter in a textbook. Its theories and findings are not specific in their implications but relate to, draw upon, and may contribute to a broad range of social psychological issues—from social influence, attitude-behaviour research, social perception, discourse analysis, social representations, non-verbal communication, and so forth. Moreover, media studies are here to stay, and social psychology must resolve its relationship with them.

Although at different points in this book I will specifically address a literature in social psychology or in media studies, each argument offered is intended to have implications for the other or to draw links between historically separate literatures whose concerns and concepts are more similar than is often recognised. The book is thus something of a balancing act, in which I will juggle with social psychology—specifically, social cognition (Fiske and Taylor, 1984) and recent developments in social representations (Farr and Moscovici, 1984) and discourse theory (Potter and Wetherell, 1987), and media studies—spanning the split between traditional sociological research and critical mass communications or cultural studies insofar as both deal with audiences (Fejes, 1984; Katz, 1980). It is hoped that the mutual boundary between these disciplines will become increasingly fuzzy and permeable in regard to audiences and interpreters of everyday social texts.

As each discipline reaches its own internal 'crisis' (see Gilmour and Duck, 1980, for the crisis in social psychology), a period of rethinking is taking place. This book is intended as a contribution to both these arenas of rethinking simultaneously. The metaphor of the text and reader will be offered as a route forward. To reduce the potential breadth of concerns, the book will centre upon viewers' interpretations of a specific genre of televison programming, the soap opera. As we shall see, this genre exemplifies many key concepts and problems. It thus constitutes a convenient point of intersection for otherwise diverse research domains.

This chapter will pursue the question of the relation between media and everyday life in several ways. First I will examine the historical changes in the relation between the two disciplines of media studies and social psychology. Secondly, the vast body of research on the impact of television will be selectively reviewed to illustrate the various approaches taken to the relationship between media and everyday social life, revealing the importance of the question of reading or making sense. And finally, recent work on social cognition, psychology's approach to sense-making, will be discussed in terms of its potential and problems, arguing for the inseparability of making sense of television and making sense of everyday life. Issues of audience interpretation or cognitive activity and the nature of the text-reader relationship are further explored in Chapter 2.

The Related Histories of Social Psychology and Media Studies

Disciplinary boundaries are often disturbingly impervious. It is amazing that social psychology should have only recently begun to recognise the importance of language in social life (Rommetweit, 1984), given the rise of socio-linguistics, of the philosophy of language, and of linguistic anthropology in the last few decades. At the same time, the boundaries are more permeable than is often recognised. Although social psychology and media studies have their own journals and, in America, their own departments and courses, their history is highly interrelated. Smith (1983) tells the history of the two in terms of a common pre-war origin and a separate subsequent development. On the other hand, Reeves *et al.* (1982) argue that most social psychological developments feed into mass communications such that the history of media studies *is* the history of social psychology, at least in America. Of course, media studies draws upon a range of disciplines, including sociology, political science, literary criticism and anthropology. Yet in terms of broad developmental stages, the links with social psychology are strong.

The development of social psychology

Social psychology may be very roughly characterised as beginning with the attitude/opinion research of the 1930s and 40s, spawned by immigration, war and propaganda agencies and concerned with the formation of public opinion, the vulnerability of attitudes to external influences, and the structures of social beliefs (see Smith, 1983). This led to the newly formed academic departments' interest in the cognitive persuasion research of the fifties, focusing on the thought processes of the target of persuasion and revealing his or her defences, motivations to selectively attend to certain messages, and autonomous processes of attitude formation (see Berkowitz, 1978). The Behaviourism of the sixties represented an abrupt break from mentalistic and semantic concerns, examining instead the dependence of people on the structures of their environment and the patterns of learning from that environment (Bandura and Walters, 1964). The seventies were beset by crises and splitting (Harre and Secord, 1972), with a profusion of critiques sometimes more destructive than constructive, although a return to cognitivism and the rise of influential new concerns was also salient. The eighties reveal attempts at new developments and convergence (Gilmour and Duck, 1980).

The development of mass communications

It appears that social psychology and media studies have shared a similar fate. Katz (1980) described mass communications research as a history of oscillation between conceptions of powerful media and powerful viewers. The mass society thesis of the Frankfurt school of the thirties and forties, with its visions of a helpless mass audience of isolated and oppressed individuals gave way to the 'two-step flow model' of the fifties, with its contrasting conception of the audience as selective, as organised in social groups with opinion leaders buffering the impact of the media and providing alternative world views (Katz and Lazarsfeld, 1955). This was followed by a return to powerful media with the experimental Behaviourist research conceiving of innocent and ignorant children, helplessly moulded into their social roles (Bandura and Walters, 1964), including antisocial roles such as aggression and fear, which again gave way in the seventies to the selective, discriminating viewer of Uses and Gratifications research, deciding what to watch according to prior needs, moulding the media to fit his or her own desires (Blumler and Katz, 1974).

While traditional mass communications theory, practised largely by American sociologists, was oscillating between powerful media and powerful viewers, a separate strand of research developed out of the Frankfurt school which took a more consistent position (see Katz, 1987). Critical mass communications (Gitlin, 1978; Gouldner, 1976; Hall *et al.*, 1980) advocated powerful media and influential texts, giving little attention to the role of the audience except as helpless pawns receiving given messages and circulating them through society (Fejes, 1984). As I shall discuss further, this approach adopted a more Marxist and literary focus, concerned with the role of the media in the reproduction of ideology and with detailed analyses of the 'true', hidden meanings of media texts (e.g. Newcomb, 1982; Rowland and Watkins, 1984).

Parallels between mass communications and social psychology

Turning now to contemporary developments in social psychology, an oscillation between active and passive may also be seen to structure the history of social psychology. However, the focus is more on the person, there being no obvious 'other' to parallel the media (although many have been nominated—such as social institutions, reinforcement agencies, real world logic). So, starting with the common concern of the mass society thesis of people helpless in the face of hegemonic propaganda and persuasion, social psychology moved through a more developed cognitivism, with selective perception, the 'new look' with its emphasis on constructive perception, and with consistency and dissonance theories, only to succumb to Behaviourism and the return of the passive individual written upon by circumstances and open to manipulation. Then came the return of the socially located individual with social identity theory (Tajfel, 1978), of the skilled interpreter with nonverbal communication and rules-roles theories (Argyle et al., 1981), of the minority influence to fight back against the conformity processes exerted by the majority (Moscovici, 1976).

Trends in media research

Most research on television is ultimately concerned with its effects upon the audience. Although the 'effects' approach (Bryant and Zillman, 1986; Halloran, 1970; Hovland, Lumsdaine and Sheffield, 1949), narrowly defined as experimental and behaviouristic, is currently unfashionable (see below), it remains nonetheless the key issue underlying all research on audiences. Thus a consideration of effects research is needed in order to trace the historical and theoretical connections between media studies and social psychology. Returning to the question posed earlier about the relationship between television and everyday life, one could regard effects research as proposing a clear distinction between the two and then examining the extent to which the former influences the latter.

There has been considerable recent interest in interpretation or decoding across a wide range of media theories (Reeves et al., 1982) which parallels the rise of social cognition within psychology (Fiske and Taylor, 1984). This can be seen to represent an undermining of the distinction between television and everyday life, suggesting instead that television is an integral part of everyday life and that the meanings or world view of the one are not different in kind from the meanings of the other. The assumption of a clear television:life distinction has caused problems for effects research, suggesting that the very question of how television affects life is an inappropriate one. Can it be replaced by the question of the relative power to contribute to the social construction of meanings not between television and life but between texts and readers?

Disciplinary rifts and divisions

As noted above, social psychology and media studies have a common origin in post-war opinion poll and persuasion research (Hovland *et al.*, 1949; Katz, 1980, 1987), where the rapid rise of the mass media posed considerable problems for the psychology of influence and attitude change as well as spawning the new discipline of mass communications, mainly in America, especially for the study of such problems both in their own right and in their more sociological context of institutional analysis and macroprocesses of information transmission and circulation in society (Curran *et al.*, 1977). If social psychology and media studies were ultimately split for practical and disciplinary reasons, an early split also emerged within media studies, this time for theoretical and political reasons, between the so-called administrative and critical schools of mass communications (Lazarsfeld, 1941; and see the special issue of the *Journal of Communication*, **33**(3), 'Ferment in the Field', 1983). The administrative school continued the government-sponsored, problem-orientated research of the public opinion and persuasion tradition, while the critical school developed the Frankfurt school's critical, Marxist approach. Rather in the manner of an unhappy divorce settlement, the administrative or 'traditional' approach took the audience as its substantive and theoretical focus while the critical school took the text.

This has since developed to the state where traditional researchers tend to ignore, and are ignorant of, the text. For example, they might ask whether watching a film excerpt containing 'altruistic behaviour' increases children's tendency to help each other without any consideration of the kind of altruistic behaviour portrayed, of what counts as altruism, of whether the narrative context casts a particular interpretative gloss on the portrayal, or how the excerpt compares with other altruistic images. On the other hand, critical researchers tend implicitly to speculate about but remain in considerable ignorance of the audience. They may obliquely refer to audience interests or experience as if these were straightforwardly known and, implicitly, as if any audience data obtained would inevitably support one's theory. The conventions of publication in each approach permit considerable vagueness about the one—either text or reader—while demanding great precision over the other.

In terms of academic sources, the traditional approach developed closely with social psychology, as a uniquely American approach, while the critical school drew upon European thought in the fields of semiotics, Marxist sociology and critical theory. More recently, the critical school has begun to modify its perspective on mass communications, acknowledging some justice to the accusations of cultural elitism—that researchers alone could determine the 'true' meanings of texts, and over-emphasis on hegemony— that the media are all powerful and thus the audience is homogeneous in its reception of the same meanings. Critical researchers have, to a significant extent, turned to the study of the audience.

The split within media studies did not, however, ultimately resolve the problem of how to study the role of television in everyday life, it merely allowed each side to proceed. Now cultural studies is beginning to feel the lack of a theory of the audience and the traditional approach has begun to feel the lack of a sophisticated theory of the text (see Berelson, 1952, for an exposition of content analysis; see Burgelin, 1972, on the problems with content analysis). The latter has also suffered from an accumulation of mixed or disappointing results regarding the effects of media exposure (see below), leading it to look towards other theoretical perspectives, and particularly that of social cognition.

Interestingly, one can identify a parallel desire for a disciplinary split within social psychology. Indeed, at the time that the critical and administrative schools were most mutually hostile, similar concerns and debates led to the 'crisis in social psychology' (see Gilmour and Duck, 1980). The concerns were, in brief, the quantitative/qualitative debate in methodology and its related epistemological concerns about the relations between description and explanation, the subject and the researcher, the subject and its context, and the concepts of objectivity and hypothetico-deductive versus inductive reasoning.

For example, Gergen (1973) criticised the ahistorical aims of social psychology, Harre and Secord (1972) criticised its positivist and objectivist philosophy of science, others bemoaned its exclusion of language, discourse and ideology, and many criticised its reductionism and its individualism. The crisis mirrored the split in media studies even to the European versus American identities of the main protagonists. Only now is social psychology belatedly developing its own critical tradition, rediscovering its symbolic interactionist roots (Farr, 1981), its folk psychology tradition in social representation theory (Farr and Moscovici, 1984), the neighbouring fields of linguistics and semiotics in a new move towards discourse analysis (Potter and Wetherell, 1987), and its political consciousness particularly in the development of feminist psychology (Wilkinson, 1986).

Drawing on the parallel with media studies, we might label these latter developments 'critical social psychology' in contrast with 'traditional social psychology'. Maybe the key difference lies in the role of the term 'social', as the former approach looks towards the relation of social psychology to the other social sciences, emphasising the essentially social nature of psychology, while the latter approach draws more on cognitive, individual psychology as applied to a social setting. The meanings of 'critical' in the sense of a Marxist orientation does not, however, characterise the European tradition of social psychology. Indeed, such moves show certain tendencies towards 'reinventing the wheel' in relation to theories of social representation and influence: they could benefit from observing parallel but earlier developments within media studies. So, as I shall discuss in Chapters 2 and 3, the tables may now be turned, so that social psychology may learn from media studies.

The Effects of Television on its Audience

The issue of whether and how television affects its audience is surely the most researched area in media studies—it is the key question for traditional mass communication researchers, and has been supported by enormous amounts of funding and public concern (Bryant and Zillman, 1986; Hovland *et al.*, 1949; Liebert *et al.*, 1982). Consequently, there has been much recent dismay over the inability of traditional sociological and psychological mass communications research to offer clear conclusions regarding the causal impact of television. Hawkins and Pingree (1983) conclude in their review that evidence for effects is weak and problematic (see also Durkin, 1985b, and Murray and Kippax, 1979). The reasons for this may be theoretical, for instance Katz (1978) points to a need for a more general integrative theory of media effects to make sense of the mixture of positive and negative findings obtained and to direct future research. Roberts and Bachen (1981) blame the 'problem-orientation' of the field, where research has been driven by issues of public concern, such as advertising, stereotyping, violence, instead of by theoretical directives. They describe effects research as 'a pot-pourri, a borrowing area, lacking in unifying theory, a collection of suburbs in search of a city' (pp. 308–9). Gerbner counsels against disappointment thus:

> If, as we argue, the messages are so stable, the medium is so ubiquitous, and accumulated total exposure is what counts, then almost everyone should be affected. . . . It is clear, then, that the cards are stacked against finding evidence of effects (Gerbner *et al.*, 1986, p. 21).

Traditionally, 'effects research' meant the exposure of randomly determined groups to different, brief, experimental materials such that specified responses in the different groups may be compared. Only by controlled exposure and random group allocation can causal claims be tested, according to this strictly experimental approach. This approach can be said to have had some success. For example, it has been shown that children exposed to violent programmes are slower to seek adult help when they witness violence among other children (Drabman and Thomas, 1975). Being forewarned about the events to come in a horror film was found to increase the degree to which subjects were frightened by the film (Cantor, Ziemke, and Sparks, 1984). Men who viewed a series of films showing violence against women came to have fewer negative reactions to the films and to see them as less violent (Linz, Donnerstein, and Penrod, 1984). Davidson *et al*. (1979) showed that five- and six-year-old girls held less gender-stereotyped attitudes after watching a low-stereotyped cartoon, compared to those who saw neutral or high-stereotyped cartoons.

Criticisms of effects research

These types of experiments have been criticised for their atheoretical nature, in which studies were merely accumulated on socially relevant themes. As with the above examples, these studies were often originally conducted within the framework of social learning theory, but in essence this theory simply states that children learn vicariously by imitating rewarded characters on television and avoiding punished actions. This begs the question of interpretation: how do children learn to connect action and consequences and how do they identify and assess the different characters? In its more recent, cognitive formulations, social learning theory has become indistinguishable from the more general trend towards social cognition in mass communications (see below). Some researchers now combine the cognitive and behavioural approaches. For example, Liss *et al*. (1983) showed how children are confused by narratives in which the heroes use aggressive actions for moral ends. So while children showed more altruistic behaviour after watching a film in which conflicts are resolved constructively and non-violently (Collins and Getz, 1976), this was not the case for films in which the 'goodies' help others using violent methods (think of Batman, Wonder Woman, Superman). Such films contravene children's simple expectations of consistency between motivation and action.

However, the experimental approach, begun by Bandura (see Bandura and Walters, 1964) with his experiments on children's aggression to 'bobo' dolls following a violent film, has been much criticised for many other reasons also (e.g. Noble, 1975). One may criticise the ecological validity of the independent variables used, in which subjects typically receive a brief exposure of an often artificially constructed (non-professional) programme segment. Thus the stimulus is stripped on its narrative and genre context, and often the only meanings studied are the closed, denotational, and acontextual aspects. Similarly, there are problems with the dependent variables used, which often bear only tenuous relationship to the theoretical construct of interest (for example, the use of electric shocks to simulate aggressive behaviour or helping an experimenter to simulate altruism). Dependent variables are typically assessed immediately after media exposure, so the longevity of many effects found is not known. Finally, critics point to the unnatural context of laboratory research, with its non-natural viewing conditions, confounding demand characteristics, and isolation of the individual. These criticisms of the experimental approach were clearly in the air at the time, for they mirror those levelled at social psychology more generally. These criticisms provoked the crisis in research (Harre and Secord, 1972) and form part of the longstanding debate on the reliability and validity of experimental (and sometimes, empirical) research, particularly for establishing causal claims.

Developments in effects research

Some researchers have attempted to overcome these criticisms without rejecting the general framework of hypothesis testing and causal argument. Phillips (1986) studied the occurrence of national suicides following highly publicised suicides of famous figures by analysing temporal correlational patterns in social statistics and media coverage. After applying appropriate controls (for example, seasonal variation, corresponding reductions in other categories of death), he found an increase of some 10 per cent in the incidence of suicides in the month following the publicity. The publicity was also found to affect the number of single, but not multiple, vehicle driver deaths, while publicised murder stories increased only the subsequent number of multiple driver deaths. This research has spawned a heated debate, mainly of a methodological nature, particularly criticising Phillips' reliance on national statistics and questioning whether other controls should be applied. Nonetheless, his findings are provocative.

A second attempt to overcome the criticisms of the experimental approach, especially those of the unnatural nature of the laboratory context, is that of Gerbner's cultivation approach (Gerbner and Gross, 1976; Gerbner et al., 1986). He focuses solely upon naturally viewed television programming extended over a long period of time. Further, he acknowledges the absence of 'true' control groups, for everyone has been directly or indirectly exposed to material related to the hypothesis under test. His third innovation is to link studies of effects to an analysis of the programmes themselves, thus making explicit the stimulus which is supposed to affect the viewers without reducing that stimulus to a brief and isolated segment. Thus his independent variable—the meanings of the television programmes—are not undermined. For example, he showed that those who watch more television ('heavy viewers') are more likely to see the world according to the social reality constructed by television than are light viewers, whose construction of reality is more in line with, say, actual incidences of violent crimes, numbers of elderly people, or extremity of racial and gender stereotyping (see Hawkins and Pingree, 1983, for a review). Thus Gerbner claims that if we redefine 'effects' as indirect, gradual, generalised, and symbolic, then television can be shown to have a consistent, though still small, effect on its viewers.

Gerbner's emphasis on texts as symbolic is important, for it exemplifies a broader trend away from literal meanings in programmes towards symbolic meanings, and thus changes both the traditional conception of programmes and of the consequent role for the viewers, where the latter is changed in the direction of increased interpretive activity (reading off connotation from denotation). For example, Gerbner argues that the over-representation of violent crime on television constitutes messages not about violence, such that one should hypothesise that viewers would become more aggressive (as Bandura, for example, hypothesised with mixed success), but instead about law and order. The action-adventure genre is seen as reinforcing and reconstructing our faith in law and order, our pleasure in the status quo, and our beliefs in social justice. That the 'baddies' are always caught or killed becomes important, legitimating viewers' beliefs in a 'just world' (Lerner, 1980). Again, a role for the viewer is introduced in having to make the causal inferences between motives, actions, and consequences.

Such arguments connect with those from the critical school of mass communications. For example, Tuchman (1979) argues that the relative absence of female characters on television is not a statement about the actual balance of men and women in reality but a symbolic statement about their relative importance in social reality. Women are 'symbolically annihilated'. Unfortunately, this move towards a more complex view of the text is problematic for Gerbner, and arguably for mass communications researchers generally, as they attempt to import a theory of the text from the critical school without otherwise modifying their own theories. For example, Gerbner tends to confuse denotation and connotation. On the one hand, he tests whether the numerical infrequency of the elderly on television is correlated with viewers' underestimation of the numbers of elderly people in the population—presuming a denotative reading rather than one of symbolic annihilation to be affecting viewers. Yet in other research he tests whether the frequency of television crime portrayals is correlated with an overvaluation of the symbolic significance of law, order and justice, rather than with an overestimation of actual crime statistics.

More damaging, Hawkins and Pingree (1983) show that while the first stage of the cultivation argument holds, that people alter their estimates of actual 'real-world' phenomena in line with the television statistics, the second stage does not: people do not appear to draw the connotative inferences suggested from these statistical distortions concerning, say, the relative importance or unimportance of certain social groups or, say, the symbolic importance of justice, given the number of crime shows they watch. The interpretative activity implicitly assumed by cultivation appears not to take place.

Notice how easily I have fallen into Gerbner's invited trap of inferring causality from correlational evidence: in fact all we have is an observed correlation (or lack of one) between media exposure and 'real world beliefs'. The validity of the causal argument rests on the attempt to control for every possible factor which might also account for differences in social beliefs between light and heavy television viewers. While one might argue that this is *a priori* impossible, Gerbner's work is also flawed by methodological disputes over his application of these controls independently. Hirsch (1980), for example, showed that simultaneous application of appropriate controls eliminates any residual relationship between exposure and social reality beliefs. He thus claims that the evidence for cultivation is artefactual, there being in each case a third underlying cause which accounts for the then-spurious correlation between exposure and beliefs. For example, the apparent relationship between exposure to media violence and fear of crime is instead explained by the neighbourhood viewers live in: those who live in high-crime areas are more likely both to stay at home and watch television and also to believe that their chances of being attacked are higher than those who live in low crime areas.

I have dwelt on this research because it represents a certain stage in the historical development of the effects argument, by introducing the analysis of the text, by pointing to an interpretative role for the viewer, and by changing our hitherto limited conception of media effects. Nonetheless, its relative theoretical naivety in the conception of the effects process (an unspecified passive process of cultivation), its reliance on the much criticised method of content analysis to determine programme meaning (which aims to index meaning by assessing the relative frequencies of discrete, acontextual, denotational units of texts, see Berelson, 1952; Krippendorf, 1982) and, like Phillips, its use of social statistics and opinion polls (also vulnerable to attack as indices of social processes), make cultivation analysis one step in a long theoretical development.

Critical mass communications and the television audience

The critical school of mass communications has explicitly avoided the study of media effects as it has all study of the audience, until recently. Fejes (1984) identifies several reasons for this avoidance. The main two are first that such research considers the concept of effect irrelevant, it being subsumed under the broader concept of ideology and studied through the non-experimental analysis of hegemonic processes (those processes by which the dominant ideology is imposed by the powerful on to the powerless masses). Secondly, that effects are in fact studied by critical researchers, only implicitly in terms of assumptions about the audience built into media research on the production and reproduction of meanings. Unfortunately, the resultant image of the audience is simplified and naive. The audience is seen implicitly as an undifferentiated mass, who passively receive the meanings of the media as given, and who are affected by these meanings in a similar fashion to the early 'powerful media' model of traditional research, namely as by a 'hypodermic needle'. Similar assumptions were tested by Gerbner's cultivation research without much success. Recently, some critical researchers have recognised that audiences are both heterogeneous and selective in their responses to television (see Chapter 2). This audience activity together with the socially located nature of the audience may serve to undermine hegemony, and certainly changes the focus from mass domination to a focus on difference between audience groupings and resistance or struggle as meanings are negotiated rather than imposed (Fiske, 1987). Hall thus points the way to the study of interpretation before that of effect or impact:

> before this message can have an 'effect' (however defined), satisfy a 'need' or be put to a 'use', it must first be appropriated as meaningful discourse and be meaningfully decoded. It is this set of decoded meanings which 'have an effect', influence, entertain, instruct or persuade (Hall, 1980, p. 130).

Fejes's own solution is that the critical school must incorporate and reconceptualise some of the classic effects paradigms, such as agenda-setting (how the media tell us not what to think but what to think about: McCombs and Gilbert, 1986), the spiral of silence (how the media tell us what not to think or talk about: Noelle-Neumann, 1974), or the knowledge gap (how the socially deprived learn less from, and thus fall further behind the already informed, Tichenor *et al.*, 1970). All these can be seen as attempts to analyse the processes of media distribution of ideological meanings through a heterogenous audience. These models can also be seen to integrate psychological and sociological levels of analysis. For example, recent explanations of the knowledge gap no longer draw upon cognitive deficit hypotheses to differentiate among social classes but on motivations and issue salience or relevance to account for the gap. Similarly, the spiral of silence assumes a general desire for conformity and consensus among the media audience to provide the mechanism which drives an issue into the spiral of silence.

The Interpretative Viewer

Out of disappointment, then, with the experimental approach as well as a delayed realisation of its theoretical impoverishment, researchers are now reconceptualising media effects as gradual, symbolic, and cognitive, affecting people's frameworks for thinking as well as the content of their thoughts. Thus media effects concern not only behaviour but also cognitions, emotions, social interactions, and attitudes. In reviewing recent traditions in media research, Katz (1980) argues that they have various things in common:

(1) The definition of reality: all are concerned with the ways in which the media constrain cognitive and perceptual organisation. They share a belief (2) in the persuasive powers of the media, although of more subtle and insidious kinds than have previously been studied: thus influence may be exerted through the imposition of salient concerns, cognitive styles and frames of reference (p. 133).

These developments can be seen as converging towards the more ideological concerns of the critical school. However, this convergence requires recognition of a more informed and heterogenous audience than hitherto conceived, with the audience playing a more active part in the creation of meanings. In advocating a move towards social cognition as the new, integrating theoretical framework, Roberts and Bachen (1981) write:

The basic link between media content and human social behaviour is forged in the interaction between information transmitted by the media on the one hand and human information processing on the other . . . differences in response may derive from variations in how similar messages are interpreted by different people or by similar people under differing conditions (p. 318).

For television to have any effects on its viewers, whether behavioural, attitudinal or cognitive, programmes must first be perceived and comprehended by the viewers. Thus this process should be studied before the problem-driven questions of function and effects are further considered. When interpreting a programme, viewers use not only the information in the programme, but also their past experience with the programme, its genre, and their own personal and social experiences with the phenomena portrayed (e.g. institutions, relationships, myths, explanations). Furthermore, they integrate these different sources in coherent and complex ways. Thus a programme's effects must depend on the ways in which viewers' representations of the programmes are a transformation of the original.

The interpretative task

Let us consider the problem of interpreting complex texts. Suppose you overhear the following conversation between a mother (Pauline) and a teenage son (Mark). The mother is visiting her son in a youth detention centre:

M   Sit down then.
P   Sorry. How are you?
M   Alright.
P   You've lost weight.
M   Anybody would in this place.
P   Tough is it.
M   I can cope.

P   They treating you alright are they?
M   It's not a hospital mum, I'm supposed to come out of here a changed person. Fit to rejoin society. It's not a cushy number.

P   No. Well—how do you feel?
M   What about?
P   About what you did?
M   Not a lot.

M   Short sharp shock—that's what they used to call these places.
P   Yeah.
M   It's about right as well.
P   Has it put you off doing it again?
M   No, I don't think so. Make sure I don't get caught next time. That's the best thing about this place, you do so much exercise by the time I get out I'll be so fit they won't be able to catch me.
P   Mark—you shouldn't do it. You mustn't do things like that.
M   Leave it out mum, I've had that rammed down my throat ever since I got here.
P   I don't understand you.
M   It's not that hard really. I was broke, so I thought I'd help myself.
P   But we brought you up right—we brought you up not to do things like that.
M   You brought me up in the East End mum.

You might conclude from this that the generation gap is alive and well, that this mother and son have failed each other and cannot communicate. On hearing many similar conversations you might wonder about the present state of the family and worry about today's youth. But how did this conversation acquire its meanings? What work did the hearer have to do to make sense of it?

Firstly, even before hearing the last sentence, one could infer from their speech, that these people are working class. The extract gains meaning from reference to a topical debate in Britain, the value of the Government's 'short sharp shock' scheme for young offenders. So the hearer can contribute that knowledge, as well as an image of the East End of London as a place to bring up children. Gender knowledge can fill out the impression of a disappointed mother, unsure of where whe went wrong, and of a defiant young man with his own code of ethics. Indeed, the hearers who do not fill in such sociopolitical knowledge will make a different 'reading' of the extract from those who do.

The conflict between mother and son can be interpreted according to two key thematic oppositions which the hearer must make salient, which both explain the conflict and give it broader relevance. The first is that of moral:immoral, where this conversation gains meaning as an exemplar of numerous cases where, to the older generation, the younger one seems immoral and to the younger one, the concept of 'morals' seems dated and unreasonable (Mark's analysis of both his upbringing and the effects of the detention centre is certainly a reasoned one). The second opposition is powerful:powerless. Mark is tough and resilient, Pauline is helpless, she doesn't understand. The couple align the two oppositions, the conventionally moral position is powerless in the face of the tougher, immoral one. The opening remarks serve as a metonymy for the whole conversation: Mark takes charge of his mother, his mother apologises and obeys.

Certain aspects of the conversation appear indeterminate in meaning. Is Mark being sullen towards a patient mother or is he being patient with an ignorant and innocent mother? Hearers may favour one side or the other, maybe depending on one's relative sympathies for men or women, the young or the middle-aged, the child or the parent, the free or the underdog. One can also see this text as open in Eco's sense (1979a) of not only containing more than one interpretation amongst which hearers may choose, but also of inviting both to be read in conjunction with each other, so one's interpretation is a product of both. Hence the conversation has an emergent meaning, which recognises both Pauline and Mark's incompatible perspectives and hence involves a statement about intergenerational or familial miscommunication resulting from mutual misperception of motives and viewpoints. Each participant sees only his or her own perspective, lending the conversation its air of hopelessness: the hearer may see both perspectives and, with or without allegiances, may see the relation between the two.

This interpretive activity called for on the part of the hearer would seem to be the same, whether or not this mother and son were real people, say one's friends or family, or whether they are characters on television; in fact this extract was taken from the soap opera, *EastEnders*. There are certain differences: if they were your friends, you may know how hard the son tried to communicate with his mother and to avoid crime; if you watch *EastEnders*, you would know of the 'heart of gold' of the mother compared to the disreputability of the son. Again, for *EastEnders*, you know the conventions of the genre (that, for example, they are unlikely to reach an understanding, that the woman's perspective will be favoured, or that this conversation is intended as a contrast with a different mother-son relationship between other characters), and this guides your inferences and expectations. But these types of sense-making are all of the same kind. Through the interrelation of the structure of the text (the conversation, whether 'fact or fiction'), and the hearer/viewers' social knowledge of everyday events, commonsense discourses and the specific conventions of the situation (whether genre/programme or everyday situation), a particular and located set of meanings are created through an active process of negotiation and integration. How is this achieved, how should we theorise this process, and where is the balance of power located between text and reader?

Theoretical approaches to interpretation

The question of the viewers' interpretative 'work' needed to make sense of a text itself presumes a transcendence of the original active/passive argument regarding the role of the viewer. For example, for the classic literary approach, such a question did not arise because the meaning of the text was given within the text itself: one could not ask whether and how viewers contributed to its construction. Nor was the nature of everyday interpretation by ordinary viewers seen as an important social process worthy of serious analysis. Unlike the literary theorist, a traditional media sociologist well might ask whether or not people in fact received the meanings available to them. Consider, for example, the uses and gratifications theorists (Blumler and Katz, 1974), concerned with audience selectivity and viewers' different motivations to attend to the media: here at least the possibility is raised that meanings available might not translate neatly into meanings received, for people may attend only to certain messages and avoid others. While the person is thus accorded some active role, it is purely motivational and not interpretative: the meanings themselves are not available for negotiation.

Each approach then, would encounter problems with my proposed account of the interpretation of the above mother/son discussion for neither acknowledges that for which there is now ample evidence, namely that people construct various and often unexpected interpretations of programmes, reading with or against the grain, depending on their own contribution and the knowledge resources available to them. Interestingly, these two approaches represent opposite cases insofar as the literary approach has, until recently, presumed unitary meaning in the text and provided no role for the reader whatsoever (reflecting an elitist interest in academic or 'true' readers but not ordinary, 'inaccurate' ones), while the uses and gratifications approach with which it is often compared (Morley, 1980) allows for as many meanings (or gratifications) as there are viewers (or uses), thereby providing no role for the text.

Most other approaches have adopted positions similar to either of these extremes: the Behaviourist omits the issue of meaning altogether, the cognitive theorist considers only the perceptions of the viewer, the effects researcher presumes a unitary and influential textual meaning, and so forth. Our task then, is to avoid these simplifying extremes and to recognise both the structuring role of the text and the constructive role of the viewer in negotiating meaning.

To elaborate the problem of interpretation, consider the task facing viewers of television drama in making sense of the characters. Characters in drama typically present a range of personality traits, each of which must be inferred from the details of the narrative, say from their interactions with other characters. This process of inference is important as characters are typically used by writers to personify different narrative themes. Thus the characters' conflicts and allegiances represent underlying messages about the relations between these basic moral or social themes. In some respects, characters often represent stereotypes about gender, class, occupation, or whatever in order to facilitate this inference process, legitimating the application of viewers' social knowledge. In other respects, characters are often constructed rather ambiguously—both in order to appeal to a wide range of viewers, who must concretise their own version of the characters, and because realistic characterisation is enhanced by complex portrayals. Much of the pleasure in viewing lies in working out for oneself what is happening and what the characters are like. As viewers come to a programme equipped with a considerable knowledge of other people, they exploit the spaces in programmes to construct their own meanings.

For example, how do viewers interpret Alexis Carrington-Colby, the character played by Joan Collins in *Dynasty*? Alexis Carrington-Colby is a glamorous, powerful and evil woman in her late forties. There are few attractive women on television of that age, so she may be seen as a positive role model, a successful older woman, who may thus increase the self-esteem of those who identify with her. Or do viewers think her too successful, rich and fortunate for an ordinary viewer to feel that she has much to do with them? This character may then be represented as an unobtainable ideal which simply depresses them and reduces their self-esteem. Or maybe she is seen as an encouraging ideal, but only if one makes the link between success and evil. In this case, one could see her as offering prizes only if one sacrifices morality and numerous feminine virtues otherwise likely to be valued by viewers such as reserve, consideration, loyalty, generosity, and so forth.

The relation between viewer and text

This example shows how the structure of the text, the experienced relation between viewer and text, the interpretation made of the text, and the consequences of viewing are all complexly bound up together. By the experienced relation between viewer and text, I mean to point to the variability in the nature of this relationship: viewers may identify with particular characters, seeing themselves as in that character's shoes; they may regard a character as a role model, imitating that character's behaviour in order to gain some of the rewards which the character is shown to enjoy; or they may recognise aspects of a character as similar to a significant person in their own lives, engaging in what Horton and Wohl (1956) term 'parasocial interaction', watching the action as if playing opposite the character, as if the character were interacting with them directly. No doubt there are yet other relationships possible between viewer and programme, and this relationship is partly a product of the text structure—different genres invite different viewer positions—and partly affects the viewer's response in terms of involvement and interpretation.

In sum, for too long audiences have been seen as passive, mindless and homogeneous and for too long people have been seen as audiences, as simple receivers or responders. But there is a danger in too wholeheartedly adopting the opposite stance: recent trends are towards the active audience, towards seeing people as initiators, constructors, creators. However, these avoid the key problem of negotiating meanings, merely replacing one simplified polemic with another. Instead the dichotomy must be transcended. If we see the media or life events as all-powerful creators of meaning, we neglect the role of audiences; if we see people as all-powerful creators of meaning, we neglect the structure of that which people interpret. The important questions concern the interrelation between the two: how do people actively make sense of structured texts and events; how do texts guide and restrict interpretations. The creation of meaning through the interaction of texts and readers is a struggle, a site of negotiation between *two* semi-powerful sources. Each side has different powerful strategies, each has different points of weakness, and each has different interests. It is this process of negotiation which is central. And through analysis of this process, traditional conceptions of both texts and readers may require rethinking, for each has traditionally been theorised in ignorance of the other.

The role of social knowledge

What then is the psychology involved in this process of negotiation? How do people use their social knowledge to make sense of complex texts as part of their everyday experiences? What has resulted from the emergence of the issue of sense-making in recent years, not only in psychology but also in a range of related disciplines from sociology to literary theory?

Let us consider further the task of the television viewer. Durkin (1985a), among others, has pointed out the common fallacy of assuming that a knowledge of television content permits inferences about effects. Indeed, this is the implicit assumption behind the vast numbers of content analytic studies conducted. Although it is, for example, now well documented that the content of television is heavily biased quantitatively with respect to gender, race, class, violence, life events and much else besides, 'frequency of message has yet to be demonstrated to be isomorphic with viewers' receptive processes' (Durkin, 1985a, p. 203). This presumed equation of frequency with importance in content analysis has been criticised as semantically naive by textual analysts (e.g. Burgelin, 1972). It is also naive in cognitive terms.

Social cognition (see later) has revealed numerous ways in which people alter or deviate from provided frequency distributions, through use of interpretive heuristics based on salience, availability, recency, relevance, prototypicality, confirmatory biases, and so forth (Fiske and Taylor, 1984; Kahneman, Slovic and Tversky, 1982). Thus clear biases in the manifest programme content may not be mirrored in viewers' own representations of the programme. Content analysis assumes that all the potentially effective messages are in the text and have now been revealed through analysis, so that all that viewers can 'do' with this content is to take it or leave it. More generally, a cognitive theory of viewers' interpretations is needed, and may be found at least in part in current social cognition. For example, what do viewers find salient, how are they selective, how do they integrate 'new' programme information with 'old' social knowledge, how do they differentiate among messages, how perceptive are they of underlying messages, and so on?

Unfortunately, while the problems of meaning and interpretation have not been explicitly recognised in much traditional mass communications research, this is not to say that issues of meaning do not arise. A study by Tan (1979) illustrates the often implicit role of interpretation in effects research. Tan showed fifteen television advertisements for beauty products to adolescent girls while a control group saw fifteen advertisements unrelated to beauty themes. Subsequently the experimental condition rated beauty as more important for 'popularity with men' and as slightly more 'personally desirable' than the control group. To understand what effect has occurred in this apparently obvious study, we need to know how the viewers interpreted what they saw in the context of their own commonsense discourses concerning femininity and sexual attraction. For example, do the experimental group now consider women to be more powerful than before, having been persuaded that beautiful women can 'twist men around their little finger', or do they now think less well of women and is their self-esteem lowered by seeing men as more powerful and critical, while seeing women as peripheral sex objects?

Again, consider the case of cultivation research, which asks whether people come to believe the television's version of reality the more they watch it. Testing this hypothesis depends on one's definition of 'television's version of reality' and hence of the meanings which viewers might construct of the programme and which might consequently influence them. For example, Noble (1975) argues that war films and Westerns are enjoyed more for their portrayal of kindness, loyalty and co-operation than for their aggressive content (or even, as Gerbner would claim, for their reaffirmation of the status quo). Both content analysis—the methodology used by traditional mass communications to reveal the meanings of programmes (Berelson, 1952)—and effects research are typically motivated by a public agenda of social concerns, notably violence, rather than by a complex appreciation of either the structure of texts or the interpretive role of viewers. As a result, commonly only the violent aspects of such programmes will be coded and only beliefs concerning violence will be examined in the viewers.

This research may thus be asking the wrong questions. A war film may increase effects related to violence (such as tolerance of aggression, fear of crime, pleasure in violence) or instead it may increase effects related to co-operation (such as need for comradeship, importance of loyalty, rejection of individualism). Further, a null result, which is common in the literature and taken to indicate an absence of effects, may mask the fact that both effects occur but cancel each other out. Or the effects may be different for different subgroups in the sample. The interpretations which viewers make of programmes mediate the potential effects of those programmes, and thus attention must be given to viewers' interpretations when studying effects.

Many of these issues—of complexity and latent meanings in texts, of varieties of audience interpretation, and of problems of research design and measurement—are minimised when studying the effects of clear-cut and manifest aspects of programmes. But they come to the fore for the many subtle aspects of textual meaning. For issues of morality, gender, value systems, or ideology, for example, television drama contains many diverse and hidden messages. It is often difficult to specify what these are, or whether apparent diversity or ambiguity masks an underlying consensus. Certainly, content analysis, designed to measure manifest and quantifiable content (Krippendorf, 1982) cannot satisfactorily reveal complex, connotative and ideological meanings. In a similar way, people's responses to such portrayals are more difficult to separate from their general social knowledge than are, say, their estimations of crime statistics. As judgements concerning gender roles, morality or values are more important to people in their everyday lives, the contribution of television in this domain constitutes a challenge to research.

The Knowledge of the Viewer

There has been a move from behavioural to cognitive research in media studies, paralleling the prominence of social cognition in recent social psychology (Eiser, 1986; Fiske and Taylor, 1984; Forgas, 1981). The key questions now concern the meanings which viewers construct of television programmes, the processes of sense-making by which they achieve this, and the social knowledge which constitutes the resource which guides and informs these processes. Social cognition is held by many researchers within traditional media studies to be a fruitful theoretical resource for pursuing these questions: it will be a part of my argument to extend this resource also to researchers from the critical or cultural schools.

Theories of social cognition

Over the last fifteen years, social cognition has become a dominant research domain in cognitive, developmental and social psychology and in artificial intelligence. It asks how people understand their social worlds and studies both people's representations of their world, or their social knowledge, and the processes by which people make sense of their world, processes involving both the construction and use (or reconstruction) of social knowledge. Deriving in part from symbolic interactionism, it argues that people's understandings of their world constitutes their reality, and thus is real for them in its consequences. The second origin of social cognition is cognitive constructivism, beginning with Bruner's New Look in the 1950s (Bruner, Goodnow and Austen, 1956), which itself originated in the Gestalt psychologists' concern with meaning as the active creation of a coherent and emergent whole from partial information (Kohler, 1930).

The study of semantic representations concerns people's knowledge of their social world, of people and events. It assumes that the social world is too complex and varied for adaptive action based on veridical and complete perception. Therefore people must be highly selective. Furthermore, information does not come ready packaged for use. It must be constructively and purposefully organised. This organisation is governed by the Gestalt principles of consistency, coherence, parsimony, and relevance, principles which together generate meaningful and adaptive representations. Thus people construct organised and abstract summaries of their past experiences which serve to frame their understanding of new experiences. Sociocognitive processes apply these representations to the interpretation of new experiences, using a variety of strategies and heuristics.

This active constructive conception of the person emphasises top-down rather than bottom-up (Bobrow and Norman, 1975; Neisser, 1976) processes, so that meaning is held to derive more from the imposition of prior social knowledge and interpretative frames than from the passive reception of given information. Thus people abstract from their everyday experiences, organise these abstractions into parsimonious and generalisable representations, and thereby create their own versions of a social world which is inherently open to interpretation. Various structures are proposed for these semantic representations or knowledge structure: frame, script, schema, stereotype, prototype, and so forth. Each is both distinct and overlapping with the others, and schema tends to be used as a generic form for knowledge structures, although it is often poorly defined (van Dijk, 1987).

The concept of schema was originally used by Piaget (e.g. 1968) to refer to the active, equilibrating, dynamic notion of knowledge representation and by Bartlett (1932) to describe the principled application of past to new knowledge. It now serves to emphasise that knowledge structures are dynamic, that meaning is constructed not given, and that there is an intimate relation between process and representation. The tradeoff people face between generality and specificity (or between parsimony and richness) is frequently understood in terms of the adaptiveness of schemata, which is useful as it is the concept of adaptiveness which links processes of knowing and interpreting to motivation, purpose, and the structure of the environment.

Social cognition as mediation

Although loosely both termed 'social cognition', one may identify two distinct theoretical perspectives present in the move towards social cognition within mass communications research. For many (e.g. Reeves, Chaffee and Tims, 1982), the role of cognition is that of mediation: television exposure can only affect behaviour through the mediating role of cognition. This links to the earlier Behaviourist formulations in which the 'organism' was inserted between the 'stimulus' and the 'response'.

For example, Berkowitz and Rogers (1986) argue that television affects behaviour only under certain circumstances, such as when the television stimulus is defined as aggressive, and Hawkins (1977) reviews work showing that television must be perceived as realistic for maximal effects. Hence, we should study the determinants of perceived aggression or realism. The adoption of Wyer and Srull's (1980) model of social information processing by Reeves *et al.* (1982) also fits this perspective. Here, social cognition is seen as a set of informed processing heuristics by which the television message is transformed into different stimuli for subsequent response.

This approach has clear analogues in recent developments in attitude theory, which are aimed at dealing with the problematically weak relationship between attitudes and the behaviours supposedly caused by these attitudes. Thus Ajzen and Fishbein (1980), for example, propose a model in which cognitive mediators, such as behavioural intention and perceived social norms, are inserted between attitude and behaviour to improve the predictive relationship. In general, this perspective retains a primary concern with behaviour. For mass communications, social cognition is inserted in order to aid predicting the relationship between media exposure and behavioural effects, such as aggressive, stereotyped, or consumerist behaviours. Van Dijk criticises this perspective:

> Despite various cognitivistic orientations in social psychology, the analysis of attitudes and attitude change has partly remained under the influence of behaviourist conceptualisations, in which messages were treated as 'stimuli', behaviours as their caused 'responses', and attitudes as the 'mediating' intermediary variables of this connection . . . [yet] attitudes . . . require systematic and explicit cognitive analysis in their own right (van Dijk, 1987, pp. 250–1).

Social cognition and constructivism

The second perspective on the role of social cognition introduces a new primary concern, that of people's social construction of reality (Berger and Luckmann, 1967). These social constructions create everyday meanings for people, and thus supersede the concern with behaviours, for it is meaning which turns behaviours into actions. On this view, we will never predict behaviours successfully, for only on the level of meaningful action are behaviours systematically determined and integrated with beliefs and motivations. To understand patterns in action, we must understand patterns in meaning or social construction of reality. Thus, cognitive effects are the effects of interest. Cognition becomes involved with television in a circular fashion: not only is television interpreted through sociocognitive knowledge and processes but also television affects this knowledge and processes. Television does not only offer role models for action, which may be variously interpreted, but it also offers images and frameworks for everyday understanding, through which we subsequently interpret other social texts. It may not only tell us what to do but also what it means to do such and such and what kind of a person you are to do this. The influence of symbolic interactionism is clear.

To use an attributional example, it becomes as important to know that depressed people see their world in terms of the frame of external successes and internal failures, for this is their symbolically constructed reality, as to see that this causes them to lack motivation for attempting further successes and hence to remain depressed. Or again, the fact that most people are not members of and come into little contact with ethnic minorities and so have little opportunity to enact overt discrimination is only part of what is interesting about discrimination. It is still of concern that most people are, nonetheless, racially prejudiced. Prejudice is integrated with their sense of self and purpose in life, their concepts of justice, of nationality, and their explanations for unemployment or the balance of payments. Prejudice is kept alive, as van Dijk (1987) shows, not through occasional discriminatory acts, but through the central role these beliefs play in the symbolic world of the majority, allowing them to form a comfortable ingroup identity through the continual telling of outgroup stories and jokes. Thus, the social construction of reality approach moves away from action as overt behaviour to take instead thought and speech as paradigm cases: thought is acting upon ourselves, speech is acting upon others as well; each serves to reproduce and reconstruct the symbolic (rather than the physical) world. As van Dijk says, 'verbal statements are also (communicative) acts, and in need of analysis like other "behaviours caused by" attitudes'.

Finally, this view of social cognition invokes an integrated, consistency-oriented view of the person: a frame of understanding derived from television viewing may lead to the reinterpretation of related social knowledge, this in turn leading to indirect and spreading cognitive effects. As argued earlier, the social construction (or reconstruction) of reality in everyday life simultaneously draws upon television and 'real-life' indiscriminately (although certain contingent differences, such as differences in source credibility, knowledge of message construction, perception of authorial intentation, may lead to different inference patterns) and serves to reconstruct them both.

These two perspectives on social cognition represent a new version of the European/American division in social psychology. It is predominantly Europeans who are rediscovering the importance of the social, of narrative, of folk understanding, of language, while American researchers have more enthusiastically adopted the information processing paradigm (although work on scripts and story grammars incorporates some narrative theory into social cognition). In mass communications, the division is less clear, with researchers often being rather unclear about the role they expect social cognitions to play. For example, many study social cognition according to the mediational perspective without ever linking their research to actual or potential behavioural effects studies, so the mediating role connects to the stimulus but more rarely to the response.

Problems with social cognition

There are various problems with social cognition, as with any research literature, which should sound a warning note to those wholeheartedly adopting it for the study of mass communications. Social cognition tends to overemphasise the top-down or constructive nature of understanding and neglect the bottom-up processes. Thus one is often left with the feeling that people can make any sense they choose an experience, with no constraints imposed by the inherent structure of that which they interpret. This is too convenient for traditional mass communications researchers, who similarly tend to neglect or underestimate the complexity of the television programme whose viewers they study. Just as the question to be faced for social cognition is how do constructive and receptive processes interact, so too media studies needs to analyse the process of negotiation between programme and viewer. However, in combination with a theory of the text, social cognition can certainly help in providing a theory of the constructive viewer, as will be argued in more detail later.

Two further problems should be briefly mentioned. Social cognition cannot adequately account for the existence of consensus in representation. As many have pointed out (e.g. Forgas, 1983), it is insufficiently social, neglecting the social context and producing overly individualistic accounts of cognition. Further, social cognition is still at an early stage of development, which makes its adoption by a new field problematic, although it also means that social cognition can learn from media studies, as argued above. Being largely an experimentally-oriented enterprise, its strategy, like that of experimental effects media research, is to explain complex phenomena by breaking them down into their constituent processes and then studying artificial simulations of each part in the laboratory. Thus we know something of people's understanding of simple scenario descriptions of others and of short folk tales (Mandler, 1984), but

almost nothing of their understanding of their family or of a complex text
such as a television programme. Moreover, it may be that when the
individual parts are recombined, we may find that the emergent properties
of the whole are still unknown.

Varieties of media effect

Following the move from behavioural to cognitive effects, researchers
now conceive of a variety of media effects. If the behavioural approach
favoured a singular and clear notion of behavioural change, the cognitive
approach has opened up a broader, more exciting, set of questions which
derive from developments in both the social psychology of everyday
understanding and in textual analysis (revealing the range of meanings and
devices which texts may employ). Thus not only the *what*, but also the *how*
of media effects is changing. The *tabular rasa* assumption of Behaviourism
allowed for the simplest and strongest conception of effects, in which
viewing induces new information or behaviour into the passively receptive
individual. As the viewers' long-term social knowledge and their constructive, interpretive capabilities are recognised, the possibility of strong and
direct effects is reduced.

Television is most likely to affect viewers in this strong sense when it
constitutes the sole, and trusted, source of information. This occurs, for
example, for programmes about cable and satellite technology or the
disease Aids. McCombs and Gilbert (1986) showed that the agenda setting
function of the news is greater for those issues for which the viewers have
no alternative sources of information. However, many programmes deal
with familiar events with which the viewers are experienced. Further,
programmes often do not provide specific information so much as
examples of ways of thinking and acting.

Television may simply reinforce viewers' prior beliefs by showing
characters who embody those beliefs being rewarded in comparison to
those who embody the opposite (Curran, Gurevitch and Woollacott, 1982;
Kreizenbeck, 1983). Thus television may legitimate or validate the viewers'
private experiences. Or television may increase the salience of ideas or
ways of thinking with which the viewer is already familiar. Thus repetition
in programmes may increase the availability of salience of certain ideas in
the viewers. Further, television may prioritise issues through agenda
setting, telling viewers what are the key issues they should think about.
Finally, television may play a restructuring role for viewers' cognitions. In
other words, through their narrative requirements for consistency,
coherences, and redundancy (Silverstone, 1981), programmes may organise people's beliefs and frames of thinking in specific, robust, often
simplified ways, creating dichotomies and oppositions, forming associations and connotations, not previously used by the viewers. In all,
television may provide viewers with 'pictures of the world, the definitions

of the situation and problems, the explanations, alternative remedies and solutions' (Halloran, 1970, p. 53). As Lang and Lang (1985) note, returning us to the symbolic interactionist framework, 'as long as the meanings read into the content are real, they are . . . real in their consequences. They become part of the culturally enshrined symbolic environment' (p. 57).

2

The Active Viewer

The Textual Approach to Meaning

Both social psychology and media studies have come to define as central the question of how people make sense of everyday phenomena, of which the media are a part. Each now emphasises people's interpretive capabilities and sees the process of interpretation as one of negotiation between a set of structured potentialities 'out there' and the person's repertoire of knowledge representations and processing strategies. This interest in interpretation has different theoretical implications for each school of mass communications—traditional and critical—and represents an issue over which a convergence may be established (Liebes, 1986a).

How did media studies examine the meanings of television programmes before the rise of the 'active viewer'? As was noted earlier, the split within media studies has resulted in many complex theories and analyses of texts conducted by the critical school quite independently of a consideration of the audience-oriented research of the traditional approach. The critical school has drawn on the domains of semiotics, linguistics, and anthropology. Theories originally developed to account for diverse cultural and societal traditions or for the structures of 'high' literature have been applied to Western popular culture, both as a cultural practice and a transformation of literary genres. Analyses of popular culture (Bigsby, 1976; Masterman, 1984; Newcomb, 1982; Rowland and Watkins, 1984) have revealed many intriguing and illuminating meanings underlying media texts.

The analysis of popular culture

For example, Eco (1979b) analysed the narrative structure underlying Fleming's James Bond novels, drawing on literary theories of poetics and structuralism. He revealed fixed sequences of narrative elements which underlie all of the novels and argued that these sequences satisfy the reader through confirmation of expectations and the reassurance of familiar, predictable happenings. These narratives also contain latent xenophobic, gender stereotyped and moralistic messages which are repeatedly played out in the novels. Through revealing the narrative structure and the latent messages, Eco's analysis represents a traditional structuralist one insofar as he unveils the underlying structural commonalities beneath the apparent diversity across all the different novels. Thus each novel is seen simply as a variant on or transformation of an underlying constant structure.

Similarly, Wright (1975) analysed the basic themes in the Western film and showed how these themes relate to, and are instantiated through, stylised narrative sequences, standardised character roles, and traditional moral conclusions. Drawing upon the structuralist terminology of bipolar oppositions, he concludes that 'in the classic Western, the good/bad opposition repeats some of the social imagery of the inside/outside dichotomy; but since it is aimed more specifically at the difference between the society and the villains, it is more explicitly concerned with values' (p. 53). Like Eco's analysis, a superficially trivial, fantasy-based genre is shown to contain basic, mythic messages concerning problems of wide-spread concern to readers or viewers. The 'real' story lies behind that of the manifest story and, further, is more or less the same as that which lies behind numerous other stories.

There are many further examples of such analyses of popular culture as containing mythic, moral, and ideological meanings concerning issues central to the culture. These meanings are encoded into texts by drawing upon structures of opposition, classic realist narrative and multiple levels of meaning, among other conventions. One could point to Patte's (1975) analysis of the Good Samaritan parable, Fiske's (1984) analysis of *Dr. Who,* Silverstone's (1984) analysis of a television programme about the moral journey of a transsexual, McRobbie's (1983) analysis of the 'romantic individualism' which underlies the teenage girl's magazine, *Jackie,* Silj *et al.*'s (1988) analysis of a range of European soap operas and Kress's (1983) analysis of the ideology underlying news reports. Each analysis is premised on an appreciation of the complexity of texts and the non-obviousness of texts. This is in line with Barthes' (1973) argument that underlying meanings are 'naturalised' or 'mystified' such that the casual reader is neither conscious nor critical of them, though nonetheless receptive.

Problems with text analysis

While such analyses are revealing, they encounter considerable problems insofar as implicitly, at least, they search for the 'true' meaning of the text. Analysts tend to deny the role of the analyst (or any other reader) and of the analyst's sociohistorical position when identifying 'the' meaning of the text. They tend to conceive of the text as static rather than dynamic, to reify their own analytic categories as features of the text, to underestimate the role of the contexts both of production and reading, seeking instead context-free universals in meaning. Finally, they often forget to see the text as a communicative moment in the cycling of meanings between culture, producers and consumers (Hall, 1980). Such problems have led to the demise of the structuralist approach and the rise of the reader-oriented approach.

The problem of what Eco (1979a) calls the 'crystalline text'—the view of the text as fixed, given and independent of the context of reading—is in some ways the same as that faced by content analysis. This latter approach to the analysis of meaning is typically adopted by traditional mass communications, as meanings are sought not in terms of qualitatively distinct structures and structural transformations which underlie the surface meanings, but instead in terms of the patterns of frequency relations between units of meaning which constitute that surface of manifest level of meaning. For example, in the domain of gender stereotyping, Tedesco (1974) found that male prime-time characters were more likely to be powerful, smart, rational and stable, while female prime-time characters were more often sociable, peaceful, attractive and happy. Turrow (1974) assessed patterns of advice giving, showing that men in prime-time television more often give directives and orders than do women. On the level of frequencies of gender-biased patterns, then, the media can be shown by such methods to portray stereotyped messages (see Durkin, 1985a; Howitt, 1982). There has been a long dispute between the latent structural and manifest content forms of analysis (Burgelin, 1972; Curran, 1976). For example, with what reliability can certain meanings be said to underlie the manifest meaning, or, how validly do frequency patterns index the symbolic importance of a theme or association?

The problem remains, however, for both structural and content analysis, that the meanings which analysts find in the text may not be those which a reader finds. Both conceive of text meaning as fixed, stable and given irrespective of the context of reception and the activity of the viewers. One may resort to explanations such as false consciousness—arguing that the viewer does pick up the meanings identified by the analyst even though the opposite seems to be true, or to simply seeing the viewer as wrong—having made a nonsense of the text by misinterpreting the real meanings. Either way, two key problems remain. Firstly, one has not explained how it is possible for the same text to be read in different ways by readers, or by readers and analysts. Secondly, one has not accounted for the actual meanings circulating in society following the reading of certain texts, one has only described those meanings that 'should' be circulating according to one's textual analysis.

These problems are exacerbated when one moves from the study of high culture to that of popular culture. Popular texts such as television programmes are specifically intended to appeal to wide audiences of varied experience and interests. Thus one cannot, as Culler advocates for literary analysis, assume that in the case of television viewers, 'an explicit formulation of one's own interpretive operations would have considerable general validity' (Culler, 1981, p. 53), for the cultural background of the analyst and reader in the case of popular culture are likely to be very different. Interpretative operations, insofar as they are determined by cultural and cognitive practices, are likely to lead to different relations between the text and the reader depending on the context of the reader and the act of reading. It is an empirical question as to whether a middle-class male academic interprets a soap opera in the same way, and using the same knowledge and strategies, as a working-class housewife. Having the text in front of you does not tell you what it means to its audiences.

Again unlike literature, the research questions in the study of popular culture are different: while the literary critic may be interested in what the text means in relation to literary theories and other texts, and while the literary historian may be concerned to discover what the text meant to its author or how it arose from its own cultural context, in contrast, the media researcher is ultimately concerned with the question of effects. What do actual, contemporary audiences 'do' with the text and how does it enter into and influence their culture? The question is not how was the text produced so much as what meanings does it produce and reproduce.

The Social Cognition of the Active Viewer

Uses and gratifications theory

What audiences 'do' with texts is the subject of the 'uses and gratifications' approach to the mass media (Blumler and Katz, 1974). This approach, which seems to take the opposite view from that of the structuralist, crystalline text, proposed a 'toolkit' model of the text, where audiences were wholly unconstrained in making what they wished of the text. Thus viewers have been found to watch television mainly for reasons of entertainment or diversion, social utility and personal relationships, reality orientation or information seeking and personal identity and values (McQuail *et al.*, 1972; Rubin, 1985; Rosengren *et al.*, 1985). Meanings existed solely in the diverse minds of the powerful and self-motivated audience. Now labelled 'vulgar gratificationism', Blumler *et al.* (1985) acknowledge that uses and gratifications has suffered a problem with the 'disappearing message' in its underestimation of the power of the text which parallels that of the critical school's 'disappearing audience' (Fejes, 1984). Each school tends to ignore the central subject matter of the other. The resulting location of meaning in the text by those who focus on texts and in the viewers by those who study audiences has meant that the division of labour has resulted in contradictory or oppositional theories of television meanings.

Active and passive audiences

The uses and gratifications school, together with the rise of social cognition in traditional mass communications, has led to the now widespread notion of the 'active viewer' of television. This parallels the rise of the active viewer in the critical school of mass communications, with the introduction of reception aesthetics and reader-response theories in literary criticism (see later). The active viewer makes sense of programmes relatively unconstrained by the structure of the text, drawing instead upon his or her interests, knowledge and experience. The concept of activity has been much used and little defined, often signifying primarily a break with past elitist conceptions of passive viewers (and superior analysts). However vaguely defined, the concept has provoked a considerable body of interesting research, often on children, whose passivity has been of great public concern and yet whose activity on viewing is most apparent if one actually watches them.

For example, following a broadly Piagetian and semiotic framework, Hodge and Tripp (1986) analyse children's developing understandings of television drama. They show how children make sense of programmes according to their level of sociocognitive development. The important point is that children do not simply have more or less complete versions of adult understandings but that they generate their own equally coherent and relevant understandings. These depend on their ability to make inferences, their social scripts and knowledge schemas, and their understandings of the difference between fiction and reality (see also Dorr, 1983, on the stages of development which children go through in developing this distinction). As knowledge guides their interpretations, children's viewing can be seen as active and the resultant meanings may differ widely from that given by the programmes. Collins (1983) takes a similar perspective, although his view of the texts being interpreted is propositional rather than semiotic. He focused specifically on the comprehension of causal links in narrative sequence, showing how children gradually develop schemas which allow them to infer the relations between portrayed motives, actions and consequences. Similarly, they must develop the ability to discriminate plot-relevant and irrelevant details. Such developments are dependent on general stages of cognitive developments and children of different ages up to around ten years old make quite different inferential connections between the events portrayed. This research provides little analysis of the structure of the texts under study, but even so, the kinds of interpretive work which viewers must do is implicit in those aspects of the text which are identified, for example ellipsis, flashbacks, parallel narratives, plots and subplots. Viewers must make knowledgeable inferences even to construct the 'true' and coherent order of events.

This approach to the 'active viewer' reconstructs theories of social knowledge as interpretive resources of viewers, as dynamic and directive rather than as accumulations of static, known facts to which television may merely contribute or override. Findings within social cognition, such as people's bias towards seeking confirmatory rather than falsifying evidence, their knowledge of standardised event scripts, or the development of story grammars may be applied not only to the interpretation of events in everyday life but also to viewers' making sense of television. As people are increasingly seen as active interpreters of everyday life they inevitably become active viewers also. This research on television interpretation suffers consequently from similar problems to those of social cognition, such is the penalty for borrowing from other domains. Hence research on the active viewer tends to be overly constructive, neglecting the role of the text, to be overly cognitive, neglecting the role of emotions and actions, to be overly individualistic, reducing the social act of viewing to the individual act of cognising.

These latter two points are to some extent overcome by Levy and Windahl's (1985) broader typology of audience activity, deriving from the integration of the social cognition of viewing with uses and gratifications theory. They identify two dimensions defining this typology. The first concerns the communication sequence, placing the act of viewing in the context of the period before viewing, in which viewers select and anticipate programmes, and interact socially concerning these plans, and the period after viewing in which viewers may selectively recall what they saw, retain certain character identifications, and discuss their impressions with others. The second dimension distinguishes three types of audience orientation towards viewing: selectively, involvement, and utility.

Nonetheless, this approach is still reductionist in its use of cognition: viewers may select but they cannot construct, meanings may be chosen or not but they are still given by the text. Further, Levy and Windahl interpret 'active' as meaning conscious, which, while fitting the ordinary connotations of activity does not fit with the constructivist school of either social psychology or mass communications. In these, the very act of making sense is inherently a constructive act, and without this act, there is no meaning, conscious or unconscious. Most important, this taxonomy suggests types of viewing activity theorised in the absence of the text, ironically more noticeable for mass communications than for social cognition, which easily regards life as a Rorshach blot. Indeed, the question of how social cognition is constrained by the structure of the environment is especially amenable to the study of the mass media, where the programme or text is readily available and hard to ignore.

Reception Theory and Reader-Response Criticism

A theory of the interaction between readers and texts, or viewers and programmes, is required. This may be provided by literary critical developments in reader-oriented theories which specifically address the centrality of the person in the interpretative process. In this section I will outline the major concepts of reception and reader-response theorists, after which I will present some of the empirical work resulting from the application of these theories to popular culture.

Arguably, some analyses of actual texts can themselves be read as attempts to specify not what texts mean, independent of their readers, but how they contribute to meaning-making by the reader. For example, in their volume analysing the popular British soap opera, *Coronation Street*, Dyer *et al.* (1981) could be said to explore not the meanings 'in' the text so much as the relationships between the world portrayed and the world in which the viewers actually live, exploring the probable viewing experiences of the audience in the context of this contrast. They identify the conventional and literary devices by which the text constructs a coherent whole which guides the viewer towards certain understandings. For example, the programme permits the viewer an awareness of certain contradictions (as in its conception of 'woman'—as both powerful and conventionally feminine) while disguising or denying others (as in the conception of 'work'—as both central and yet invisible). The programme is shown to result from the resolution of two conflicting aims: to be 'realistic', to connect with the experience of viewers, to be authentic, and on the other hand, to be entertaining and fit the conventions and requirements of the medium and the genre. These conventions concern narrative form (for example, cliff-hanger, speed of events, interplay between multiple plots), production requirements (for example, finance, schedules, deadlines, ratings), characterisation (for example, consistency, development, depth), and a general notion of viewers' pleasures (for example, nostalgia, conservativism, range of positions for identification, balance between serious and comic), and so forth. In essence, an analysis of the structuring of the text, its context of production, dominant themes and genre conventions themselves embody an implicit representation of the interpretative role of the reader, specifying what knowledge they must bring to bear, what inferences are required for coherence, and the concerns that should motivate their reading.

The text-reader metaphor

Within literary theory, several schools of thought have recently focused on the relationship between texts and readers. These theories are applicable to programmes and viewers and, even, to social situations and their participants. In Germany, a variety of theorists offer what together is termed 'reception aesthetics' or reception theory. In Italy, Eco (1979a) has theorised the 'role of the reader' and in America, diverse literary critics have adopted the reader-response approach to texts (Suleiman and Crosman, 1980; Tompkins, 1980). There are problems in relating these approaches to the predominantly Marxist critical school (see Collins *et al.*, 1986; Curran *et al.*, 1977; Hall *et al.*, 1980). In some ways, reader-oriented theories are opposed to Marxism, apparently offering a view emphasising psychological reductionism, an undermining of hegemony and separation of interpretation from materialist theories of production and context (Holub, 1984). However, these different approaches are compatible in their similar use of semiotics or literary criticism for textual analysis and in their interest in theorising the role of the reader or audience. I will turn to the empirical work arising from this convergence later but will first consider these reader-oriented theories, focusing specifically on the work of Iser, Jauss and Eco.

Reader-oriented theories (see Hohendahl, 1974; Holub, 1984; Suleiman and Crosman, 1980; Tompkins, 1980) begin by recognising the dual problems of unlimited semiosis and divergent readings: in both theory and practice, one cannot specify a unique, fixed and bounded meaning which lies inherently 'in' a text; and different readers may make very different, but equally meaningful and coherent, readings of a text. As Iser says:

> The work itself cannot be identical with the text or with its actualisation but must be situated somewhere between the two. It must inevitably be virtual in character, as it cannot be reduced to the reality of the text or to the subjectivity of the reader, and it is from this virtuality that it derives its dynamism. As the reader passes through the various perspectives offered by the text, and relates the different views and patterns to one another, he sets the work in motion, and so sets himself in motion, too (Iser, 1980, p. 106).

The role of readers has always been implicitly central to those theories of literature in which the work is evaluated in terms of its defamiliarising function, its ability to challenge habitual perceptions, or the imagery to which it gives rise on reading. In particular, Igarden's (1973) phenomenological approach can be seen as a key precursor of reception aesthetics, for he developed a conception of the text as a 'schematised structure' to be cognitively completed or concretised by the reader. Without this concretising process, the text is indeterminate, not yet meaningful (i.e. 'virtual'), awaiting the reader's exercise of phantasy (and thus producing Eco's 'realised text', 1979a). Holub (1984) traces the origins of reception theory to the bringing together of this phenomenological approach with that of semiotics, this latter providing a social theory of the contextualisation of meaning with which to ground the phenomenological approach within contexts of production and consumption.

The reception theories of Iser, Jauss and Eco

Reception theory argues that as a communicative act, the text cannot make sense independently of an interpreting reader, and the analyst's role now is to elucidate the 'model reader' (Eco, 1979a) or the 'implied reader' (Iser, 1980) or the 'horizon of expectations' (Jauss, 1982) presumed by the text, and to determine where and how the model reader (and, ideally, the actual reader) is required to contribute in order for the text to hold together. 'The author thus has to foresee a model of the possible reader (hereafter Model reader) supposedly able to deal interpretatively with the same expressions in the same way as the author deals generatively with them' (Eco, 1979a, p. 7). In this way, texts can represent communicative strategies.

Iser also is concerned with the process of reading, focusing on the 'mental images formed when attempting to construct a consistent and cohesive aesthetic object' (Holub, 1984, p. 84). At any one point in reading, these mental images form the 'wandering viewpoint', the point at which the reader is phenomenologically present in the text. It represents the reader's construction of meaning thus far ('retention') and also the resource against which expectations are formed and future reading is evaluated ('protension'). The process is guided by principles of consistency and coherence, and the resultant mental images can be seen as a Gestalt.

The role of the reader

Eco draws more on semiotic concepts, particularly that of the code, in his analysis of the 'role of the reader', and thus he emphasises more the socially located nature of the act of reading:

> The existence of various codes and subcodes, the variety of sociocultural circumstances in which a message is emitted (where the codes of the addressee can be different from those of the sender), and the rate of initiative displayed by the addressee in making presuppositions and abductions—all result in making a message . . . an empty form to which various possible senses can be attributed' (Eco, 1979a, p. 5).

However, the reader is affected by the reading just as she or he affects the textual meaning through the constructive process of reading: 'A well-organised text on the one hand presupposes a model of competence coming, so to speak, from outside the text, but on the other hand works to build up, by merely textual means, such a competence' (Eco, 1979a, p. 8). The model reader of a text can be discovered by analysing textual codes, use of stereotyped overcoding, co-reference, rhetoric, inference, frames, genre and so forth, all of which comprise textual strategies or conventions by which the reader is invited to interpose his or her cultural competence into the interpretative process in order to make sense of the text. Iser analyses texts in terms of two key processes, the location of gaps or 'blanks' which require inferential completion by the reader and the use of negation, in which the reader's preconceptions and social norms are first recognised and then questioned or undermined by the text.

Openness and closure

Eco introduces a distinction unique in reception theory which has become very influential, namely that between open and closed texts (1979a). He exemplifies these through the analysis of Joyce's *Ulysses* and

Fleming's James Bond novels respectively (1979b), although he notes that most texts fall somewhere in between, having both open and closed aspects. Open texts envisage a variety of interpretations or textual realisations. Moreover, they deliberately manipulate the interrelations between these different readings, thereby creating irony, allegory and satire. Closed texts, on the other hand, aim for a particular and specific reading:

> They apparently aim at pulling the reader along a predetermined path, carefully displaying their effects so as to arouse pity or fear, excitement or depression at the due place and at the right moment. Every step of the 'story' elicits just the expectation that its further course will satisfy (Eco, 1979a, p. 8).

However, because they tend to be aimed at the average reader, closed texts (whether road signs or a Fleming novel) can give rise to unforeseen interpretations ('aberrant readings') because of the sociocultural circumstances of actual readers. Consequently, they may become indeterminate in meaning.

This mapping of high culture on to open and popular culture on to closed texts would seem elitist. Allen (1985), Fiske (1987), Seiter (1981), and others have has disagreed with Eco, arguing strongly that certain aspects of popular culture, especially soap opera, are fairly open in important respects. For example, soap operas resist closure in their absence of beginnings and endings, and they not only specify multiple viewpoints on the events portrayed, but also thrive on the interplay between these viewpoints. Any text draws upon cultural meanings, does not (cannot) fully specify contexts, and gains its meaning from paradigmatic selections (Fiske, 1982) where the reader must supply the paradigm of selected and non-selected options at any choice point. Certainly, the model reader is less theoretically interesting the more closed the text, and as a semiotician, Eco focuses on the more interesting cases. But for a media researcher or psychologist, if a highly popular television text merely requires repeated rehearsal of stereotyped knowledge, this must be studied for its experiential consequences.

Problems with reader-oriented theories

The concept of the open text has been enthusiastically adopted by researchers of popular culture in the last few years. In the process, the concept has become somewhat blurred in meaning. Specifically, it is most frequently used as a synonym for indeterminacy. For example, Buckingham (1987) writes 'Soap operas can therefore be seen to possess a greater degree of "openness" or "indeterminacy" than many other television genres' (p. 36). Thus empirical evidence of divergent readings is uncritically taken as evidence for an open text. Yet this is quite different from Eco's original use of the concept, and is in fact the opposite of Eco's meaning. As described above, closed texts are more indeterminate because of their inability to control or anticipate actual social conditions of reading, while the breadth of vision and demanding nature of the open text makes unexploited interpretative resources and hence unanticipated readings far less likely:

> As for aberrant presuppositions and deviating circumstances, they are not realizing any openness, but, instead, producing mere states of indeterminacy. What I call open texts are, rather, reducing such as indeterminacy, whereas closed texts, even though aiming at eliciting a sort of 'obedient' co-operation, are in the last analysis randomly open to every pragmatic accident (Eco, 1979a, pp. 6–7).

Certainly, there are theoretical and practical problems in distinguishing openness from indeterminacy unless one invokes the concept of authorial intention. For mass culture texts, authorial intention is especially hard to specify. Yet this issue is critical for the issue of power and influence. If a text intends multiple interpretations, then empirical observations of divergence in interpretation among readers or viewers may indicate a powerful role for the text and provide evidence of communicative success. If the text intends a single interpretation, the divergence indicates aberrant readings and a powerful role for the viewer which, from the author or text's viewpoint constitutes communicative failure. Eco's argument that different texts are structured so as to implicate readers in different ways is too important to put aside, for the point concerns the communicative relation between text and reader. To treat openness and indeterminacy as synonymous is to lose the possibility of an author who intends openness (and structures the text to ensure multiple readings) and hence also the possibility that divergence indicates communicative success on the part of the text.

There is a further ambiguity in reception theory concerning the nature of the role of the reader. In some writings it would appear that the role of the reader comprises filling in the gaps left by the text and intended by the text for the reader to complete. In other writings, however, the role of the reader is seen as truly constructive, so that the reader may provide, or contribute to, the frames which structure the emergent meanings. In some senses then, the role of the reader in reception theory is relatively passive compared, say, to a sociocognitive view of interpretation, in which the social knowledge of the viewer would provide them with interpretative frames independent of and possibly different from those offered by the text. The use of the term 'invitation' (e.g. Buckingham, 1987) evades this problem, for the force of the term 'invite' is conveniently vague: is the force of the invitation such that one can or cannot refuse to follow the text?

Finally, there is a problem in specifying the structure of this virtual text or schematised structure: if there was a problem before in specifying the 'crystalline' text independently of the reader, then the problem is not eliminated for we must now specify the nature of the virtual text. Some would argue for the impossibility of specifying even the virtual text (Fish,

1980), while others would change the nature of the question:

> Instead of taking the proliferation of interpretations as an obstacle to knowledge, can one attempt to make it an object of knowledge, asking how it is that literary works have the meaning they do for readers? . . . a proper description of a literary work must refer to the meanings it has for readers . . . such a semiotics would be a theory of reading and its object would not be literary works themselves but their intelligibility: the ways in which they make sense, the ways in which readers have made sense of them (Culler, 1981, pp. 48–50).

The Convergence of Research on the Empirical Audience

The possibility of an integration between theories of texts and of readers is an exciting one in relation to developments in media theory. A key question becomes that of the actual contribution that readers of viewers make to the negotiation of meaning. As these viewers are unknown to typically middle-class analysts, being from the whole spectrum of diversity in gender, age, ethnicity, class, and religion, the empirical study of audiences would seem to be called for. Such a study holds out the promise of combining the energies of traditional and critical mass communications on the same problem, that of audiences making sense of programmes. It would involve introducing a theory of the text-reader relationship in answer to the 'lack of theoretical integration' and 'disappearing message' currently causing problems for the traditional study of audiences. In their aptly titled paper, 'Reaching out', Blumler *et al.* (1985) acknowledge that 'we must therefore build into our outlook an explicit recognition that texts are not infinitely open and may allow a limited number of possible readings' (p. 260). And from the critical 'side', Hall notes that

> there seem some grounds for thinking that a new and exciting phase in so-called audience research, of a quite new kind, may be opening up . . . the use of the semiotic paradigm promises to dispel the lingering behaviourism which has dogged mass-media research for so long, especially in its approach to content (Hall, 1980, p. 131).

Resistance to convergence

Carey (1985) endorses this move towards audience-oriented research by critical scholars, but wishes to reject a convergence with traditional mass communications. He calls for a major reorientation in mass communications research, arguing that 'the search for a positivist science of communications' (p. 27) should be abandoned because 'the central tradition of effects research has been a failure on its own terms' (p. 28). His proposed alternative, cultural studies, draws 'more on the vocabulary of poetry and politics and less on the vocabulary of metaphysics and determinism' (p. 29) and emphasises the issues of class, ideology, and power. He justly points out that 'the positivist resistance to cultural studies, beyond the ever-present desire to maintain a distinction between hard science and soft scholarship, between knowledge and opinion, is grounded in a deep political instinct' (p. 32).

Allen (1985) resists this move towards convergence between cultural studies and traditional mass communications because of the inherent reductionism, ahistorical approach, and oversimplification of the latter. Culler too (see also Holub, 1984) argues that 'well-intentioned empirical research can miscarry' (Culler, 1981, p. 52) and that 'there is little need to concern oneself with the design of experiments [because] there already exist more than enough interpretations with which to begin' (p. 53). While many literary interpretations of high culture texts exist, this is not true for popular culture texts: these interpretations must be obtained empirically. More importantly, in seeking convergence with the critical school, the traditional school is in a mood to admit problems and engage in rethinking which could be productive, while not throwing out the findings obtained and methodologies used hitherto.

Schroder (1987) identifies five problems with the traditional approach which hinder convergence. He argues that the traditional approach focuses on: individual, behavioural, and short-term effects rather than long-term societal effects; on attitudinal change rather than the more common consistencies which must also be accounted for; on attitudes and opinions as individual entities rather than as part of structured belief systems; an overestimation of the importance of interpersonal relations in mediating the influence of television; and he argues finally, 'they are still clinging to the familiar quantitative methodology, although it appears to be unable to capture the multidimensionality and complexity of the media's symbolic structures, as well as the ambiguities and contradictions of audience experiences' (1987, p. 13).

To balance these criticisms, Schroder also discusses the need for reorientation within the critical or cultural studies approach:

> the critical tradition will have to abandon its insistence on powerful media effects, and the accompanying tendency to regard the media text as a one-dimensional entity, rather than as a multiplicity of meanings to be decoded by the audience. . . . It has become necessary to examine how the audience actually selects, perceives, decodes, and makes sense of media texts (pp. 16–17).

However:

> Social scientists, on the other hand, fully self-sufficient in the gathering of empirical data and firmly grounded in sociological understandings of the media audience, need cultural studies insights in order to tackle any analysis of textual structures (p. 28).

In favour of convergence, one can additionally note that empirical data has some independence from its methodology and so can sometimes be informative despite doubts about its methodology. The traditional approach can benefit from critical analysis of its scientific assumptions and, conversely, it would be redundant for cultural studies to reinvent empirical methods and existing psychological findings about 'actual' viewers. But most important here, cultural studies can provide the theory of the text for traditional mass communications. This may be extended to much of social psychology, because this too suffers from a simplistic conception of social stimuli: the idea of the social world as text and of social life as practice should have wider currency (see Chapter 3).

Empirical reception research

Notwithstanding the above doubts, many researchers have begun empirical research within cultural studies. Reception theory raises too many interesting empirical issues to be ignored: what are real readers' 'horizons of expectations', how do they fit the schematic structures provided by texts, what differences do different sociocultural backgrounds make, do ordinary and specialist readings concur?, and so on. Indeed, having begun such research, it is becoming clear that one of the best arguments in favour of empirical research is that often actual audiences surprise the researchers who study them. The recent empirical research is, in many ways, necessarily exploratory, asking basic and yet unanswered questions concerning the nature of readers' and viewers' interpretations of popular culture. Using ethnographic, psychoanalytic or literary critical perspectives, several authors (e.g. Ang, 1985; Radway, 1984, 1985) are beginning to generate interesting insights into what real people 'do' with texts.

After studying viewers of the British soap opera, *Crossroads,* Hobson begins to challenge the emphasis on programmes *per se* as objects of analysis, and to think in terms of 'flow' (Newcomb, 1988; Williams, 1974):

> it became clear through the process of study that the audience do not watch programmes as separate or individual items, nor even as types of programmes, but rather they build up an understanding of themes over a much wider range of programmes and length of time viewing (Hobson, 1982, p. 107).

She concluded that watching soap opera was part of the women's everday lives, and *Crossroads* was commonly watched during household activities. Viewers were active rather than passive during viewing: they were involved in the programme not bored by it, they could be critical of the programme rather than mindlessly accepting at face value whatever was shown; and they built up complex knowledge about the programme's history and characters. Finally, she argues that the programme served various functions for the women: it provided examples of strong women; a means of structuring their day; a topic of conversation; a time which was defined as 'theirs'; and it raised important issues for them which touched their own experiences of life.

Like Hobson, Ang (1985) focused on a single programme, *Dallas,* and used an open ended methodology to examine viewers' experiences of the programme. Her analysis is based on some forty letters written in response to a magazine advertisement which requested viewers to explain their responses to *Dallas.* Ang's analysis of these letters is concerned with two key issues: pleasure and ideology, especially feminist ideology.

Both Hobson and Ang interpret their data in relation to research questions with illustrative excerpts from the viewers' accounts presented verbatim. Ang argues that viewers' experiences are always ambivalent and contradictory, very different from popular assumptions about the straight-forward nature of soap opera viewing. She focuses on the sociocultural and psychological nature of viewers' 'consumption' of *Dallas,* making the role of the viewer a mediator in the transmission of ideological meanings. Involvement with characters was found to be as central to the experience of viewing. Realism, not commonly associated with a glamorous American soap opera like *Dallas,* was found to exist not at the literal but the symbolic level of meaning. In other words, the characters are experienced as emotionally human, if not literally realistic. As she puts it, they are judged in terms of emotional realism, not empirical realism. Viewers recognise the parallel between the 'structures of feeling' represented in the programme and as experienced in their own lives: 'this structure of feeling can be called the *tragic* structure of feeling; tragic because of the idea that happiness can never last for ever but, quite the contrary, is precarious' (1985, p. 46).

Much of Ang's research raises rather than solves questions. For example, does soap opera have a radical or conservative effect on viewers? What is the relation between (and the viewers' position on) the ideology of mass culture (i.e. mass culture is bad, alienating, cheap, etc.) and the populist ideology (i.e. each to their own, people's experience as primary)? These questions place empirical work on soap opera in relation to theoretical debates. Unfortunately, Ang's empirical data are often only suggestive. They place issues on the research agenda, but they do not take us much further either methodologically or substantively.

Morley (1980) relates his research on audience decodings of the *Nationwide* programme to the structure of the text, as analysed in Brunsdon and Morley (1978). Decoding becomes important, Morley argues because:

> before messages can have 'effects' on audiences, they must be decoded. 'Effects' is thus a shorthand, and inadequate, way of marking the point where audiences differentially read and made sense of messages which have been transmitted, and act on those meanings within the context of the rest of their situation and experience (1980, p. 11).

Morley examined the intepretations made of the popular current affairs programme *Nationwide* by internally homogeneous groups from a variety of class and labour positions—trade unionists, students, engineering apprentices, bank managers, and so forth. He compared the groups' interpretations to each other and to his prior analysis, examining in particular, their match or mismatch with three hypothetical interpretative frameworks or modes of text–viewer relationship, namely dominant, oppositional, and negotiated.

He concludes that firstly, dominant, negative, and oppositional codes are all used by viewers, although often in combination or in inconsistent ways. Secondly, social class relates to code use, although this relation is complex. Viewers thus vary in how critical or accepting they are of a television text. Much of the programme was perceived uncritically as 'obvious' or 'natural'. At other times, viewers consciously recognised textual mechanisms of 'preferring' or directing interpretation. Some viewers made very little sense of the programme, being alienated from its discourse. Others made sense of the programme but in divergent ways.

Morley discusses the problems of interpreting the interpretations and analysing a large body of unstructured interviews. Perhaps wisely, he refrains from reducing the data to quantitative categories and presents instead large sections of the material verbatim. Unfortunately, Morley does not attempt to reveal the structural relations between the individual interpretative statements that he quotes other than to point out whether they support or contradict the next quotation. Nonetheless, this is provocative research which paves the way for future studies of audience interpretation and establishes the commitment of cultural studies to issues of actual textual interpretation.

In another study, Radway (1984, 1985) investigated the readers of popular romance novels, relating the women's interpretations to the texts themselves and to the readings made by literary critics. She locates her work within semiotics and reader-response theory, being concerned with:

> textual meaning as the product of a complex transaction between an inert textual structure, composed of verbal signifiers, and an actively productive reader, who constructs those signifiers as meaningful signs on the basis of previously learned interpretive procedures and cultural codes (Radway, 1985, p. 340).

She argues further that:

> Different readers read differently because they belong to what are known as various interpretive communities, each of which acts upon print differently and for different purposes (Radway, 1985, p. 341).

Her interviews revealed that in many ways, the romance readers interpreted the novels according to their interests and attitudes towards language. For example, she shows how, despite the frequently weak and subservient behaviour of the heroines, the readers believed them to be strong and independent because they were explicitly described thus at the beginning of the novels. This reflects, she argues, not the stupidity of the readers, but their belief that words are selected for accuracy and that the original statements remain fixed and true: consistency is sacrificed for the belief in the factual nature of language. Together with other examples, this suggests a different form of literacy from that of literary critics.

Similarly, although the novels repeatedly used secondary foil characters to contrast with the central couple, the women refused to acknowledge their roles, perceiving only action which furthered the ideal conclusion for the hero and heroine. Radway argues that these novels show their readers how the domestic life is the way to true happiness while the women justify the time devoted to reading by believing that the novels, through their factual or historical content, further their self-improvement.

A further project is the research on cross-cultural reception of *Dallas* among diverse ethnic groups in Jerusalem, America and Japan conducted by Katz and Liebes (Katz and Liebes, 1986; Liebes, 1984; Liebes and Katz, 1986; Katz, Iwao and Liebes, 1988). Initially started to examine the notion of cultural imperialism from American programmes in other countries, this research has compared the interpretations of the same programme made by many viewers of different cultures and religions:

> We are not attempting to demonstrate 'effect'; rather, we are interested in those processes that are prerequisite to possible effect, namely, understanding, interpretation, and evaluation, both explicit and implicit (Liebes, 1984, p. 46).

The study of viewers is related to the text by detailed consideration of the cultural, mythic, and moral messages and themes in *Dallas*. They frame the research within Newcomb and Hirsch's (1984) notion of cultural forum: television drama provides a forum for viewers' discussion and negotiation of issues of cultural, moral and personal significance, particularly those issues which are unresolved or contentious. In many ways this research provides a series of illustrations and confirmations of the points discussed under the cultural studies and soap opera sections of the previous chapter. In a later paper, Liebes and Katz (1986) attempt a more structured approach by postulating that viewers of different cultural backgrounds manifest different degrees of 'critical distance' from the text. This suggests two qualitatively different modes of interpretation, the critical and the referential, which contrast with, say, Morley's (1980) oppositional and dominant, although clearly the two distinctions have much in common. Nonetheless, as with Morley's work, there is an implicit evaluative bias in Liebes and Katz's work in favour of the critical (or oppositional) reading, which is rather suspiciously to be found more commonly in American than Russian Jews (or, for Morley, among the left wing rather than the right). There is a clear need for theories which would relate cultural groups to textual interpretations so that audience decodings could themselves be interpreted in the context of a prior knowledge of the culture. This would permit the testing of predictions of decodings given cultural or social background, thus avoiding both a presumed reductionism of decoding to cultural group or the *post hoc* reasoning often resorted to in order to account for group differences.

There are various other empirical studies of audience decodings which should be noted in this context. For example, Buckingham (1987) studied adolescents' reception of the British soap opera *EastEnders,* Seiter *et al.* (1987) examined the reception of soap opera in America, Schroder (1988) has interviewed viewers of *Dynasty* in Denmark, and Herzog (1986) has used projective measures to analyse the role of fantasy in the reception of *Dallas* in Germany. Each of these studies is searching for an adequate methodology to capture the richness and complexity of viewers' response to the fictional media, typically soap opera. And each in some ways produces data which challenge prior assumptions about the audience based solely on a consideration of the text. In general, however, both theoretical and methodological frameworks are lacking in response to this new challenge to study the audience in relation to both a sophisticated textual analysis and an appreciation of the resources and activities of the viewers.

The Active Viewer and the Effects of Television

Thus far this chapter has explored the convergence of cultural studies and traditional mass communications on the concept of the 'active viewer'. The concept has considerable implications for the theory of the text, indeed theories of texts and viewers are inextricably related, implicitly if not explicitly. The concept of the active viewer also has implications for the nature of the viewing experience or mode of interaction with the television, and for the effects of viewing. Both these implications require further development in the context of a more integrated theory of viewing motives and effects, on which work is now beginning (Rosengren *et al.,* 1985). Any theory of viewing must adopt some conception of texts and take some stand on the relative activity or power of viewers with respect to texts. One problem, then, in the move towards a more integrated and complex approach to viewing television is that existing theories of media effects tend to embody different conceptions of the viewer and, consequently, of the text.

Assumptions about audiences

Gerbner's theory of cultivation (e.g. Gerbner and Gross, 1976; Gerbner *et al.,* 1986) tacitly adopts a passive conception of the viewer. His use of content analysis implies a theory of the text as containing given meanings, although on a connotational or ideological rather than a literal level (unlike the passive viewer and given, denotational meanings of the Behaviourism or social learning theory approaches; Bandura and Walters, 1964). Thus Gerbner does not conceive of divergent interpretations on watching violent meanings for such contents can only cultivate an endorsement of the moral and legal status quo. The role of the viewer is limited to the veridical perception of statistical frequencies and their connotative associations, as the hypothesis is that the more one views, the more one adopts the television reality. The viewer does not construct his or her own meanings, and has freedom only in the choice to be a heavy or light viewer.

Similarly, the agenda-setting (McCombs and Shaw, 1972) and spiral of silence (Noelle-Neumann, 1974) theories imply a relatively passive viewer, for the effect of the media is conceptualised as telling viewers what to think about or what not to think, or talk, about. Recent developments which link this approach to uses and gratifications research (McCombs and Weaver, 1985) imply a more active viewer, as problematic results within these paradigms are revealed to be a function of the mediating role of viewers' motivations and, hence, programme selections. Again, the knowledge gap hypothesis (Tichenor *et al.*, 1970), which originally posited that the media generated a differential distribution of knowledge as a function of cognitive differences between viewers being passively applied to television, is being likewise reconceptualised. Thus differential motivations to seek out and acquire information about current affairs become important mediators, again a more active conception of the viewer. In any of these theories, except cultivation, very little is said of the text (Fejes, 1984): content analysis is used merely to index issue mention, salience, and history. How issues are framed, combined, conventionalised or evaluated is not analysed.

Modes of viewing

Rubin (1984, 1985) has developed uses and gratifications by categorising the different possible motivations for viewing into broadly active or passive modes, a development of McQuail, Blumler and Brown's (1972) notion of different modes of 'media-person interaction'. On factor analysing associations between different viewing motivations, Rubin found two main factors, instrumental (seeking knowledge, reality orientation, social utility) and ritualised (habitual, mindless viewing). He suggests that the active: passive distinction should be studied as a link in a larger causal chain which connects text to effect via the mode of media–person interaction, for him, instrumental or ritualised. In support of this proposal, one may note tentative evidence for the mediating role of viewing motivations or modes in the process of media effects. Carveth and Alexander (1985) showed that ritualised viewing motives are more conducive to media effects. On the other hand, Hawkins and Pingree (1983) found the opposite in their cultivation study, showing that the cultivation effect observed held only for those viewing for instrumental motives.

While the mode of viewing is clearly important, such research will find contradictory results as above if the concept of effect is not pluralised, as argued in Chapter 1. Maybe cultivation effects occur only for viewers actively seeking out information about the world from the media; otherwise their social reality beliefs will not be influenced. Other effects processes may require ritualised viewers, with their defences down and a willingness to absorb images uncritically. Or maybe one should examine the text more closely in relation to prior beliefs of the viewer. The process of reinforcement, for example, implies that the text mirrors existing social knowledge (rarely checked for in reinforcement studies) while attitude change implies a discrepancy between text and knowledge which may only exist in certain cases. One may speculate that the former process would be favoured by a ritualised mode and the latter by an instrumental model of viewing.

The contribution of social psychology

In attempting to integrate the variety of effects processes with both the mode of viewing and the relationship between textual meanings and viewers' social knowledge and beliefs, one may draw on a recent, cognitively-oriented theory of attitude change proposed by Petty and Cacioppo in their 'elaboration likelihood' model (Petty *et al.*, 1981). This theory makes a parallel distinction between active and passive viewing: central versus peripheral modes of processing. While the mechanistic imagery is unfortunate, this theory begins to make just the distinctions needed by theories of media effects. They propose that persuasion or attitude change is a function of the degree of cognitive elaboration of the message, where characteristics of message, source, and audience determine the likelihood of this elaboration process. This cognitive elaboration must be self-generated, for when arguments in favour of a position are provided by the text, this is far less influential than when the audience must generate their own arguments. The central route to persuasion involves the thoughtful weighing up of relevant arguments, while the peripheral route involves affective associations and simple inferences from contextual cues. Hence, for central route persuasion, the quality of the arguments are more important, for they are carefully considered, while for the peripheral route contextual cues such as source credibility become more important. While Petty and Cacioppo argue that attitude change is more persistent, resistant to counter-argument and predictive of behaviour if achieved through the central route, one could also argue that the ubiquity and constant reiteration of peripherally processed messages serves to keep even more temporary effects continually alive and reinforced. They proceed to examine in detail the differing conditions under which the two modes of persuasion occur. Again, the relevance to elaborating the active/passive viewer distinction is clear. The kinds of determining conditions concern the focus of attention (focused or distracted), the repetition of messages (this results in persuasion only if good arguments, otherwise the problems with the argument become salient), the degree of personal involvement with the issue (favouring critical processing and hence the possibility of central persuasion), the degree of personal responsibility for the consequences of following the position advocated, and so forth. Thus the context of persuasion, the structure of the message and the degree of cognitive activity of the person together determine the amount and nature of the persuasion which may result.

Another related distinction in social psychology comes from Langer's

(Langer *et al.*, 1978) mindlessness theory. Langer's mindful processing resembles central route processing or the active viewer and mindlessness resembles the peripheral route and the passive viewer. Each mode has its own dynamics and determinants. Langer's theory connects theories of attitude change to theories of social knowledge, such as Schank and Abelson's (1977) script theory. Here, the existence of well-established representational knowledge structures favours passive processing, in which the person does not perceive anything which contradicts preconceptions, and merely retraces former steps, reruns old experiences and treats the novel as the familiar.

This connects with research on young children comprehending television drama. Collins and Wellman (1982) asked how those who did not understand the narrative as adults did, lacking the required scripts and schemas, did in fact make sense of the narrative. He found that the youngest children were easily distracted by some aspect of the narrative which cued a script that they did possess. They did not perceive the story to be nonsense so much as perceived a completely different story. From the point of introduction of the misleading cue, they 'went off' on their own familiar track, irrespective of the story itself. Older children made more use of mindful or central processing, more closely monitoring the development of the narrative so that those who still lacked the appropriate schemas were at least aware of their lack, and scanned the narrative in an attempt to 'get back on track'. In sum, there are a variety of developments in social psychology which can inform research on the active viewer of television, help to specify the nature of the interpretive resources of the viewer and analyse the determinants of active versus passive viewing.

The Genre of Soap Opera

As mentioned at the outset, and as is implicit especially from the trend towards empirical research within cultural studies, the genre of soap opera has played a central role in the development of reader-oriented, 'active viewer' theories within media studies. The reasons for this are several, but basically stem from the various consequences of soap opera being historically a feminine genre (Fiske, 1987). As a devalued genre, soap opera has somehow evolved outside the critical masculine gaze, and is structured instead according to the 'rhythms of reception' (Modleski, 1982) of its predominantly female, home-based viewers.

Soap opera conventions

Soap opera, peculiar among television drama genres, has no heroes but a multiplicity of equivalent characters. Hence it invites not an exclusive and passive identification but rather an active and participatory involvement or parasocial interaction (Horton and Wohl, 1956). Following the interrupted and interruptable, fragmented structure of the housewife's day, soap opera offers simultaneous multiple narrative strands. Again, like the viewer's repetitive and never-completed daily tasks, the narratives resist closure. Soap operas thus contrast with the more masculine action-adventure shows (Fiske, 1987), which focus mainly on the beginning and, especially, on the ending of stories, in which dramatic tension is structured around the knowledge of an inevitable and final resolution to the events. Instead, soap opera consists of 'endless middle'. Narratives do not so much begin and end as weave in and out of each other, evolving from previous stories, remaining unfinished, full of the potential for future development or transformation. Soap opera thus cannot offer clear and singular solutions to the personal and moral problems portrayed. For example, there can be no 'happy ever after' for marriages never last. Rather they explore a multiplicity of relevant perspectives on the issues (for example, the problematic and conflicting expectations of modern marriage), which implicate but are not resolved by cultural myths, social knowledge, and commonsense discourses. There are no objective truths, no answers, no permanent securities, no uncompromised actions, no absolutes.

Hence, soap opera is unusual among highly popular culture genres in providing a considerable role for the viewer. The viewer's knowledge and experience is a relevant contribution to the text, his or her perspective may be as valid as any portrayed, the relatively strong and 'realistic' women in soap opera further legitimates this active role for the viewer, and the complexity and multiplicity of the text (in terms of both diachronic—or temporal, and synchronic—or simultaneous structures) invite the viewer to impose a certain order or closure according to his or her own notions of what is likely or desirable or meaningful.

As soap opera has played such an important illustrative and interesting role in arguments about the active viewer, and as the empirical research to be presented in later chapters concerning the relations between text and reader was conducted using soap opera, this genre will be explored here as an orientation for the rest of the book. As will be argued in Chapter 3, audience-oriented researchers often give short shrift to the specific conventions of the genre whose interpretations or effects they are studying. In aiming for generality, their ignorance of the text and its genre has in fact had detrimental effects on both the sophistication of previous hypotheses and the interpretation of previous findings in the literature.

Soap opera: History and form

Soap opera has changed in form over its history, beginning with the daily American radio soap operas which served as an advertising vehicle for soap manufacturers, and resulting in a diversity of forms in different media and different countries. Although much has been written on this issue (Buckman, 1984; Cassata and Skill, 1983, Cantor and Pingree, 1983;

Intintoli, 1984; Wober, 1984), I will here adopt a pragmatic definition which follows that of the viewers. Thus the term 'soap opera' is used to refer to a genre of programmes, typically on television, although radio soap operas still exist. They manifest most or all of the following features. They are transmitted at regular and frequent times, often daily. They are aimed predominantly at female viewers, and thus occupy daytime or early evening rather than prime-time slots. They use a fairly constant and large cast and continue for years, building up a faithful audience. They have cheap production values (except American prime-time shows) and are regarded as low prestige entertainment. Soap operas tend to concern the day-to-day activities, the minutiae of the everyday lives of characters who centre on a small community and/or a large family. They attempt simulation of real time and realistic events, with several interweaving narratives whose resolutions overlap rather than coincide with episode bounderies. They make use of the 'cliff-hanger' to ensure continued viewing and focus predominantly on female characters and 'feminine' or domestic concerns.

The American soap operas transmitted in Britain (e.g. *Dallas, Dynasty,* and *Falcon Crest*) are prime-time, expensive, and melodramatic, while the homegrown British soap operas (e.g. *Coronation Street, Brookside,* and *EastEnders*) are early evening, cheap, and everday in subject matter. The former concern the wealthy, the latter concern the working class poor. Nonetheless, in terms of involvement, treatment of moral and political issues, narrative structure, and viewer loyalty, the American and British soap operas are often similar.

The genre has been ridiculed for many years not only by popular opinion, but also by academics, whose distanced and often patronising stance surely hinders their understanding of soap opera viewers:

> One would have to have a passion for sameness, amounting to mania if after six years of viewing *Coronation Street* or *Hawaii Five-O,* one still looked forward eagerly to the next episode (Himmelweit, Swift and Jaeger, 1980, p. 96).

Allen (1985) has argued convincingly that soap operas only present a vision of endless 'sameness' to a non-viewer: to those who know the programme well, a wide range of subtle, complex and historically informed meanings are involved. It is these which create the interest and the experience of viewing soap opera. Specifically, he distinguishes between soap opera's repetitive and simplistic synagmatic structure (the chronologic level of narrative sequencing) and its highly complex paradigmatic structure (the structures of choice and possibility which exist at any one point in time).

The soap opera audience

In Britain, soap operas dominate the audience ratings, attracting massive audiences on a regular basis, and they have become the most popular genre on British television (Wober, 1984). Table 1 shows the viewing figures for three soap operas, revealing demographic variations in audience composition. *Coronation Street* is watched by about one-third of the British population, by rather more women than men and by more older people, especially those from the lower socioeconomic classes. *EastEnders,* watched by a little under one-third of the population, is also watched

TABLE 1. *Viewing figures (adults over 16 years) for three soap operas, expressed as percentages of the total population: IPA Social Class by Age and Sex*

Social class		ABC1			C2DE		
Age (years)		16–34	35–54	55+	16–34	35–54	55+
Population (in millions)							
	Total						
Total	42.305	5.746	6.144	4.359	9.015	7.681	9.360
Men	20.014	2.793	2.962	2.016	4.513	3.771	3.959
Women	22.291	2.953	3.182	2.343	4.502	3.910	5.401
CORONATION STREET (% population)							
Total	33	18	21	27	28	35	56
Men	27	15	15	24	21	28	50
Women	39	22	27	30	35	42	60
EASTENDERS (% population)							
Total	29	28	26	17	33	35	27
Men	23	22	20	13	26	30	24
Women	33	33	32	20	39	40	29
DALLAS (% population)							
Total	20	18	17	16	19	20	24
Men	15	12	12	14	14	17	19
Women	24	23	22	17	24	24	28

Note 1: Figures obtained from Audience Composition Report, BARB/AGB, U.K.

Note 2: Figures are calculated on the basis of audience figures for quarter-hour periods (not complete programmes) averaged over the 4 weeks ending 26/10/86 for the following time periods: *Coronation Street,* ITV (Monday 19.30–19.45); *EastEnders,* BBC1 (Tuesday 19.30–19.45); and *Dallas,* BBC1 (Wednesday 20.00–20.15).

by more women than men. However, *EastEnders* attracts a younger audience. It too is watched more by those of lower socioeconomic class, although this difference is less marked than for *Coronation Street.* One-fifth of the population watch *Dallas:* again, the audience contains more women than men, although the age and class differences are marginal.

Myth and morality

The popularity of soap opera appears to rest on its undemanding nature and its preoccupation with everyday human concerns. It thus can be said to bear a close relation to the simplified and conventionally acceptable aspects of our culture, namely myth and ideology. As with myths and folktales, soap opera and television drama generally fulfils the social functions of justification for and celebration of conventional wisdom and practice in the face of challenge or uncertainty (Allen, 1985; Dyer *et al.,* 1981; Gerbner *et al.,* 1986; Silverstone, 1981). The texts are organised to ensure the clarity of the message and their purpose is to explicate, to embody cultural truths, and to reveal the simple wisdom we can rely upon which underlies the superficial confusions in which we become embroiled. In this sense, soap operas are like myths and folk tales, conventional, conservative and moral.

Soap opera, like more 'serious' television drama, attempts to encompass the unpleasant and problematic aspects of our human relations. However, the success of individual solutions to problems is lauded to the exclusion of sociopolitical solutions (Dyer *et al.,* 1981). 'Unless politics are personalised the soaps can't handle them' (Buckman, 1984, p. 31). Attempts at social relevance or realism are particularly important to the British soap operas: this is endorsed and valued by both producers and viewers. For example, Jack Barton, a former producer of *Crossroads,* says that 'with some of the more serious social comments we've made and issues we've dealt with, in each case they were very carefully thought about and researched, and they have had positive results to the community' (quoted in Hobson, 1982, p. 47). Similarly, Julia Smith, producer of *EastEnders,* has stated that 'I've always thought that you can do an awful lot of information-giving through soap opera. One of the things we try to do with a programme is to make a lot of people ask why' (quoted in *The Times,* 19/2/85).

The viewers clearly gain pleasure from this social realism, saying, for example that 'more people are watching British soap operas because they are now dealing with delicate public issues and are not afraid to delve into these problems' and that 'they portray so many things which *are* happening in the world today and do not shrink away from real life but instead face us with the problems that *do* happen' (viewers quoted in Livingstone, 1988a).

Thus, soap opera serves some of the same functions as cultural myths, connecting with basic human concerns, explaining complex social pheno-mena, providing categories for thought and moral precepts to live by. As another viewer comments, 'we can relate to the situations and sometimes sort your own problems out through listening and doing what the character portrayed has done'.

The notion of soap opera containing latent social messages is often regarded with suspicion or ridicule. Yet consider the representation of motherhood in *EastEnders* (Liebes and Livingstone, 1989). In 1987 this programme featured as central characters, a traditional working class matriarch whose power is waning, two teenage single-parent mothers, one of whom finds refuge in prostitution and the other in an unhappy marriage, a woman whose baby dies of a cot death and is subsequently infertile, an alcoholic mother of an adopted daughter, a health visitor (official mother?), a black woman whose ambitions break up her family, a woman who has had adopted the child born from a rape attack, the religious mother of the local criminal, and so forth. How can the programme, with its inevitably unequal distributions of unhappiness, misfortune and injustice, and its inevitable identification of different motherhood positions with characters of different cultural background, avoid offering complex messages about motherhood?

Stereotyping in soap opera

In his analysis of the world of soap opera, Buckman (1984) concludes: 'All problems on the soaps have to be personalised, and the personalities involved must conform to stereotypes whose views reflect majority thinking' (p. 146), and 'Stereotypes are central to soaps, the foundation of the narrative structure which forms the basis of the genre's appeal. . . . Only when the liberated woman has become a stereotype herself will she be able to take her place in soap opera' (p. 168). He is not proposing a conspiracy theory to brainwash the masses, but instead draws upon cognitive arguments (involving schemata and heuristics) familiar to psychologists. Thus as the genre developed:

> the writers and producers . . . in their rush to get something together, they grabbed at the wisdom they and their audience knew so well, because it was there, it was easy, it was something everyone could swallow without effort, because—being based on good sense—it was something they could justify, if anyone asked them (p. 24).

Cantor and Pingree (1983) examined gender stereotyping using content analysis and showed that the genre tends to support the status quo, glorifying women committed to children rather than a career, associating the less stereotyped characters with negative images, portraying women as people who converse within the family while men converse as professionals and so forth.

Again, in relation to the conservativism of the genre (indeed of television generally), Kreizenbeck (1983) examined the portrayal of morality and sexuality in soap opera as a cautious balance between entertainment and a desire not to shock or alienate the audience. This is achieved through moral judgements offered for actions, so that the 'good' women are family-oriented, non-sexual, and place their careers second, while the 'bad' women are openly seductive, use sex as a weapon, and are often punished for pursuing their careers by unwanted pregnancies:

> The soap opera, by presenting characters who flaunt the values and morals of the audience, strengthens that audience's resolve to hold on to these abused ideals . . . the family is the soap source of spiritual and emotional strength (p. 176).

Yet soap opera is absorbing, human drama, and consequently the stereotypes and moral judgements are fairly subtle and not always obvious at first glance. While stereotypes are often to be found underneath, on the surface exists the wealth of personal details that viewers find satisfying and which contribute to their view of characters as 'like real people'. For example, one viewer says 'I know that after a while the characters do become real people and we are concerned for their well-being just as we are our friends and colleagues' (Livingstone, 1988a). And indeed, after watching the same programme for years if not decades, the accumulating histories and interactions of the characters are bound to complicate any simple or stereotyped perceptions.

Soap opera: An open text?

Having argued that soap opera serves important mythic functions in contemporary society, there are also certain respects in which soap opera deviates from mythic form, constituting what Eco (1979a) would call a more open text. Firstly, mythic narratives centre upon a single agent (the 'hero'). The essence of soap opera, however, is the absence of a central figure. Instead, the drama involves a cluster of interrelated characters who, at different times, come to the fore or retreat to the background.

Secondly, the main theme of soap opera is not that of individual quest but that of human relationships, and preferably a tangle of relationships centrally involving several characters in each story. Soap operas are not primarily concerned with universal problems whose origin and resolution are beyond human control, with external forces (personified as they might be in the figure of the villain) which require magical or superhuman strength to combat. Their concern, for which they require multiple agents, is instead with the all-too-human problems which most of us experience, and thus with what is essentially confused and contradictory. All is not always made clear, endings are not consistently happy, disagreements may endure. This argues from an indeterminate textual structure.

Thirdly, myth assumes a single perspective in which the viewers/readers, hero, other characters and story-teller all share the same understanding of, say, the goodness of the hero, the value of the quest and the wickedness of the villain. In soap opera, this is clearly not the case, and the multiple, often conflicting understandings create the interest, tension, irony, and humour.

Fourthly, closed texts are typically bounded by an identifiable and discrete beginning and ending to each story. In soap opera a problem may be hinted at and the requisite conditions for its occurrence established some time earlier than the event itself. Problems rarely arrive 'out of the blue' and narratives may also disappear with no clear resolution, merely a stalemate and a shift in textual focus. It is a specific feature of soap opera that it should emulate, albeit in selected areas, the lives of the viewers, and so it is concerned to parallel the slow, confused, erratic and often mundane development of events experienced by its viewers in their day-to-day lives (Porter, 1982). For example, Sutherland and Siniawsky (1982) show that, although soap operas tend to punish those who violate moral standards and thus support the status quo, nonetheless 'many of the resolutions were left open to viewers' interpretations' (p. 73).

Jordan (1981) argues that the conventions of closure do not clearly operate in soap operas because the conventions behind particularly British soap opera are mixed, incorporating aspects of social realism, of the American genre of soap opera, and of romantic 'women's' fiction (Buckman, 1984). Thus conventional ideology of class and gender cannot be straightforwardly upheld in soap opera. Born in the days of social consciousness and documentary realism (1960s), British soap operas, in contrast to their American counterparts, cannot be said to simply convey capitalist ideals of money, status, security, ambition, and individual gain, but instead they concern the historically more subversive values of traditional communities which are suspicious of the technological and competitive concerns of the outside world with its claims to science and its lofty disregard of folk wisdom, co-operation, and loyalty to the community. Similarly as regards gender, the conventions of soap opera, developed for a largely female audience, require strong, active women, in direct contradiction to conventional gender roles, as shown in most other television programmes (Durkin, 1985a).

In sum, soap opera is a genre which provides relatively open texts, and thus can be expected to provide a substantial role for the viewer, in that there is no single hero figure, no single perspective expressed, no discrete bounderies to the narratives. On the other hand, soap opera is closed in that it reassures us in our age-old beliefs in the power of the individual, in traditional values of stability, community, patriarchy, and resistance to change. It systematically excludes certain phenomena in its apparently general treatment of everyday concerns, and it is closed in that conclusions may be reached about the moral superiority of one of the expressed views (usually the 'establishment' view).

In soap opera, the variety of perspectives expressed are individually personified in the various characters. Each issue (abortion, marriage, loyalty, etc.) is given an open treatment because different characters each express a different perspective on the issue (Kershaw, 1981). The viewer is presented with a range of often conflicting viewpoints, and the interest lies in their juxtaposition, in the fact that often there is no simple answer, and in the space for the viewer to interpose his or her own views on the issue. Such open discussions frequently take place in the local pub, which serves as the central meeting place of the community. Here suspicions, hints and uncertainties are transformed from private individual concerns into subject matter for public debate.

Openness, familiarity, and longevity all enhance viewers' personal involvement with and loyalty to a soap opera. This involvement is supported not only by the ratings, but also by research on the role that soap opera plays in viewers' lives (Rubin, 1985; Taylor and Mullan, 1986). These show that soap opera is felt to be emotionally satisfying, thought provoking, informative, to provide social comfort and so forth. A variety of social psychological needs may thus be met. One viewer notes that 'when you're watching soap operas you can experience a full range of emotions from anger and despair to sheer joy, excitement and relief' (Livingstone, 1988a). Cognitively, these needs are met differently according to the openness or closure of the text and the consequent role for the viewers in the construction of meanings.

Viewers watch soap opera for many years and become involved with the characters. Thus they build up complex character representations which should reflect the viewers' balance between programme structure and social knowledge. The characters in soap opera become real for people and thus constitute an extension of their social networks and part of their everyday lives.

3
The Role of the Text in Social Psychology

Introduction

Social psychology and media studies have not only a common history but certain parallel developments over the last few decades. In the area of audience research, these parallels may facilitate a convergence between traditional, psychological, empirical approaches with critical, textual approaches to audience interpretation. Later in the book, empirical research will be presented which demonstrates the viability of this convergence. I first wish to broaden the argument by exploring the notion that this convergence between traditional and critical media studies can benefit not only audience research but also the source disciplines. In this chapter, I will consider the contribution which developments in media studies could make to current problems in social psychology, focusing mainly on the potential role of the concept of the text, derived from semiotic theory and as used by critical mass communications, and also on notions of influence or effect from traditional mass communication theory. In the next chapter, I will consider the reverse argument, that social psychology can contribute to media studies by offering a theoretical and empirical resource for studying the viewer. In short, I am arguing for increased permeability of disciplinary boundaries, and increased theoretical 'borrowing' from neighbouring domains. There are a set of related but often unrecognised problems facing social psychology at present which may be substantially aided by borrowing from textual or semiotic theories developed within literary, cultural, and media studies. The first problem concerns the continued use of stimulus-response terminology within psychology and hence uncertainties about the nature of that-which-is-perceived, the object of social perception. The second problem is that of ecological validity—the assumption that theories can be extended to encompass the complex from initially simple experiments. Thirdly, there is an inability to cope with natural discourse and hence a tendency towards individual reductionism. I shall argue in this chapter that these problems would be better approached by replacing the notion of the stimulus with that of the text. Then I will explore the semiotic approach to the text. The various ways in which this concept is more productive than that of the stimulus will be illustrated by analysing a television narrative so as to reveal aspects of the narrative which cannot otherwise be accounted for. The notion of the text, it will then be argued, is not so foreign to social psychology, for many textual concepts can be seen to have direct psychological analogues which make social cognition appropriate for theorising the role of the reader in everyday textual interpretation. Finally, I shall attempt to show how concepts of both textuality and media effects can contribute to more recent developments in social psychology, specifically social representations and discourse theory.

From Stimulus to Text

The limitations of the 'stimulus'

Rommetweit (1984) has argued that psychology, particularly information processing psychology (Broadbent, 1958), has adopted a 'monistic' outlook, stemming from early stimulus-response behaviourism. By this, he means that psychology assumes that the objects of perception and representation have invariant, singular and unequivocal meanings. Thus, the object of perception, still frequently referred to as a stimulus despite the general move from behaviourism to cognition, is presumed to be fixed in meaning, something 'out there' and prior to and unchanged by the act of perception. This 'objective' meaning is seen as unitary: there are no multiple or diverse meanings permitted, although the case of ambiguity (conceived simply as having two distinct meanings) is studied as an interesting exception which implicitly proves the rule. The meanings are unequivocal in that they are not debatable or uncertain but are definite and determinate, even though we may not know them as such.

This typically unstated view of the stimulus has profound implications for the psychological study of the perception, especially of social perception. The strict separation of the perceiver and the perceived has encouraged a mirror or correspondence theory of meaning, in which perceiving constitutes the act of paralleling, through representations, the intrinsic meaning of the object (Grant, 1970). It has initially led to a receptive, passive theory of the perceiver, still present in theories which reformulate the stimulus as 'real world logic' (Rosch and Lloyd, 1978) or 'patterns of correlations' (Hamilton, 1981). Hence perception can be active only in the possibility of biasing or inaccurately translating external structures into mental structures, as if using a distorting lens. More recently, the tendency to ignore or avoid specification of the structure of the stimulus, has led to a revival of William James's 'blooming, buzzing confusion' (1890). Here the stimulus is held to be so unstructured and amorphous as to encourage an overemphasis on the constructive processes of perception and representation to create meanings. This view, which contrasts with the passive, stimulus view, nonetheless exists side by side with the latter view, so that, typically, social cognition can both be overly constructive and yet talk of the (rarely-described) stimulus.

The stimulus in empirical research

As van Dijk notes, 'arguments in messages were identified (or produced in experimental materials) in an intuitive way [in persuasion research]' (1987, p. 259). They were either 'not analysed at all, or characterised in intuitively plausible categories'. The many aspects of texts identified by textual theories, such as the role of context, levels of textual meaning, rhetorical devices, the role of genre, and so forth, are typically ignored. Given concurrent developments in related fields, this ignorance is surprising. 'We witness another major shortcoming of classical persuasion research, that is, its neglect of the systematic structures and contents of persuasive messages. After all, the ordering of arguments, choice of words (style), or the strength of appeals . . . are only some (even rather marginal) aspects of persuasive discourse. Little inspiration was taken from insights in linguistics, or the beginning of discourse analysis in anthropology, semiotics, and literary scholarship, to define the precise nature of persuasive messages' (van Dijk, 1987, p. 257).

Thus the impoverished conception of the persuasive message, namely as stimulus rather than text, has limited the range of experiments which could be conducted on the effects of such messages. Also, 'it is now easier to see why so many experimental results were inconclusive, or why firm experimental findings hardly received satisfactory explanations' (van Dijk, 1987, p. 257). A similar argument could be advanced for the disappointing results in mass communications effects research, where, aside from the problems of establishing causal direction and controlling for selective perception, the nature of the television programme—particularly its structured or generic nature—is rarely examined. 'Experimental materials' are constructed with merely an intuitive notion of their meaning, with an assumption that their meaning is singular, fixed, unambiguous, and unaffected by context of viewing or of programme editing. Clearly, if these assumptions are misguided, then research based on them will be similarly misleading in its conclusions.

In general, psychologists have evaded the problem of specifying the stimulus/text prior to interpretation by dealing only in such limited or 'obvious' texts that no academic reader thinks to challenge their interpretation. Yet, for example, no rules are provided for defining the 'ambiguous' stimulus which is much used within cognitive psychology to demonstrate the disambiguating effects of competing interpretive labels or frames. Indeed, the function of pretesting of experimental materials is to check that both academic readers and experimental subjects will all interpret the materials consensually and as intended. Any ways in which readers differ in their interpretations is rejected as error, and the materials which produced this undesirable response are disregarded. If there existed specifiable rules concerning the structure of experimental materials, so that one could construct these materials according to given, prior principles, the whole enterprise of pretesting would be unnecessary, and many interesting materials which fail the pretesting requirement of consensual and singular interpretation need not be rejected. It is this implicit appeal to common-sense interpretation by readers which has meant that many features intrinsic to everyday texts, such as multiple or open meanings, meaning as negotiation between speaker and hearer, conventional structures and rhetoric have been or even have to be systematically excluded from study. And yet, as Rommetweit (1984) argues, 'vagueness, ambiguity, and incompleteness—and hence also: versatility, flexibility, and negotiability— are inherent and essential characteristics of any natural language' (p. 335). The consequences of the attempt to avoid such multiple and negotiable nature of meanings is that the stimuli or texts studied are divorced from their social context, the very context from which they gain their meaning and become worthy of study: 'the semantic system inherent in our everyday language is *orderly* and *borders on our knowledge of the world*, yet precisely for that reason it is *ambiguous* and *open*' (Rommetweit, 1984, p. 333).

As an example of an apparently innocent statement by a researcher committed, implicitly at least, to the stimulus approach, consider the following introduction to his work by Collins (1983): 'I discuss some characteristics of the television stimulus and describe some recent findings about children's comprehension of social information conveyed in typical programs' (p. 126). Although in fact Collins' research is reformulable in other, more productive terms, one can criticise almost every word in this sentence. For example, both 'stimulus' and 'information' imply given and singular meanings (the stimulus is singular, information is static). This is supported by the passive and asymmetric notion of 'conveyed' (like its alternative, transmitted, it implies that the meanings are transferred from programme to child without an active role for the child, Hall 1980). The meanings of programmes are reduced to a list of characteristics, to be considered independently, rather than as interrelated structures. 'Compre-hension', which implies correct or incorrect reception, but not constructive or divergent interpretation, is to be studied simply in terms of 'findings', in the absence of a theory. The notion of 'typical programmes', finally, serves to deny the importance of genre or programme conventions and history, in the structuring of meanings. Without wishing to castigate Collins, I would emphasise how the very language of information processing psychology tends to deny the complexity of everyday texts. These latter have been excluded by appealing to common-sense concepts which mystify this complexity, in the very discipline overtly devoted to defamiliarising the obvious.

The object of perception as text

I have argued that social psychology has an impoverished notion of that-which-is-perceived in the course of everyday social interaction. The object of perception is conceived either as a stimulus, that which is closed, singular and fixed in meaning, or as a 'blooming, buzzing confusion', that which is wholly open, multiple, and variable in meaning. Even more problematic than the adoption of one or other of these extremes is the implicit commuting between the two, a confusion which arises from the conventions of psychological theorising which permit an avoidance of specifying the object of perception. The concept of the text, which I shall discuss in the next section, has been adopted by the humanities and some social sciences because it lies between the extremes of open and closed, it is a historical and cultural construct rather than an *a priori* given, and it breaks down and complicates the simple linear relationship between stimulus and response, speaker and hearer, subject and object.

We may consider not only written or mediated materials as texts, but also conversation, nonverbal communication or interaction rituals and routines as texts. In beginning his book on television culture, Fiske (1987) argues that just as everyday life is heavily constructed or coded, and here one could think of symbolic interactionist and ethnomethodological work (Garfinkel, 1967; Goffman, 1971), so too is television neither transparent nor obvious in its meanings. I wish to emphasise the opposite: if we can fruitfully analyse television as text, considering its technical and generic conventions, context of production, cultural codes of gender, authority, class, its levels of meaning, its modes of address to the reader, and its preferred ideological readings, then similarly we can consider social life as text, and analyse social meanings in terms of the codes and conventions by which they are constructed.

There are some moves in this direction (Hodge and Kress, 1988; Gergen and Gergen, 1986; Murray, 1985) whose developments should be welcomed within mainstream social psychology. It should be noted, however, that much of traditional mass communications has used the psychologist's 'stimulus' rather than the semiotician's 'text' in the past: the argument is really that psychology can draw upon the semiotic text as used by literary theory, critical mass communications, and only following recent developments, by traditional mass communications—learning from the benefits accruing to the traditional approach resulting from such developments. Nonetheless, all media theory has paid more attention to programmes/texts/stimuli than has psychology—indeed, they are hard to ignore.

A Semiotic Approach to the Text: Illuminating Audience Interpretations

There are many introductions to semiotic and structuralist approaches to texts. These approaches are becoming increasingly diverse, as they encompass or relate to developments in psychoanalysis, sociolinguistics, philosophy, feminism and literary criticism (Eagleton, 1983; Fiske, 1982; Hawkes, 1977; Weedon, 1987). I propose therefore to develop the case for the role of the text in social psychology by illustrating some of the most clearly fruitful concepts through one specific analysis.

This section will thus not offer an exposition but rather an examination of how the key concepts of semiotics reveal aspects of texts not considered by a stimulus-bound approach. These concepts can be seen as compatible with, rather than foreign to, social psychological thinking on the interpretive activity of the person or reader. I will be considering semiotic concepts as they relate to reception theory or reader-oriented approaches as discussed earlier. The focus will be on the knowledge that they presume or the work that they demand of the reader. Together they offer an analysis of the text not familiar to but potentially fruitful for social psychology.

Let us consider the structure of a particular soap opera narrative, analysing it in such a way that it can be related to people's interpretations of that narrative. A soap opera narrative was chosen in part because this genre serves as the theme throughout the book for raising theoretical debates about the role of the viewer, textual openness and viewer involvement. Also, as discussed in Chapter 1, soap opera is likely to be interpreted in a similar way to everyday texts such as conversations, gossip, social events and situations. I will here draw upon a more detailed textual analysis of this narrative (Livingstone, 1987a) and a fuller account of a sample of regular viewers' subsequent free recall of this narrative (Livingstone, 1989c).

Narrativity

Events are frequently organised according to a familiar narrative structure. The concept of narrative has been recently taken up by some researchers in social psychology (Sarbin, 1986) and communications (Lucaites and Condit, 1985). An analysis of the narrative structure of the particular text to be considered here will also serve as a means of presenting the text to its present readers.

Various partially compatible schemes exist for understanding narrative, prompted by Propp's (1968) initial scheme for folk tales. Propp realised that apparently diverse stories all draw upon a constant, underlying structure. This structure has a standard set of character roles (hero, villain, magical helper, etc.) and a standard event sequence (setting, discovery of a problem or lack, hero sets out on a journey, and so on, until the goal is reached and overcoming of the lack is celebrated). The narrative under study will be analysed through a combination of Burke's four stage classification of narrative events (1970) and van Dijk's (1987) classification of the smaller elements which can be seen to make up each stage. I use van Dijk here because he offers a very similar analysis to that of Propp in specifying the elements of a narrative by which the hero attempts to solve a problem, hindered by various obstacles and villains and helped by magical agents. Yet van Dijk's approach seems more applicable to genres other than the classical folk tale for it permits more variation and recursion. Secondly, it is formulated through an analysis of story grammars in cognitive psychology and thus is more immediately accessible to social psychology. Van Dijk draws upon story grammar research to relate the structure of a narrative to its comprehension—for the interpretative structures of comprehension mirror the generative structures of production. Thus he proposes that people understand and retell narrative by breaking down a story into ordered components (Table 1).

TABLE 1. *A scheme for narrative structure (from van Dijk, 1987)*

Summary: a preface to the story providing information about relevance and interest.

Setting: this provides general information as to location, time, and participants.

Orientation: this indicates the special circumstances which led to the complication.

Complication: events contrary to the goals or expectations of the protagonist; interesting interfering events and actions.

Resolution: this functions together with a complication to comprise an event core or happening; actions performed in response to the complication with or without success.

Evaluation: this may appear discontinuously throughout the story and provides information about the personal opinions or emotions of the story teller.

Coda/Conclusion: provides information about the relevance of the story for the present communicative context.

This scheme, as van Dijk shows through his analyses of narratives concerned with racial prejudice, fits the telling of short stories or conversational anecdotes very well. Elements may remain implicit or transformed in some stories. Further, the complication/resolution pair is often repeated several times. A problem arises for the telling of longer stories or more complex stories, as with both a soap opera and other everyday narratives. If the complication/resolution pair is repeated several times, it becomes a mere listing of events, and structural relations among these event pairs are thus lost. The reduction of a structure to a list is a common problem in social psychology, for which a more structural or semiotic approach can provide the remedy. This may be achieved by combining this lower-order scheme with Burke's more abstract scheme for dramatic narrative. Burke, a literary critic, proposed a scheme which captures the key mythic functions of narrative. He highlights the dramatic tension created by a disequilibrium in the original setting which brings about the main happenings. The complication/resolution pairs are seen as attempts to reduce tension by re-establishing normative equilibrium. The four stages in his scheme are disruption of equilibrium, guilt, restitution, and redemption.

In the disruption stage, certain norms of the social order are challenged and a state of intolerable disequilibrium results. This is followed by the guilt stage in which the social problem is personified and its psychological implications—agency, intention, responsibility, blame—are developed. This stage, unimportant in the hero legends, where good and bad are clear, is central to soap opera, where multiple agents are located in a web of human relationships and actions are morally complex or ambiguous. The attribution of guilt or responsibility becomes a key problem in an ambiguous or complex world in which mythic certainties are absent. From the readers' or viewers' perspective, this stage is the most interesting and relevant. The stage of restitutory action attempts to eliminate the source of disruption and re-establish equilibrium. The redemption stage translates the consequences of the personal actions of the restitution stage back into the social domain by celebrating the moral implications of the new equilibrium. Thus a cyclic process occurs where a sociostructural phenomenon (typically, rule-breaking) is transformed to an individual phenomenon of agency (for example, guilt and personal responsibility) and then back to a sociostructural one (e.g. rules mended and penance done). This is typical of soap opera, often criticised for personalising political or structural issues and for offering individual solutions to social ills (Buckman, 1984), It may also be common in other everyday narratives, as people frequently focus on the personal rather than the sociopolitical (possibly a version of the fundamental attribution error). Mythic narrative, from which other narrative forms draw some of their conventions, thus explores threats to the status quo, ultimately creating a heightened appreciation of the status quo by showing how one overcomes moral or social challenges to the state of equilibrium.

The present narrative, from the popular soap opera *Coronation Street* (transmitted in autumn, 1984), involves an initial equilibrium in which Ken Barlow (mid-forties) is married to Deirdre Barlow (mid-thirties) and works as a journalist alone with his secretary Sally Waterman (mid-twenties). It explores threats to the valued state of stable married life, particularly that of the younger and independent woman. By sacrificing the latter to the former, marriage is in some ways symbolically strengthened and celebrated. In other ways, however, the institution of marriage can be seen to be undermined through questioning, doubt, and portrayed alternatives (here, romantic affairs). The development of the narrative is shown in Table 2.

TABLE 2. *Narrative structure for* Coronation Street *story (adapted from van Dijk (1987) and Burke (1970))*

Opening/setting/orientation

1	complication	Sally is transformed into a sexy young woman
1	resolution (u)	Sally begins an affair with Billy (publican) (i.e. no longer 'available')

Disruption: Sally comes between Ken and Deirdre

2	complication	Ken becomes jealous, hostile, fascinated by Billy and Sally
3	complication	Deirdre becomes anxious about Ken and their marriage
4	complication	all the community gossips about Ken: the problem becomes public
2/3	resolution (u)	Deirdre plans a holiday for her and Ken to take Ken away and reaffirm their marriage
5	complication	Sally and Ken are tender, discuss an affair (i.e. a development of 2, provoked by 5)
6	complication	Deirdre is upset, challenges Ken (i.e. a development of 3)
6	resolution (u)	Ken denies all, Deirdre doesn't believe him
7	complication	Ken and Sally kiss in the office (i.e. a development of 5)
7	resolution (u)	Ken and Sally agree to stop (unsuccessful because Deirdre's suspicions already aroused)

Guilt: Deirdre blames Ken, Billy blames Ken and Sally, the community considers how to lay blame

8	complication	Sally ends her affair with Billy (becoming available again)
3/6	resolution (u)	Ken and Deirdre go on holiday (unsuccessful as they do not talk through the problem)
9	complication	Billy becomes revengeful, spreads rumours (provoked by 8)
10	complication	all the community discusses rumours, gossip (provoked by 8 and 9)

Restitution: Deirdre and community try to stop Ken and Sally; Ken and Sally try to silence Deirdre and the community

6/7	resolution (u)	Ken and Sally decide to ignore all the gossip
6	resolution (u)	Deirdre challenges Ken to discover the truth
6	resolution (u)	Ken denies to Deirdre that anything happened
11	complication	Ken and Mike (Deirdre's former lover) fight
9	resolution (u)	Deirdre tries to stop Billy's gossip
7	resolution	Sally confronts Deirdre, tells her the truth
12	complication	Deirdre thinks she was deceived and is angry

Redemption: Ken and Deirdre reaffirm marriage successfully; Sally leaves the community

12	resolution	Ken tells Deirdre he loves her; they make up
6	resolution	Deirdre apologises to Ken for thinking worst (thus taking the blame for her accusations)
6	resolution	Ken forgives Deirdre
7	resolution	Sally leaves the community for new job (thus taking the blame for the complications)
13	complication	Deirdre's suspicions aroused because Sally felt she needed to leave.

Note: each resolution is numbered according to the complication it attempts to resolve; (u) indicates an unsuccessful resolution.

Recalling the narrative

Mapping out the structure of this narrative allows us to understand how such a narrative is commonly understood. Here I will refer to the ways in which some viewers who regularly watch this soap opera and viewed the particular narrative under natural circumstances actually recalled these events (Livingstone, 1989c). The analysis of the narrative provides a model not only for structuring the viewers' 'retellings' (Liebes, 1986b) but also for comparing their accounts as they differ on meaningful points of interpretation.

For example, while one viewer recalled all the complications first, and then dealt with their respective resolutions (c1, c2...cn, r1, r2...rn), while another paired complication and resolution in turn, thus telling a more orderly but less dramatic story (c1,r1,c2,r2...cn,rn). Importantly, both viewers balanced their stories, matching resolutions to complications and thus ultimately resolving all dramatic tensions generated in the telling. Some viewers altered the sequence of events in their stories in the direction of emphasising Burke's four part scheme of narrative structure. For example, one viewer ignored the gradual development of the narrative through Ken's growing attraction for Sally and begins with the dramatic act of disruption: 'It started with a kiss in the office, then they discovered they fancied each other.' Several other viewers changed the 'unsatisfactory' position of Ken and Deirdre's holiday (which occurs during the guilt stage) to the end of the story. Thus the holiday can function as a celebration of narrative resolution which is otherwise lacking and the holiday gains in meaning. For example, one viewer labelled the holiday according to its reconstructed function: 'and they decided to take a second honeymoon to celebrate their reunion'. Similarly, another viewer ends: 'Deirdre and Ken sorted it all out, went on holiday together.' This indicates both the importance of Burke's analysis in providing a higher-order scheme for that of van Dijk and also the psychological reality of this scheme for organising the build-up and dissipation of dramatic tension.

Most stories included references to both the disruption and the redemption stages, for these contain the most dramatically exciting events. But several viewers were vague about the intervening events which constituted the bulk of the narrative. For example, one viewer jumps from a series of disruptive events to saying 'I can't remember how it all finished but we haven't seen much of Sally since, and K and D seem to be all right now', thus skipping to the redemption stage. Another provides considerable detail of events as far as the holiday and the kiss, and then summarises 'somehow or other Deirdre became aware of it all and Deirdre and Ken sorted it all out', thus recognising the existence of the gossip but forgetting the details. However, the narrative stage of restitution is not in fact omitted in the retelling; it is seen to play an essential linking role, but is summarised as uninteresting. This tendency towards underplaying the middle stages in favour of the more dramatic stages (while still telling a balanced and coherent story) exemplifies one type of selection in interpretation.

Divergence in focus

A second type of selective interpretation concerns the relative importance accorded to the six key relationships around which the narrative is structured. The narrative would have been an 'eternal triangle' with Ken, Deirdre and Sally, but for the inclusion of Billy. He complicates the plot by having an affair with Sally because he had had an affair with Deirdre before her marriage to Ken and thus has a relationship of rivalry and hostility with Ken. The addition of this character thus doubles the pair-wise combinations through which the morality and excitement of adultery can be explored. The narrative contains each of these six interactions in both directions:

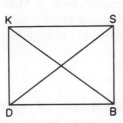

Ken and Sally consider an affair
Ken and Deirdre's marriage is in question and they argue
Sally and Billy start and end an affair
Deirdre and Billy have a past affair and present gossip to deal with
Ken and Billy are hostile rivals
Deirdre and Sally are rivals and then fight

Despite having seen the complete narrative, viewers differ in their treatment of these six interaction pairs. For example, one viewer makes no mention of Billy at all, relating only events which connected Ken, Sally and Deirdre, and thus simplifying the structure back to the 'eternal triangle' myth:

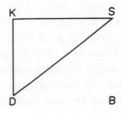

Another omits the relation between Deirdre and Billy and that between Deirdre and Sally. This viewer thereby underplays Deirdre's role in the narrative and centres on the alternative triangle of Ken/Sally/Billy. Here Ken and Billy are the central rivals, in contrast to Sally and Deirdre: the role of the men is thus emphasised over that of the women:

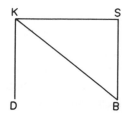

It would appear that viewers undermine the genre conventions of *Coronation Street* as a soap opera by simplifying the interconnected web of interactions between a relatively equal set of characters and by prioritising certain characters over others. This latter phenomenon is even clearer in the tendency to ignore the roles of the secondary characters such as Mike (with whom Deirdre had an extra-marital affair) or Hilda (the main gossip) or Bet (the jealous barmaid), all of whom were important, though not central, to the original narrative.

Genre knowledge

This discussion of narrativity has incidentally raised a number of other semiotic concepts. It has clearly made use of the notion of *genre,* in which a set of texts are related to each other by common use of certain recognisable conventions of construction. For example, the soap opera genre depends upon the use of multiple, simultaneous plots, unending narrative strands, the absence of a hero, a focus on dialogue rather than action and the use of domestic and romantic plots. This contrasts with what Fiske (1987) calls more 'masculine' genres, such as the action-adventure programme, police shows or Westerns, where the emphasis is upon single or at most dual plots, clear endings, one or a pair of heroes, action and external/social plots. These conventions are crucial to understanding the determinants of viewers' readings. For example, one viewer misrecalls the above story, claiming that on discovering the 'affair' Deirdre attempts to leave Ken for her mother's house. The point is that this viewer is nonetheless staying within the bounds of, and thus her knowledge of, the generic conventions of soap opera. Her knowledge of these conventions is clear from the fact that neither she nor any other viewer misremembers that, for example, Deirdre shoots Sally in a fury or that Sally is discovered to head a drugs ring or that the story becomes one of Deirdre finding herself alone and joining a feminist collective: all of these would be perfectly possible according to conventions of a police drama or a feminist play. One might extend the concept of genre to everyday situations: consider describing your actions of yesterday to a policeman in a police station, a friend at a party, or your mother on the telephone, Again, each situation has its own conventions which structure the nature of the communication for both speaker and hearer.

Syntagm and paradigm

A second aspect of narrative concerns that of choice points, or the *syntagmatic,* sequential structure of the text. Barthes (1977) argues that narratives are constructed of a series of choice points, with a *paradigm* or set of alternative possibilities available at each point. Thus there are two sources of variation in a structure: the selection made from a fixed set at any one point in time, and the order in which these selections are strung together over time. The ordering is organised so that the narrative creates tension for the reader which rises during pollution, guilt and purification and is reduced by redemptive actions. There are also tensions created at each choice point. For example, a tension is set up in the narrative concerning interruption and interruptability. In one scene, Deirdre interrupts Ken and Sally in the office when they 'happen' to be innocently engaged in their work. When they finally do kiss in the office, they are not interrupted. But as the relationship between Ken and Sally is largely conducted in the office where they engage in both innocent and guilty interactions, and as the office is continually interrupted, often by Deirdre or Billy, an inevitable tension is set up which makes each office scene an exciting one. It is not surprising then that one viewer succumbs to the continual teasing suggestions by 'recalling' that 'Deirdre walked in on them in the middle of an embrace': after all, suggestion can influence memory in a range of ways. As the narrative hinges upon secrecy, interruption and interruptability creates key points of tension. As the text contains only one possibility on each occasion, either interruption or privacy, then it is the viewers' awareness of both possibilities—of the paradigm available—which creates the perception of choice and hence of tension.

The text may tease in other ways and this contributes to the pleasure of reading. For instance, one viewer responds to textual provocation concerning the existence or not of a sexual relationship between Ken and Sally in saying: 'Ken managed to get close emotionally to Sally, and this developed into a lusty affair!' This could be dismissed as wishful thinking, but clearly also represents an attempt at closure in response to the continual teasing of the text (will they/won't they?).

Levels of meaning

A third semiotic concern is the way in which the narrative developments are carried by different levels of meaning. For example, how is it that Sally is transformed into a sexy, young woman at the beginning and how does her resultant affair with Billy affect Ken and Deirdre's marriage? The first question exemplifies the notion of levels of meaning, the second exemplifies the notion of polar oppositions by which transformations in meaning are effected. Before the narrative begins, Sally is portrayed as efficient, although not exactly prim. One day, she undergoes a dramatic change, appearing in turquoise mini-skirt, a low-cut tee-shirt, and lots of make up. She flirts with Billy, dimples and laughs with the men around, and is noticed by all. These changes on the manifest or denotative level convey a new, connotative meaning of sexuality and availability. This change in one character signals a reordering of other characters, as all are locked into an interdependent system. For example, the text reminds viewers of the recent lack of romance between Ken and Deirdre, challenging Ken to reaffirm his masculinity by joining in with the other men in admiring the new Sally. On an ideological level, the change reverses the usual British soap opera association between sexuality and morality, in which typically the sexual characters are immoral and the asexual ones are moral. Temporarily at least, viewers are encouraged to pity or criticise Deirdre for having let herself go, to sympathise with Ken for his interest in Sally, and to admire Sally for her open, vivacious and attractive femininity. Ultimately, the narrative revalues the more conservative equilibrium of a stable marriage by introducing a new opposition of maturity which can be used to replace that of sexuality. Once more the text encourages its readers to admire Deirdre—now seen as mature rather than unattractive, and ridicule Sally—now seen as immature rather than sexy, thereby justifying Ken's decision to leave Sally and to stay with Deidre. Thus the narrative achieves its direction, transformations and tensions through manipulation of key thematic oppositions which themselves are coded through relating denotational to connotational and ideological levels of meaning. Audiences must be skilled in decoding these transformations and associations.

Openness and closure

The concept of textual openness (Eco, 1979a) has been discussed in the previous chapter. Here I wish firstly to exemplify the concept through analysis of the above narrative, showing how integral is openness to the structuring of the text and to its generic conventions. Secondly, I will show how essential is this concept to understanding the role of the reader, by examining viewers' responses to the openness of the text. Thirdly I will break down the concept according to the different strategies through which the text achieves openness. Although openness is particularly considered integral to the genre of soap opera, research interest in this genre leans heavily on the association between soap opera and daily life, so that by analysing soap opera one may discover the forms of, or at least hypotheses concerning, openness and interpretative activity in daily life.

The concept of openness greatly complicates both the processes of meaning creation and the nature of the meanings created on reading, compared to those implied using a singular, closed, and transparent notion of the 'stimulus'. Yet, because the concept of structure is retained, an open text is not a vague or dissolved text, into which readers may freely introduce any meanings that they wish. Openness may be examined through several structuring aspects of the text: cultural forum, multiple perspectives, boundaries and participants. In brief, a text may permit multiple readings firstly insofar as it constitutes a forum—offering a range of moral or cultural positions on an issue (Newcomb and Hirsch, 1984). Further, it may offer a range of characters with which one might identify and from whose perspective events can be viewed. There may be an indeterminacy of boundaries to the narratives, so that viewers may vary in their constructions of where and why the narrative begins and ends. Finally, the text may carry different implications for cause and responsibility attributions, depending on the perspective of speakers, hearers and overhearers (Goffman, 1981). All these contribute to the structuring or organisation of textual openness.

Cultural forum and moral perspectives

I will begin with the notions of forum and of perspectives taken together, as typically the range of moral positions is constructed and offered through personification in the variety of particular characters. Much has been written on the role of soap opera as contemporary mythology (Allen, 1985; Buckman, 1984; Dyer *et al.*, 1981). Soap operas offer rhetorical, normative and common-sense solutions to issues of personal or community threat. For this reason, soap operas deal in topical social and moral problems and, because of their meaningful and acceptable solutions, are seen by viewers as relevant, helpful and realistic (Livingstone, 1988a). In terms of text structure, this means that a programme must identify a relevant moral issue, engage the viewers' emotional sympathies and involvement, encompass a wide range of explanatory discourses which constitute the paradigm of competing interpretive frameworks for viewers, and resolve uncertainty by selecting or preferring a single, culturally normative resolution to the threat portrayed or uncertainty identified.

Soap opera can be seen both to fit this pattern, repeatedly raising and resolving moral problems, and also to deviate from this pattern through the competing convention of textual openness or indeterminacy. Soap operas appear to deviate from the narrative structure of hero legends and folk tales (as analysed by Propp, 1968; see also Silverstone, 1984) insofar as no single character takes the hero role and thus the narrative cannot be simply viewed from a single perspective. Viewers identify with or engage in parasocial interaction with a subset of all characters in a variety of ways (Horton and Wohl, 1956). The pleasure of viewing lies partly in the interplay between different characters and, symbolically, between different viewpoints or rhetorical discourses. Hence, the interpretation of the narrative cannot be straightforwardly derived from an analysis of the text.

In this particular narrative, ten explanations for the potential adultery were offered by or could be said to be available in the text (see Table 3). Each references a complex and common sense, 'naturalised' (Barthes, 1973) discourse concerning, say, male virility, feminine seduction, boredom in marriage or life expectations. Each also identifies a causal agent as the prime mover of the narrative and may or may not make an attribution of personal responsibility for the consequences of that agent's actions. The explanations are to some extent mutually exclusive. Insofar as different positions are personified in different characters, to whom both viewers and programme have established particular loyalties, the explanations may be seen not as pluralistic but as structured in dominance (Hall, 1980)—some being more favoured or 'preferred' than others.

One could argue that the explanations of male menopause (and doubts about sustained virility) and of attraction as arising inevitably from prolonged close contact in the office are the most preferred. In support of this, we can note that they are the most frequently offered and they also appear to be sustained to the end of the narrative (hence at the end, the husband has still admitted no responsibility, the wife has apologised, the mistress has left under a cloud of immorality). Thus, the programme would appear to identify a discourse of male virility doubly threatened by events: through the husband's age and through the close contact of an attractive woman. For example, Ken says to Sally: 'I suppose I'm a classic case really . . . the onset of middle age. The male menopause. Y'know, you must have heard all the jargon.' This speaks to the viewer, inviting them to insert their own social knowledge to fill out his perspective. And as he later says to Deirdre: 'Well you're right about one thing. She is there, in the office, and she's not exactly ugly.' We are left with a renewed faith in his manhood and possibly a suspicion of men who do not experience such challenges and respond with seduction.

Viewers' selectivity in the use of explanatory rhetoric

As I have argued earlier, viewers do not necessarily interpret the text by following the preferred reading in a mode of passive acceptance. The present analysis of viewers' recall of this narrative supports this claim empirically. Specifically, in concretising their personal versions of the text, with its wide range of possible, unequally favoured explanations, viewers interpreted the narrative as follows (see Table 3; and Livingstone, 1989c). Like the text, between them they made a wide range of interpretations of this potential affair, although in the main, each viewer adopted only one or two explanations for their story.

The set of explanations offered by viewers overlaps highly with those of the text. Thus both text and viewers (taken together) identify explanations for adultery concerning the desire to live life to the full, that Ken became obsessed with Sally, that Ken and Deirdre have problems in their marriage, that close contact generates attraction, that the 'other woman' seduces the innocent husband, that the potential adultery was motivated by revenge for Deirdre's adulterous affair, and that Ken was jealous of Sally and Billy. Three textual explanations were ignored by viewers, namely that society has lost the old values (a reference to the nostalgic perspective of *Coronation Street*), that Ken was threatened by the 'male menopause', and that Ken was immature. A further three explanations were introduced by the viewers which had not been offered by the text itself, namely that Ken acted out of revenge for Deirdre's past affair with Billy, that Ken seduced Sally, and that Ken was carried away by his feelings for Sally.

The preferred reading which I identified above was barely recognised by viewers. Instead viewers opted for the explanations of seduction, revenge, and jealousy, with the common secondary explanation of the husband being carried away by his feelings. For example, one viewer says: 'Sally was at that time having an affair with Billy Walker. This made Ken jealous, as his wife Deirdre was associated with Billy Walker some years ago.' And another: 'We had weeks of Ken being worried about his feelings for Sally changing from those of a boss to those of a potential lover, and it eventually culminated in him kissing her and embracing her in the office.'

Thus, viewers appear to interpret the text in the direction of maximising drama and emotional tension. Explanations which point to the husband as agent and which resist responsibility attributions are rejected in favour of explanations with female agents (wife or mistress) and clear personal responsibility. This is achieved through actively connecting the present to past narratives. For example, although the text made little reference to Deirdre's previous adulterous affair with Mike, and made no explicit reference at all to her even earlier affair with Billy, these were introduced by viewers 'in the know' as clear motivating forces behind the characters' present actions. For example, one viewer notes that 'Sally also had an association with Mike Baldwin, who Deirdre had had an affair with during their marriage (Ken and Deirdre's).'

A range of perspectives is offered by the text, which readers variously adopt, and which one can imagine also being offered in many everyday gossipy conversations. It is this diversity in perspectives offered which also moves the plot. Thus Ken and Deirdre's different perspectives lead each to seek restitution in different ways. Ken interprets adultery as the sexual act,

TABLE 3. *Explanations for adultery offered by text (espoused by specific characters) and viewers (a sample of regular viewers asked to recall the narrative)*

Explanation	Proposer in text	Viewers (freq.)	Causal agent	Responsibility attribution
people have no values now	H	—	social decay	no
must live to the full	H	1	S and K	yes
obsession	S	2	no	
marital problem	S	2	K and D	yes
male menopause	K,S,Bt	—	K	no
husband's immaturity	K	—	K	no
close contact	B,M,K,D	1	K	no
woman seduces	S	5	S	yes
revenge for Mike	D	2	D	yes
revenge for Billy	—	3	D	yes
jealousy	S	3	K	yes
husband seduces	—	1	K	yes
carried away by feelings (generally an additional explanation)	—	8	K	no

Note: S=Sally (secretary), K=Ken (husband), D=Deirdre (wife), B=Billy (publican), M=Mike (factory boss), Bt=Bet (barmaid), H=Hilda (local gossip).

and so considers that no rules have been infringed while Deirdre interprets adultery as infidelity in thought, as compounded by subsequent denial and deceit, and thus considers that the marriage contract is at risk. Clearly, these two positions represent equally viable cultural understandings—the conflict between them therefore constructs a real problem for the viewers and thereby creates a need for resolution to be satisfied by the text. In the narrative, Ken opts for denial and an attempt to put it all behind him and say nothing. For Deirdre, this functions as evidence of guilt and continued deceit, and it hinders her own strategy of revealing the truth through talk, whether to Ken or others in the community. Viewers may follow either character, depending on their sympathies, and thus different viewers may see events differently. Alternatively, the viewer may make the truly open reading, in Eco's sense, by negotiating the interplay between the two strategies and becoming involved in the resulting tension and conflict.

Multiple meanings

This brings us to a further way in which the text may be open. Here I draw upon Goffman's critique of the speaker–hearer model in his discussion of 'radio talk' (1981). He attacks the common model of communication as the transfer of a single meaning from speaker to hearer through his exploration of the complexities of everyday contexts of communication. Consider, he says, the position of the eavesdropper, of the third party under discussion, of the subject of an ironic aside or of the party being subtly colluded with during a three-way conversation. Their positions, and thus the meanings which they construct from the conversation, differ substantially from each other and from the speaking participants. In this everyday, complex situation, the 'message' is unclear, the hearers are multiple and stand in very different relations to the utterance, the intended and unintended meanings may differ, and so forth. Soap opera provides a classical example of this. Imagine the routine combinations of collusion, secrecy, eavesdropping, irony and deceit which comprise many soap opera conversations, and add in the position of the viewer who identifies with certain characters and who knows what some characters don't know, including who is listening at the keyhole. Here, we have a complex interplay of participants to the communicative act. These not only make the simple notions of speaker, message and hearer inapplicable but also multiply the meanings which could be derived from the text, depending on perspectives adopted, knowledge available and complexities perceived.

Narrative boundaries

Soap opera narratives, like everyday conversations and situations, manifest a systematic refusal to impose clear beginnings and endings on events. This genre convention has specific implications for audience involvement and interpretations. For the soap opera, this openness or uncertainty is held to have emancipatory or complicating implications for readings (Allen, 1985; Curti, 1988; Feuer, 1984; Kuhn, 1984; Fiske, 1987). This is due to the normative nature of closure (Barthes, 1973) which is resisted by the text—marriages cannot end happily ever after; apparent resolutions of conflict are only temporary; problems cannot be neatly solved; simplicity is undermined by subsequent complications. Interestingly, the psychological literature on story grammars and narrative comprehension points to the reader's need to impose closure upon narrative openness. Such an imposition of closure is held to serve as one of people's central sense-making operations (e.g. Mandler, 1984). However, such strategies on the part of the reader have been studied only in relation to closed texts (like folktales) by psychologists.

'In the beginning . . .'

Let us examine the beginning of the narrative being analysed. Despite the obvious contradiction of identifying a beginning to a text while simultaneously acknowledging the openness of these boundaries, the present narrative can be said to begin at the coincident occurrence in the programme of the reappearance of the husband and wife (absent for some weeks) and the physical/symbolic transformation of the secretary (the dramatic change towards a sexy appearance and flirtatious manner). Yet the initial boundary to the narrative remains ambiguous and unclear.

For example, the husband notes that the main plot (the potential affair between him and his secretary) was brought about by the subplot (the actual affair between Billy and Sally): Ken says to Sally: 'it wasn't until you started seeing him [Billy] that I realised how much I cared'. The text gives no indication of when this 'caring' began, for it was not manifest until Sally began her affair with Billy and Ken himself realised his feelings. Consequently, the text invites viewers to project backwards in time, identifying with Ken and reinterpreting past events. The narrative also begins very slowly, progressing through a number of stages which mark developments in awareness. First Ken is harsh towards Sally with no apparent reason; then the community guesses that his harshness masks attraction; then Ken realises his attraction to Sally; finally Deirdre and Sally become aware of it. Only then is the disruptive event apparent, and the narrative proper can begin to pass through Burke's narrative stages. As is typical of both soap opera and other narratives, the prior equilibrium is unstated and must be inferred, drawing on existing understandings of the viewers.

Most of the viewers begin own recalling of this narrative in a similarly vague and open fashion. For example, one viewer begins: 'We had weeks of Ken being worried about his feelings for Sally changing from those of a boss to those of a potential lover, and it eventually culminated in him kissing her and embracing her in the office. Prior to this he had taken her to the Rovers several times for a drink/meal, etc. supposedly to discuss a story.' Another begins with a state (whose origin is not given) rather than an event: 'Ken was interested in Sally but was allowing her to "make the running".' For another viewer, the narrative also begins with a state, not an event: 'It seemed that Ken was a little unsettled in his marriage at the time.' This statement is impossible to assess in terms of recall accuracy for it depends on the viewer's perception of this marriage, and of what counts as being unsettled. The text had previously portrayed the marriage as routine and 'normal'—this may or may not be interpreted as unsettled. The portrayal had both an absence of romance and an absence of disturbance: thus the text was indeterminate and requires viewers' understandings of 'normal marriage' to resolve this indeterminacy.

One viewer imposed clear closure on this indeterminacy by starting the story with a discrete, disruptive event: 'It started with a kiss in the office.' Other viewers imposed closure by inferring that Billy's affair with Sally was the origin of Ken's feelings for Sally, where concern and interest developed first into jealousy and then into attraction. In conclusion, about the viewers accepted the openness of the text, imposing no boundary at the beginning of their stories. This suggests that they gain pleasure in the conventions of the genre. The remaining viewers sought to impose closure, following their social knowledge of the structure of classic narrative rather than the generic conventions of the programme. Interestingly, in their task of imposing closure, the viewers were forced to seek explanations for subsequent events by imputing either a problematic marriage, or jealousy, or sudden overwhelming attraction to account for the initiating event: presumably this inference structures their perceptions of the events which follow.

'And finally . . .'

A similar pattern emerges in the relationship between the text and its readers in the ending of the narrative. The text again follows the conventions of soap opera in avoiding a closed ending. The final scenes proceeded thus:

D:K – I call it a lie, Ken. What do you call it?

K:D – It was the truth. I did not have an affair with Sally. I did not make love to her.

D:K – You did show a lot of restraint, didn't you, both of you.

K:D – Yes.

D:K – Then it was a lie. You fancied her and you said you didn't.

K:D – I never said that. I said there was nothing going on.

D:K – There was something going on, you were fancying her.

K:D – Oh, I give up.

The debate over competing perceptions of events, and over definitions of fidelity, past conversations, and deceit, is never resolved. Rather the participants drop the debate under the pressure to retain their marriage. They proceed instead to the redemption/celebration stage without true restitution:

D:K – What's she got that I haven't got anyway?

K:D – Not a thing . . . you're beautiful. And I love you.

D:K – Yeah well, just watch it in the future, eh? Keep your eyes on your work.

K:D – Oh I will, believe me.

Deirdre then apologises:

D:K – I'm sorry, Ken . . . [they hug] . . . for making a mountain out of a molehill. I was jealous.

Although this appears to resolve the debate in Ken's favour, this too is undermined when Ken attempts to reassure Deirdre by informing her that Sally has offered to leave her job and the community as a 'noble gesture':

D:K – But according to you and her, nobody's done anything wrong, so
      why should she feel noble . . . You can only take the blame for
      something if something's happened, if you've got something on
      your conscience. Has Sally got something on her conscience, Ken?
K:D – No!
D:K – Well it sounds like it to me. It sounds very much like it. [she walks
      out of the room]
K – I don't believe it!

This is the last we see of any of the characters for several weeks, and the
lack of resolution thus remains. Several weeks later, in an apparently
unconnected story, Sally sells a confidential story to a rival paper, as Ken
had refused to print it, and consequently she leaves the community (and
the programme) altogether to work on the rival paper. Much later still,
Billy takes to drink, fast cars and womanising. He too leaves the programme in disrepute.

As with the issue of narrative beginnings, the viewers' social knowledge
of narrative structure would suggest the need for closure, this knowledge
competing with the conventions of the genre which leave stories hanging.
Here, the apparently independent stories which follow concerning Sally
and Billy are in some ways set up by the present narrative, in that both
Sally and Billy have become superfluous and disreputable characters
(being rejected in romance). Their departure provides a period of calm for
Ken and Deidre to re-establish their marriage without complications
before the next problem is posed for them. So, how do viewers end their
stories? In several stories, Ken and Deirdre's holiday was moved from the
middle of the story to the end, to create a 'happy ever after' conclusion.
Sally's move to her new job was seen to provide a clear conclusion: either
Sally is thereby confirmed as the disreputable loser, or at least the source
of temptation has been removed. For example, one viewer ends: 'Later,
Sally was written out of the series when she wrote a story for another
newspaper when Ken had refused to print it in his own—so honour was
satisfied.' And another ends: 'In the end I think Billy Walker left and Sally
moved on to another job. This makes things easier for all concerned,
especially Ken and Deirdre'; for several viewers, Billy's move from the
series also served to impose closure and is thus brought forward and
explicitly connected to the present narrative.

Ken's decision not to pursue the affair was also used to provide the end
of the narrative, although again this occurred near the beginning and
provoked, rather than resolved, his problems with Deirdre. Hence one
viewer ended: 'I think Ken thought better of it, and it was mutually
decided that they should not take the affair (he and Sally) any further, as
there was too much at stake for Ken.' Several viewers simply noted that
Deirdre and Ken are now happily together, a 'happy ever after' ending;

Some kind of concluding event is nonetheless inserted. For example, one viewer added an agreement between the couple, and another added a cognitive realisation: 'Ken and Deirdre returned to normal relationships— Ken realising it was only a passing infatuation'. Again, both of these readings could be said to be 'in' the text or not—what is important is that while the text is partially open, these viewers made their own sense of the narrative by imposing a kind of closure.

The central perceived role of Deidre's previous affair with Mike Baldwin led one viewer to identify the fact that Ken and Deirdre were now even as the end of the story, for a balance of injustice has been achieved. Another viewer completely invented a series of events which serve to conclude the story. Although they clearly did not occur, the story still fits the conventions of the soap opera genre very well: 'Many stories went round the street, and eventually (of course) Deirdre found out and confronted Ken. He broke down as Deirdre was about to leave (for her mother's home no doubt), and they decided to take a second honeymoon to celebrate their reunion.'

Finally, several viewers simply did not end their stories, thus remaining true to the conventions of the genre, irrespective of their cognitive structures for narrative representation. For example, one viewer wrote: 'Billy Walker was sexually involved with Sally Waterman. Ken Barlow became jealous at this and attempted an affair with Sally himself. Deirdre found out with the result that Billy Walker found out as well. This incident became a focal point for the gossip-artistes for several weeks, mostly centering around the public house whenever any two of the parties involved were present. I seem to recall that Billy Walker was somehow trying to blackmail Deirdre into having an affair with him as well.' Another simply could not remember an ending and did not impose one. Another commented on motivations for events but not events themselves, and thus tells a story about feelings, for which there is little closure.

In sum, there was the same pattern for endings as for beginnings. Some viewers followed the genre and the text and avoided closure in their stories, others imposed closure, using aspects of the narrative which are clearly present, which were plausible but unclear (i.e. serve as raw materials for an interpretation), or which were clearly absent.

The application of semiotics

In this section I have tried to show two things in some detail: the applicability of key semiotic concepts to the analysis of an everyday social text; and the advantages of drawing upon the same set of concepts in understanding people's responses to or readings of such texts. The analysis of the text and its readings in everyday life are intimately related. The less rich or revealing our approach to the former, the more insensitive or misleading will be our understanding of the latter. In conclusion, I have argued that a literary or semiotic approach—drawing on concepts of openness, multiple levels of meaning, genre conventions and narrativity—is far more valuable than a stimulus-bound approach. Meanings are not given prior to interpretation, they are not singular or unambiguous and they are heavily determined by the conventions of the genre to which they belong. The application of ideas from literary or mediated texts to the texts of everyday conversation and interaction is an exciting prospect.

Reception Theory and Schema Theory: Parallels and Potential

One aim of the above section was to demonstrate the potential for rapprochment between semiotic and psychological concepts. In this section, the parallels between these two theoretical domains will be made explicit. These parallels underpin the argument of this chapter that social psychology would benefit by replacing the stimulus with the text. They also underpin the argument of the next chapter, that cultural and reader-oriented studies would benefit by exploring a social psychological concept of the reader.

The concept of the schema

The early influence of the Gestalt school on both social psychology and on European theorising in literature and social science has resulted in certain consistencies or overlaps in conceptualisation. Most notably, the concept of the 'schema' is integral to both approaches. As social psychology moves towards social cognition, the concept of the schema becomes increasingly important. The schema is a representational concept which is often used to replace concepts such as stereotype, attitude, belief, or opinion, although distinctions among these and other concepts (for example, frame, prototype or script) are much debated. The advantage of the concept lies partly in this generality, that it allows us to treat all sociocognitive representations equivalently, and also in the fact that it is dynamic and process-oriented. Following Piaget (1968) and Bartlett (1932) the schema is flexible, adaptive, efficient, and holistic. It operates by assimilatory and accommodatory processes whose parameters have become the subject of much research (e.g. Crocker *et al.*, 1984; see also Abelson, 1981; Eiser, 1986; Fiske and Taylor, 1984; Palmerino *et al.*, 1984). Some would argue that the concept encompasses that of script or frame insofar as a schema designates a structuring device, a way of imposing sense on disorder, by providing a generalised structure with spaces or slots for the specific details of the situation faced. Past experience is represented by the provision of default values for each slot which may be adaptively presumed or inferred for most situations. The script, then, is a sequential or narrative schema, while the frame is static or situational.

The schema as thus described corresponds closely to the use of the term—and of related terms like Iser's (1980) skeletal structure—by reader-oriented theories in literary criticism. These theories differ in one key area. Social cognition conceives of the person operating the schema, with the target of perception providing the specific fillings for the slots available. On the other hand, reception theory sees the text as providing the schema, with carefully located gaps, in order that the reader should fill in the gaps on the basis of his or her own experience. Each approach has an interactive notion of reading or interpreting, with meaning being constructed through the dynamic of interpreter and interpreted. Yet each theorises the schema and shows little interest in how the gaps are filled, whether the schema is attributed to the knowledge of the person or the structure of the text. Reception theory says little about the reader (see Chapter 4) and as argued above, social psychology knows little of the text, whether from the media or everyday situations. Neither approach seems to conceive of both the interpretive resources of the reader and the virtual structure of the text as being schematic, organised, and yet incomplete, awaiting the other for the negotiation of meaning.

Oppositions and dimensions

Various other concepts within social cognition also have their parallels in textual or semiotic concepts. For example, while psychologists postulate that people simplify and abstract their worlds by representing surface diversity according to a few, latent, polar dimensions, so too do text analysts postulate that the surface diversity of textual forms can be related to transformations upon a few underlying oppositions. Again, a common history—rooted in structuralism—is responsible: the early structuralist notions of binary oppositions, of linear dimensions, of transformations and of simplicity underlying diversity have been influential in both psychology and literary criticism, although each has since developed these ideas according to their own concerns.

Narratives and story grammars

A final parallel concerns narrative. As discussed in the previous section, psychology is groping towards a conception of narrative structure, recognising that people's expectations, inferences, and desires for consistency are all informed by a notion of narrative. Hence the development of both script theory, and more pertinently, story grammars. Hence, this research could be criticised in the way that Billig (1987) critiques modern persuasion research for its ignorance of Greek theories of rhetoric and Lunt (1987) critiques attribution theory for its ignorance of the philosophy of causality. Just as they argue that, by beginning with empirical, inductive research instead of reading the philosophical literature, psychology has painfully learned a small proportion of that already discovered, so too could one argue about story grammar research that it has now come to understand a small part of that already known by narrative theorists such as Propp. The psychologist may make two defences: the first is the psychological reality claim, that we need to discover whether people really do think as these theories suppose; the second is the argument that one must start small and build up the complexity of one's theory (incidentally quite the opposite of the falsificationist's conjectures and refutations which psychologists typically endorse for theory construction).

In his review of story grammar research, Bower (1976) discussed his difficulties on reading James Joyce compared to a detective story. Reading between the lines, as readers inevitably do, it seems that Bower suggests that Joyce fails to make sense because he avoids straightforward narrative structure, and thus need not be studied: the recognition of narrative structure is equated strictly with the process of making sense. Hence, as detective novels 'make sense' through their clear dependence on linear narrative, they should be studied in preference, as Bower and his colleagues then proceed to do. Ironically, Bower chooses as his target the author whom, for Eco, constitutes the major theoretical challenge. According to Eco's analysis (1979a, 1979b), Bower has opted to study the closed text alone. He loses not only an understanding of how some people do in fact make sense of Joyce but, more importantly, he loses an understanding of the relationship between Joyce and a detective story (for Eco, 1979b, the James Bond novels) or between an open and a closed text, with their different implications for the role of the reader.

Psychologists seem not to notice that they study only closed texts, for the very concept of closure requires an appreciation of the differences between open and closed texts. Psychology omits study of the open, the ambiguous, the polysemic, and consequently too, omits study of this area of the role of the reader. Yet the notion of the open text is increasingly being extended to phenomena other than high culture, for example, to the soap opera and certain other media genres. It might also be applied to those everyday situations whose meanings are far from closed and whose sequences are not always tightly scripted but invite the negotiation of meaning from participants.

The reader and the information processor

Schema theory and reception theory offer a somewhat different conception of the person—as information processor and as reader respectively. While the 'information processing' metaphor has increasingly accommodated an active, sense-making conception of the person, thus bringing it closer to the similarly reconceptualised reader of literary theory, it still differs from the 'reader' of reception theory in several ways. The information processing metaphor tends towards reductionism rather than contextualism in seeking explanations. It invites the study of simple and artificial materials as information because of the assumptions of closure and the neglect of structure. It rejects the processing of certain aspects of texts, such as openness, myth, narrative, genre, or ideology, useful as these may be, seeing them only as error or noise because they do not fit the assumptions of information processing. Finally, it tends to give the person excessive power because it does not offer a corresponding theory of the information or object of perception (compare with the integral and heavily theorised relation between reader and text) and thus cannot recognise how 'information' may constrain or guide information-processing.

Consider, for example, the case of making sense of the television news (Livingstone, 1988c). If we consider the television news to be most important on a denotational level, then an information processing approach may be the most appropriate. For example, one can ask whether people learn politicians' names, recall the dates of events, identify the events referred to or understand the sequence of events. But if we consider the news also important, if not more so, on a connotational or mythic level, then a reader-oriented approach in which the person is regarded not as a processor of information but an interpreter of texts becomes appropriate. Thus one may ask how people understand the news in terms of who are the good guys and bad guys, why they think events occurred, what were the possible alternatives available or the choices made, who is seen to hold the real, underlying power or what meaning the event reported has in the context of its given narrative frame. The text approach raises questions about people's interpretations which go beyond the information processing approach, for they are dependent upon a more complex conception of the text itself. For example, we may ask whether people understand metaphor in the news, where they identify the beginnings and conclusions of narratives presented, how their interest relates to points of tension or cliffhangers, whether they see the news as so different from drama, what kinds of linking inferences they make concerning motives, responsibility, causation, and so forth.

Texts, Discourse and Social Representations: Developments in Social Psychology

Two recent developments in social psychology have explicitly attempted to move away from the information processing metaphor, with its associated notion of the stimulus and its tendency towards cognitive reductionism. Despite their advances on earlier research, these developments tend to reinvent the wheel as regards text theory. Indeed, they stand to gain from encompassing not only considerations from textual or semiotic theory but also from developments in media theory more generally.

The Theory of Social Representations

As introduced by Moscovici (1973, 1981, 1984), 'social representations' are 'cognitive systems with a logic and language of their own. . . . They do not represent simply "opinions about", "images of" or "attitudes towards" but "theories" or "branches of knowledge" in their own right, for the discovery and organisation of reality' (Moscovici, 1973). This concept can be seen as the application of Piagetian notions of cognitive dynamics, with some influence from symbolic interactionism, to Durkheimian collective representations. The concept has been very popular in recent years and has generated both empirical work and theoretical analysis (Farr and Moscovici, 1984; Farr, 1987; Harre, 1984; Litton and Potter, 1985). The definition of a social representation was left deliberately vague by Moscovici to await theoretical development, but it is a concept intended to interrelate socially given meanings with both psychological thought processes and interindividual group processes. Its key advantages lie in the attempt to theorise these relationships between different levels of analysis, often ignored by social psychology (although see Doise, 1987, for a recent analysis) and to offer social psychology a theory of social meanings which precede and transcend individual cognition.

Central to many social and cognitive psychology theories of representation is the implicit assumption that the individual personally constructs representations from observing naturally occurring patterns of correlation or covariation in the outside world. Attribution theory (Heider, 1958; Kelley, 1972), Implicit Personality Theory (Bruner and Tagiuri, 1954; Rosenberg and Sedlack, 1972), and prototype theory (Rosch and Lloyd, 1978) all make this assumption. One might protest that this would appear to contradict the earlier argument in this chapter concerning the lack of specification of stimuli and the treatment of them as inordinately open by social psychology. Rather, these points are compatible, evidencing psychology's confusion about the stimulus. Firstly these correlational patterns are rarely specified except in experimental materials. Secondly, there is an ambiguity about the relationship between the construction of a representation and its subsequent use.

Representations are often held to be constructed individually through receptivity to patterns in the real world and then are used assimilatively, by imposing the representation on to subsequent percepts. For example, implicit personality theories are abstracted inductively but then imposed constructively in later perception. According to such views, personal experience is somehow conceived as operating prior to social meanings and as the generator of personal meanings which are social only in that they are shared, for each person has abstracted from approximately the same world. Moscovici's approach contrasts directly with the above. He argues that meanings are less often individually constructed than socially given, available in the symbolic environment in a 'ready-made' form from the social group or milieu. Moreover, even when individuals construct divergent meanings, the available social representations comprise the building blocks, the means through which the world is perceived. 'While these representations, which are shared by many, enter into and influence the mind of each they are not thought by them; rather, to be more precise, they are re-thought, re-cited and re-presented' (Moscovici, 1984, p. 9). The social representation thus offers a social conception of meaning which links levels of analysis through the use of cognitive constructs conceived as operating on a group level—for example, groups are seen to assimilate and objectify representations in the same way as Piaget's children. Such an integration of levels is needed for social psychology, just as an integration between reception theory and social cognition around the schema concept is needed for research on the interpretation of texts.

Social psychology and discourse analysis

The second development in recent social psychology is the introduction of discourse analysis. Although discourse analysis has flourished in the recent interdisciplinary atmosphere in academia and has been taken up by a wide range of theorists, it has been brought into British social psychology mainly by Potter and Wetherell (1987) and their collaborators and into cognitive psychology most notably by van Dijk (1987) although see also Beaugrande and Dressler, 1980; Brown and Fish, 1983; Kintsch, 1977). The British social psychological approach has competed with social representation theory for centre stage, and like the latter theory, has offered a more social and meaning-oriented approach to social psychology. Specifically researchers have focused long-overdue attention on the role of language in everyday life—both as constructor and repository of meanings. The quarrel with social representation theory concerns the role of cognition. While Potter and Wetherell appear to endorse a linguistic Behaviourism (although see van Dijk's explicit inclusion of cognition in his approach to discourse analysis), Moscovici repeatedly uses cognitive concepts. The quarrel also concerns the primacy of language in symbolic systems, resembling the long-standing debate in semiotics of whether language is the model for, or merely one of, the other symbolic systems (Hawkes, 1977). Because of Potter and Wetherell's rejection of a sociocognitive approach, it is unclear how discourse analysis relates to psychology more generally: here it compares unfavourably with the reinterpretation of traditional concepts within social representation theory (Farr and Moscovici, 1984).

If social representation theory suffers from being too general, vague and overarching, the discourse approach has the opposite problem, being concerned with, for example, specific sentence transformations or local features such as lexicalisation (or word choice) and agency (Trew, 1979) rather than larger textual units such as narrative—again, this problem does not apply to the approaches of van Dijk (1987) and Kintsch (1977). Discourse analysis especially seems so far to be concerned with closed rather than open or indeterminate meanings, and with answering new, discourse questions rather than old, psychological questions.

Nevertheless, linguistic features of texts such as agency are indeed communicative and are common textual manipulations. For example, Trew compares an active, standard subject-verb-object sentence such as 'the police shot the rioters' with a passive, agent-deleted sentence such as 'the rioters' were shot'. He argues that the latter serves to shift attention and implicit causality and blame on to the rioters and away from the police. In a study of newspaper articles, Sigman and Fry (1985) showed that this analysis has psychological reality for the audience and that attributional patterns are indeed affected by discourse transformations. Thus like social representation theory, discourse analysis reintroduces ideological issues into social psychology (Billig, 1982) and, if we look to developments in discourse theory outside social psychology (Atkinson and Heritage, 1984; Coulthard and Montgomery, 1981; Fowler, 1981; Halliday, 1978; Hodge and Kress, 1988; Lewis, 1987), there are many more benefits to come.

Social psychology and the open text

Although discourse analysis especially has related linguistics to psychology via the concept of a 'linguistic repertoire', neither this nor social representation theory approaches the complexity of semiotic concepts of the text, most notably in the area of openness. If we consider the nature of everyday discourse and representations, it is apparent that both these social psychological approaches concur with other theories in the discipline. Thus they perceive these sources of meaning—discourse or representation—as closed, singular, and unambiguous stimuli whose true, underlying structure is to be revealed by the researcher. In this, they resemble the early structuralist position criticised by recent semioticians for the assumption of a crystalline text to be revealed by a critical elite. Neither social representations nor discourse tend to be seen as polysemic or multiple, as constructed according to generic conventions, as comprising different levels of meaning, as incorporating such devices as metaphor, narrative, or preferred readings, and most importantly, no distinction is made between the virtual and the realised text. In other words, the theory of meaning applied is inadequate, and has not followed the semiotic move (Culler, 1981) from studying the meanings 'in' the text to studying how it is that texts make sense to their audience.

It is the absence of the virtual/realised distinction (Eco, 1979a) which is most telling and from which social psychology stands to gain the most from semiotics. This absence is readily comprehensible, for the distinction becomes important only when one conceives of both open texts and aberrant readings: it is unnecessary if texts are closed and readings are as intended, for then the virtual and realised text are the same. However, without this distinction, there can be no role for the reader—that which realises the virtual text, which concretises the skeletal structure, which negotiates with the text in deriving the empirical meaning. My point then, is that social representations and discourse analysis lack a theory of the reader because they lack the theory of the open text. This explains why their relation to psychology is unclear.

Social representations and mass communications

Halloran's argument that 'the media's function is the provision of social realities where they did not exist before, or the giving of new directions to tendencies already present' (1970, p. 31) strongly resembles Moscovici's view of the function of social representations. This raises the question of the relation between social representations and media theory more generally (Livingstone, 1987c). Consider the following study on media images of the family.

Booth (1980) discusses how television deliberately attempted to alter people's conceptions of relationships in order to halt the substantial increase in broken marriages after the war. In 1953, a four-part drama-documentary entitled *The Pattern of Marriage* was broadcast by the BBC with the explicit aim of re-establishing the 'happy family' life of viewers. The programme portrayed an ordinary couple surmounting, successfully, their marital problems, so as to guide viewers through their own problems and thus maintain the family as the basic structural unit of society. Booth argues that the programmes were essentially evasive and conventional, avoiding treatment of the social causes of marital breakdown, and advocating traditional morality as a sole curative.

As television explicitly focuses upon the intra- and inter-personal levels of experience, it appears to omit, or more accurately, disguise, the sociopolitical level, for either benevolent or manipulative ends. Television drama has developed a set of generic conventions, and viewers a set of interpretative expectations, which dictate that macro-level concerns are treated (for they cannot be excluded) through the medium of the intimate or personal. Porter makes a similar analysis of soap opera representations: 'It is important to realise, however, that like pastoral devoid of irony, soap opera reflects and communicates a *form of social seeing* that legitimates a preoccupation with solely private lives. As such, it continues to make a major contribution to the domestication of American woman' (1982, p. 131, my emphasis).

The notion of 'a form of social seeing' certainly suggests social representations should relate to the media. Moscovici (1984) barely considers the media at all, even though this theory constitutes the most complex and provocative theory recently offered by social psychology concerning the nature and status of culturally given representations of

everyday phenomena. We must ask how straightforwardly social representation theory can be applied to television representations, for the media
would seem an increasingly common way in which social representations
enter the currency of everyday life. As communicative acts, media and
social representations may be rather different, so that the media may not
be 'just another source' of representations. Let us briefly consider the
differences. Moscovici, indeed social psychology generally, is often vague
about the origins of the social representations whose psychological or
group-identity consequences are studied. Yet television representations
have a relatively clear source, although the sources upon which they
themselves draw are the very social representations whose origins remain
unspecified or hidden. Programmes are constructed according to a unique
set of criteria, and the meanings which they make available to viewers must
in part reflect those constraints. These criteria variously concern institutional constraints (time, finance, facilities), medium constraints (technology, scheduling), professional constraints (legality, decency, artistic
merit), viewer constraints (ratings, conservativism, presumed intelligence), ideological constraints (morality, consumerism) and literary
constraints (genre, cohesion, narrative structure).

On the other hand, one could regard the media as prime examples of
social representations which usefully and clearly illustrate in a relatively
concrete form many of the features attributed to social representations.
One can analyse the institutions and communicative intent which produce
media representations, the programme structure and, with more difficulty,
the cultural environment and the viewers' interpretations. Drawing on the
vast body of media research may facilitate development of a comprehen-
sive theory of social representations and clarify present shortcomings of the
theory. Unfortunately, we do not at present have either a representation-
based or an interpretation-based categorisation of types of social representation, leaving the typicality of media representations uncertain.

A further dilemma in the integration of social representation theory and
the study of television representations is where one locates the social
representation in the complex communicative process that Hall (1980) has
termed the 'production cycle'. Consider that we must integrate what the
production team wanted to communicate, the television programme made
as a consequence, and what viewers perceived. Which of these is the social
representation, and what are the consequences of selecting any one of
these? While a psychologist might identify a consensus in viewers'
interpretations as the social representation, it seems more usual to identify
the initial presentation of the phenomenon (the book, the programme, the
rules our parents teach us) as the social representation. The ways in which
people make salient or interpret these phenomena is then a matter of the
use of rather than the construction of social representations. This use
constitutes a further problem for it draws upon social knowledge which

may also be regarded as social representations. The argument concerns the status of social representations in the various processes by which meaning is constructed. The many ways in which our symbolic world is endlessly created and recreated in all its variety are such that there is no one role for representations. Consequently, if the term social representation is not to be overextended, merely a fashionable gloss for any work concerning the construction or power of meaning, then it is this entire communication process which must be examined. A theory of social representations will inevitably involve this implicitly, so we should attempt to be explicit. Otherwise, we may fail to distinguish between social representations created by a powerful few for the general public and those which are, instead, emergent from people's ordinary activities.

On issues of the locus of social representations Moscovici's work is weak. Social representations appear from a nebulous social source, in a coherent and intrinsically meaningful form, and force themselves into the consciousness of the defenceless masses. Indeed, but for the deletion of the source, Moscovici often reads like the hypodermic model of critical and early traditional mass communication theory, which held that the process of media influence is analogous to the wholesale injection of pre-produced images (Curran, Gurevitch and Woollacott, 1982). Thus Moscovici has claimed of social representations that 'they impose themselves upon us with irresistible force' (1984, p. 7). Yet people's considerable personal experience, plus access to a wealth of cultural myth and rhetoric may allow them to distance themselves from television representations. Further, the totality of media or other social representations do not constitute a coherent and harmonious whole, and consequently their omissions, ambiguities and contradictions allow considerable leeway for individual interpretation and selection. Together, this must make us question the power of television to impose its new social realities so forcefully upon the viewers. The degree to which television delimits or stimulates ways of thinking remains an open question.

As suggested above, it is because the theory of social representations— and many of these arguments can be applied to discourse analysis as well— fails to distinguish between the virtual and the realised text, or as discussed here, between the social representation as programme and as reading, that this hypodermic notion is available. After all, in media effects theory, as discussed in Chapter 1, it is the role of interpretation and cognition which makes the relationship between content and effect problematic. Indeed, it was only after years of oscillating between conceiving of powerful media and powerful audiences (Katz, 1980) that traditional media research thought to analyse empirical audience response. With social representations theory poised at the beginning of this process, postulating its first hypodermic model, it would seem profitable to learn from this media research history. Indeed, the development of more complex and plural notions of effect provides just one example of how many of the arguments concerning social representations have already been rehearsed and developed in the field of mass communications.

The role of the reader in social psychology

In conclusion, if social representations and everyday discourse operate through the immediate perception of given meanings with no role for the reader, then not only will effects be powerful and direct, but also there can be no theorising of the relationship between reader and text. It is the realisation of the distance between reader and text in media theory which has generated a variety of theories concerning the nature of the relationship between them. One interesting notion among these is the recognition that readers may critically distance themselves from a text by being aware of the text as a constructed product rather than a transparent medium (Katz and Liebes, 1986; Liebes and Katz, 1986). Thus they may speculate about a text's persuasive intent, the manipulative techniques it exploits, or its inherent confusions and contradictions. How do people see a text, a social representation, a section of discourse? As what kind of offering, as what type of genre? Do they approach it passively or actively, mindlessly or mindfully? Do they relate to it critically (as a construct) or referentially (as a window on the world)? Do they make a dominant, negotiated or oppositional reading (Hall, 1980; Morley, 1980)? Do its codes match their own? The assumption of the person is of one who makes dominant, referential, passive readings, just as the assumption of the text is of a closed, influential text. The openness of the text, the power of the audience, and the variety of relationships between text and reader are all omitted from social representation and discourse theory and may be gained from learning from the contribution of semiotic and reception theories to the study of the mass media.

4
The Resourceful Reader

The Psychological Role of the Reader

Reader-oriented theories in literary criticism and cultural studies place considerable emphasis on the negotiation of meaning that takes place between reader and text, viewer and programme (Hohendahl, 1974; Holub, 1984; Suleiman and Crosman, 1980; Tompkins, 1980). They view texts not as repositories of meanings but as sets of devices which guide the negotiation of meaning by the reader. Texts are analysed for gaps which require connecting inferences, for conventions which require experience, and for invitations to the reader to elaborate, contrast or negate aspects of the text. Yet despite their professed intentions, reader-oriented theorists focus predominantly on the text rather than the reader. Consequently, critics may be prompted to ask whether these analyses differ significantly from the approaches to textual interpretation which they superseded (Allen, 1987; Holub, 1984). Literary theorists still tend to proceed as if the meaning negotiated between text and reader can in fact be determined by analysis of the text alone.

To give one example, when Mander (1983) writes about *Dallas,* she moves almost imperceptibly between an analysis of the programme structure, as in 'the writers of *Dallas* are able to suggest . . .' or 'the implicit suggestion of the show is . . .' and assumptions about viewers' perceptions, as in 'the impact of *Dallas* on the popular imagination is . . .' or '*Dallas* puts us in contact with . . .'. Is the implied reader so strongly inscribed in the text that actual readers have no option but to follow? How much is the text a set of instructions for the reader to apply and how much is it a set of invitations or suggestions, with preferences indicated rather than directives? This is, of course, another version of the open:closed question, and thus it appears that the reception theorists and their followers, while moving more towards the reader than most, do so within a conception of the text as closed. Thus much of the interpretive role of the reader peculiar to the open text, or the open features of all texts (Eco, 1979a), is not considered.

Eco considers the role of the reader more explicitly by analysing the relationship between the codes of the text (deriving from the author, the genre and the cultural context of production) and those of the reader (deriving from the reader's experience and sociocultural position of reception). It is because the reader's codes are as important to him as those of the text that Eco retains the notion of miscommunication or aberrant reading. Readers do not simply fill in the text as directed—inevitably an instance of successful, but relatively passive communication—although this is most true for the closed text. Nor do they do what they wish with the text—again, always successful communication because on this view the criteria of communicative success are solely located in the reader. Rather, as a function of the degree of mismatch between the codes of the text and reader, readings may be either aberrant or permissible, and for open texts at least, permissible readings are multiple rather than singular.

Underestimating the role of the reader

It is nonetheless true that far more is written of implied than actual readers and of the texts which readers interpret than of the resources with which they interpret the texts. Yet readers are not only provided with a role in the text but they come to texts with the interpretive resources with which to fulfil that role. They bring with them expectations, knowledge, interests and understandings. The contribution of the reader may have been implicitly excluded by literary critics simply out of ignorance of readers and out of a reluctance to muddy disciplinary boundaries too far. Just as psychology has tended to ignore the complex structuring role of texts, for they are not within the psychologist's domain, so too are readers often ignored by even those professing to include them. Further, just as psychology has tended to reinvent the wheel, creating its own theory of texts, so too do reader-oriented researchers, especially those in cultural studies who are faced with actual audiences, tend to reinvent a theory of readers.

For example, from his group discussions with adolescent viewers of *EastEnders,* Buckingham (1987) concludes that viewers draw upon three categories of knowledge, or more accurately, that the text makes three categories of invitation towards the viewer. The first category of implied knowledge concerns an understanding of narrative—how viewers piece together sequences of events, make comparisons across narratives, and predictions about future events. The second category is that of character knowledge, in which a wide range of sometimes shifting perspectives are offered to viewers for them to identify with. The third category is that of commonsense discourse, in which people relate the programme to their own general social knowledge. This scheme makes sense, dividing a text according to its major aspects of narrative, character, and discourse or context.

My point is that theories of the interpretation of narrative and character/ persons exist in abundance within social psychology and social cognition which could serve to conceptualise and elaborate these simply-conceived categories. We need not begin at the beginning by observing groups discussing a favourite programme to discover that characterisation is an important area or that people have expectations regarding narrative development. Further, the 'discourse' category can be mapped neatly on to the field on 'common-sense' social psychology (Eiser, 1986; Farr and Moscovici, 1984; Forgas, 1981; Heider, 1958). If we do this, we may then subdivide this broad category into the domains of, say, attribution and ordinary explanation, morality and responsibility judgements, group categorisation and prejudice, gender stereotyping, situational rules, sociolinguistic knowledge, and so forth. Each of these domains has been the subject of intensive study in social psychology and together they may offer a developed theory of the resources of the reader. Moreover, for children especially, psychological theories of child development, cognitive and social, could be exploited to make sense of the viewers' interpretations of texts in terms of their developmental stage.

Indeed, the ethnographic focus on adults rather than children is informative, revealing Culler's (1981) assumption that we can assume adults to be just like us, the critic. In any case, such assumptions about children are patently false, and the need for a psychology of child development becomes imperative. Children do not share adults' knowledge or experience of social phenomena, of narrative form (Collins, 1983), of media conventions such as the flashback or ellipsis (Rice, Huston and Wright, 1987) or of moral judgement (Gilligan, 1982; Kohlberg, 1964). Interestingly then, the main semiotician to have studied children's interpretations of the media empirically teamed up with an educational psychologist for the research (Hodge and Tripp, 1986). They needed to draw on Piagetian theory to account for interpretative differences between children of different ages. So, as soon as we see the viewer as separate from the critic, the need for a psychology of the viewer becomes obvious.

Theorising the role of the reader

In the previous chapter, conceptual parallels between social cognition and reception theory were discussed, and there are other parallels one could think of, say between Piagetian structuralism and the schematic analysis of texts, or between cognitive categorisation theories in psychology and in the cognitive anthropology which underlies audience ethnographies. It should be possible to use social psychology to theorise the interpretive resources of the viewer. While much social cognition in particular is couched in 'information-processing' terminology, which is in some ways opposed to the 'text-reader' metaphor, many of the findings may be translated into this new discourse and not rejected. For example, Snyder and Uranowitz (1978) showed how people's memory of a narrative was radically altered if the central character was later said to be a lesbian. Although presented in information-processing terms, this study is not about information-processing in the sense of people processing given, external information, for the study shows that the stereotype of the lesbian is a set of meanings not located 'in' the term 'lesbian' but which form part of people's everyday understanding. Such studies show not people's receptiveness to the 'information' provided but rather their active use of commonsense discourses in the construction or reconstruction of the meaning of a narrative.

A further problem with the undertheorised reader of cultural studies is that, looking from the perspective of the text, the reader appears highly disjointed. At one point, a gap is filled, later an inference is made, then an elaboration attempted. One must see the same process from the reader's perspective to perceive the goals of consistency, the attempts at coherence, the determinants behind textually provided selections, the establishment of a 'mental model' (Johnson-Laird, 1983) of the text up to the point that reading has reached, and to see how expectations are derived from this reading-to-date (Iser's 'wandering viewpoint'; 1980). If Gestalt-like concepts such as schemas serve to organise the knowledge representations which constitute the reader's resources, then Gestalt-like principles of coherence, parsimony and order constitute the principles which inform the construction and application of these resources to new material, together constituting the role of the actual reader.

Everyday explanations

As an example of how viewers' social knowledge is studied by social psychologists, consider Lunt's recent work on the causal modelling of belief systems. Lunt (1988, in press) elaborated the single perceived cause-effect links which have been studied by attribution theory—the study of ordinary explanations—by revealing people's conceptions of the causal relations which hold between multiple causes of phenomena such as loneliness or unemployment. These causal models show how people construct and represent their understanding of complex social phenomena, organising all the different potential causes into a specific model of their interrelationships. The resultant perceived patterning of causal relationships between, say, personal and social, controllable and uncontrollable or stable and unstable causes itself suggests narrative expectations and inferences (Lunt, 1987). These would, presumably, inform people's interpretation of events surrounding a lonely person in a television drama (for example, they would expect people not to try and make contact with those with unpleasant personalities, for the lonely person to become pessimistic about his or her chances of making friends and so they become shy, fear rejection and stop trying to make friends themselves; for these are all causal assumptions people make about the social world in general). The consensual and coherent nature of people's belief system would, if compared to a particular narrative, clearly reveal areas of conflict between social knowledge and the text. In other words, understanding the readers' social knowledge would tell us the inferences that people are likely to make to fill gaps in the story and the kinds of expectations that they would generate. Thus we could predict whether the text would validate (agree with) or negate (conflict with) their preconceptions. Hence, detailed knowledge of people's ordinary understandings and representations provides insights into the process of interpretation and generates hypotheses about the balance between viewer and programme in the negotiation of meanings.

Person perception

A second example of research on social knowledge concerns the perception of other people in everyday life. Beginning in the new cognitivism of the 1950s, Osgood, Suci and Tannenbaum (1957) examined the ways in which people created meaning out of diversity by relating each new object of perception to a common and abstract scheme. By investigating people's perceptions of others, of personality terms and of themselves, Osgood *et al.* found widespread use of a three-dimensional scheme on to which all meanings could be mapped, these dimensions being evaluation, potency and activity. For example, on meeting a new person, one would seek to identify their location on all of these dimensions. As the dimensions are independent of each other, one would not infer from one (say, that the person seems pleasant) to another (say, that the person is a strong character). However, inferences can be made from aspects of personality which relate to the same dimension (knowing that someone is energetic means one can infer that they are also likely to be excitable and to take the initiative)—these index the same underlying dimension (say, how active the person is). On this scheme, people may be compared, attributes integrated and organised, and expectations derived.

Gender knowledge

A similar scheme has been found for the perception and interpretation of gender. Initially studied under the rubric of gender stereotyping theory, Broverman *et al.* (1972) showed impressive consistency in people's assumptions about the typical or average man and woman. For both interpretation and prediction, people regularly reduced the complexity of personality impressions to an oppositional masculine—equals— instrumental and feminine—equals—expressive scheme. Bem (1974, 1984) broadened these findings by introducing a gender schema theory to parallel that of implicit pesonality theory. She argued that gender relates not only to stereotyping but to most if not all domains of everyday perception, so important are gender distinctions to our culture. Gender knowledge cannot be either ghettoised as of limited scope or denigrated as simply negative in impact, for it provides a crucial lens through which the social world is interpreted. Ashmore and Del Boca (1986) attempted to link gender schema research more explicitly with that of Osgood *et al.*, showing how the theme of gender typically is related to the potency dimension (so that masculine is dominant/hard and feminine is submissive/soft) in popular use.

Such schemes, then, provide a tried and tested resource for the viewer making sense of the new characters in a drama. Viewers are not presented with a ready-made personality but rather are required to construct an image given from gradual and fragmented incidents from which one or another aspect of the character may be inferred. It is not only the text but also the reader which ensures that the evolving representation is coherent and accords with what one knows of other people. Alone, each incident could give rise to numerous interpretations: it is only in the context of previous interpretations that a coherent model is gradually constructed and refined.

The application of social knowledge

People operate various strategies which direct this constructive process. These can be related back to Piaget's notions of assimilation and accommodation (1968). For example, an assimilative strategy is one which seeks out only information which confirms prior expectations and neglects anything else. Accommodatory strategies may be exemplified by the seeking of novelty when aroused. As noted earlier, most of social cognition has revealed assimilative or constructive processes. Thus an understanding of readers' knowledge is needed for studying them. Other strategies include the 'fundamental attribution error', in which people tend to neglect situational explanations for the actions of another in favour of a dispositional explanation (they show the reverse pattern in explaining their own actions, and possibly the actions of those on television with whom they have identified). People's categorisation processes tend to operate such that they minimise within category differences and magnify between category differences. This might have interesting implications for television viewing insofar as the ways in which people categorise characters (for example 'us' and 'them' or 'goodies' and 'baddies') will guide their interpretations of the characters' subsequent actions.

Some research has begun to relate sociocognitive knowledge structures to the interpretation of television characters. Both the following examples, interestingly, reveal the constructive nature of these interpretive processes, again warning against inferring effect from content analysis and neglecting actual audience interpretations. Drabman *et al.* (1981) studied children's understanding of counterstereotyped drama, specifically a narrative involving a male nurse and a female doctor. Using a narrative recall paradigm, they found that, particularly with increased time after viewing, the children frequently reversed the gender pattern to fit with their prior knowledge of 'how things should be'. Thus they tended to recall the narrative as having concerned a female nurse and a male doctor. Secondly, Reeves and his colleagues (Reeves and Greenberg, 1977; Reeves and Lometti, 1978) used multidimensional scaling to show that children organised their perceptions of favourite television characters according to a scheme very close to that of Osgood *et al.*, as proposed for the perception of people in everyday life. Children's free trait descriptions of fourteen television characters revealed the following dimensions, in order of importance: humour, strength (the potency dimension), attractiveness (the evaluation dimension), and activity. Moreover, as fits with Ashmore and Del Boca's research (1986), the male and female characters were perceived to differ only on the strength dimension. This suggests that children apply both gender knowledge and implicit personality knowledge to their interpretation of television characters, irrespective of the way in which these characters may have in fact been presented in the programmes.

In sum, I am arguing that the television audience be regarded as active, knowledgeable and skilled in their role of interpretation. And, consequently, a theory of the resources of the reader/viewer is required to further developments in reader-oriented theories of textual interpretation within cultural studies as well as to facilitate traditional mass communications' move towards social cognition. The potential of the psychology of social perceptions and representations has only been indicated here as a fruitful approach for the empirical study of the television viewer. The remainder of this chapter will argue that in two further areas, the empirical study of the viewer, particularly within the cultural studies school, can benefit from a knowledge of social psychology. The first area concerns the theorising of the viewer not only as a resource of knowledge nor simply as a representative of a particular demographic category, but also as a social actor in an interpersonal context. The second area concerns the methodologies with which audiences may be studied, for here social psychology has developed a wide variety of methods for discovering people's understandings, many of which may be applied to the television viewer and the very variety of which suits the eclectic mood of current media research.

Locating the Television Viewer in a Social Psychological Context

I have argued above that the social knowledge of viewers with which they construct meanings, can be usefully understood using social psychological concepts, especially given the conceptual parallels between social cognition and reception theory. For many researchers, these concerns are not at issue, as a straightforward sociological mapping of readers to demographic categories is preferred. This may be seen as a battle between sociological and individual reductionism, where the individual reductionism may be represented by either sociocognitive psychology or psychoanalysis (e.g. Holland, 1975).

Sociodemographic differences among viewers

In his study, Morley (1980) identified different readings with different social class or labour positions. Divergences within a particular class were taken to reflect people's negotiations of their class position or response to membership of contradictory positions (e.g. black trade union worker), but not as a reflection of different personal life experiences. Similarly, Katz and Liebes (1986) look to cultural identities as the source of interpretative repertoires to elaborate the role of the reader and Radway looks to the category of gender. While all of these studies are both innovative and interesting, as Fiske (1987) notes, the picture becomes complicated as one multiplies these social categories (for example, gender, generation, class, ethnicity, religion).

As different social categories are associated with different cultural traditions, different relations to the dominant ideology, different group concerns and so forth, their members thus approach the same text in different ways. Provided social categories are not seen as the sole determinant of viewers' interpretations, the social psychological and sociological positions are compatible in two ways, and need not be mutually exclusive, as sometimes implied.

Social knowledge structures and processes can be seen as the psychological instantiation of sociological categorisation. For example, gender stereotypes and schemas constitute the psychological processes through which sociological gender is both experienced and recreated. After all, social knowledge is the individual cognitive operation of received social representations about oneself, one's own group and other groups: it is fundamentally social, and need not be reduced to a notion of individual or asocial experience. Secondly, the psychological can be thought of as taking over where the sociological analysis leaves off. For example, although the sociological level of analysis may explain why viewers are generally conservative, uncritically accepting dominant ideology messages, the psychological level accounts for the processes by which this occurs. This would point to processes of seeking consistency, of dissonance reduction, of biases in favour of assimilation over accommodation, of confirmatory biases, and so forth. All these make the detailed linkage between the structure of, say, the television news (which masks contradiction, enhances consistency, provides simple frames for the perception of coherence) and the ready acceptance of such structures by the viewers. The psychological analysis may also reveal how and why viewers often fail to detect even those remaining contradictions and ambiguities which critical analysts identify within the news.

Psychological differences among viewers

The psychological level of analysis may identify sources of difference within sociological categories. For example, as media researchers return to the study of the family (Lull, 1988; Morley, 1986) as the main context within which television is interpreted, various factors become relevant—the social psychological and clinical literatures on family dynamics and relationships, the construction of the self concept and of gender identity, the socialising roles of parents, the importance of the concept of control and its relation to attributional styles, motivation, and depression, to the negotiation of boundaries of privacy and self-disclosure, and so forth. Consider the following example (Livingstone, 1988d) from an ethnographic study of the domestic use of information and communication technologies (Silverstone *et al.*, 1989). Two women from very similar 'working-class-made-good', West London backgrounds, both housewives and mothers with a small home-run business, illustrate the very different ways in which people incorporate household technologies into their representations of themselves and their family relationships.

For one woman, the technologies signified domestic power: while she identified all the family technologies clearly in terms of personal possession (who owns what), she assigned the higher status technologies (e.g. home computer, colour television, answer phone) to herself, the intermediate status technologies to her children (colour and black and white television, occasional use of the computer) and the lowest status (radio), unused (stereo) or external technologies (car compact disc player, portable telephone) to her husband. Thus despite her lack of economic and occupational status compared with her husband, she has used the technologies they own to establish her power, at least in the domestic sphere. For the second woman, household technologies are also a sourse of competence (she, not her husband, can work the video recorder). However, they provide merely a means to an end (for example, the fact that her children do not 'get on' is dealt with by providing each child with separate access to a television and video) and indeed, are perceived as an unfortunate evil. Technologies are not valued for their contribution to a modern identity but rather they are deplored for their destruction of family conversation, the pleasures of early courting with her husband before television took over his life, and unfettered teenage freedom. Such pleasures she perpetuates through nontechnological activities, romance novels and going to the park. While both gender and class are important categories for understanding these two women, they are inadequate for capturing either the richness or the variability of the meanings they place around the role of technology in their lives. One must also consider the sources of personal control in their lives, their means of constructing a personal identity, their coping strategies for dealing with their relatively powerless position, their social mobility ambitions, the problems their children have, and so forth. Certainly the technologies do not come with ready-made meanings and prescribed uses attached: they too must be read, with their many uses (readings) varying according to people's experiences and desires.

In conclusion, there is a danger of seeing viewers as either representatives of sociological categories or as isolated individuals lacking asocial context: here lies a role for the social psychology of the family and of socialisation and of social knowledge. Many misunderstandings have arisen from the alignment of the psychological and the individual, for in fact, all of psychology except that specifically labelled individual difference psychology is concerned with general, social constants across individuals which can nonetheless be understood as operating at the level of thoughts, motives and actions. The concept of the stereotype serves as a good example: most research argues precisely that everybody uses stereotypes, and that the differences between people are less interesting than the role that such stereotypes play in the common, normative processes of sense-making. At the most, individual differences serve to reveal the variable operation of a constant phenomenon: the individual level is used to reveal the social, by showing the boundaries and parameters within which social phenomena are constructed.

Social Psychological Methods and the Study of Audiences

Social psychology has developed a variety of methodologies with which it can now contribute to developments in audience research. From the tentative or cautionary statements framing the forays into audience research by critical researchers (consider Morley's 1980 postscript to his audience study and his 1981 paper or Ang's 1985 caveats about her conclusions), it is clear that a range of methods is needed. Those developed within social psychology are somewhat misunderstood by these researchers who frequently avow their hostility to positivism first and foremost (e.g. Allen, 1985).

A common assumption is that psychological methods impose a rigid, *a priori* structure on to people's responses, and further, that any meaning remaining in these responses is destroyed by the application of quantitative analysis. While both rigidity and quantification can indeed be destructive (as too can looseness and lack of systematicness), it is not the case that such methods are the sole approach of social psychology. As discussed earlier, social psychology has suffered its own crisis, centering on methodology and related epistemological problems. Since then, partly by returning to earlier developments (e.g. Piaget, 1968; Bartlett, 1932; Kohler, 1930, all of whom avoided statistics; Lunt and Livingstone, 1989), psychologists have developed a range of methods which can be likened to the Rorschach (or 'inkblot') test. The key points about the Rorschach test were that it was deliberately implicit as regards the researcher's own questions and constructs and that it required an interpretative, qualitative approach which could only subsequently be translated into quantification. This change in methods is part of the trend towards understanding everyday sense-making activities rather than establishing causal processes, although often the two can be related.

Recall and recognition paradigms

Consider the renewed interest in Bartlett's original work (1932) on remembering within recent social cognition. Even at the time this was considered to be a radical challenge to Ebbinghaus' controlled experiments which used deliberately meaningless materials (for many years these researchers examplified the differences between social and cognitive psychology). Bartlett's studies revealed the dynamic processes of remembering, using a version of the children's game 'Chinese whispers' in which people's progressive 'retellings' of an original story are interpreted. These memorial processes were guided by Gestalt principles of coherence and meaningfulness over the incomprehensible, such that the unfamiliar was reinterpreted in terms of the familiar, the trivia was neglected in favour of the gist, the meaningless was ignored, the narrative sequence was fitted to temporal order, and causal connections were favoured over merely associative or sequential links. This paradigm of narrative remembering has become a central method in schema theory, with two versions, one based on free recall, the other on recognition.

To take an example related to the media, Owens, Bower and Black (1979) studied what they termed the 'soap opera effect' in narrative interpretation. People were asked to read a 'soap opera type' of short story, for example, about a student worried that she might be pregnant by her professor. This was written deliberately ambiguously so that without prior knowledge of the student's concern, the story would lend itself to a different reading, merely that of a series of uneventful happenings in her day. With knowledge of her cause for concern, the same story takes on dramatic tension and interest, as her visits to the doctor, her meeting with her professor at a party, and so forth, unfold. Using the recall paradigm, Owens *et al.* discovered that people made numerous 'false intrusions' in their retelling of the story only if they knew of the possible pregnancy. They had filled out the story, elaborating it in the direction of increased coherence, relevance, and meaningfulness, in accordance with their knowledge of the central character. In the recognition paradigm, similar memorial processes were revealed through the analysis of 'false recognitions', in which people believe that they had read statements consistent with their knowledge but in fact absent from the story, because the statements mirrored the implicit inferences which they had made on reading.

In addition to exemplifying one type of activity of the reader or viewer in elaborating a narrative, this study demonstrates the concern with revealing implicit inferential and memorial processes on the part of the reader and with using interpretative, qualitative analysis on the part of the researcher.

Personal Construct Theory and the repertory grid technique

A second, well-established methodology is that developed by personal construct theory (Kelly, 1955) for the similar purpose of eliciting the spontaneous and complex structures of thought. These are conceived as systems of oppositional constructs, which people use implicitly to make sense of everyday phenomena. Developed as an idiographic and thera-peutic technique, the 'repertory grid' uses a Rorschach-type approach, here based not on a notion of memorial elaboration but on that of conceptual structuring through similarity and contrast (Banister and Fransella, 1971). For example, in the study described above concerning the domestic use and understanding of communication technologies (Living-stone, 1988d), much of the analysis was derived from the use of personal construct methods in an interview. Thus people were asked to discuss the ways in which they felt the different technologies which they possessed were different or similar to each other and why, in terms of their and their family's use of the technologies. Using the triadic method, they were asked about the technologies in groups of three, and asked to describe the ways in which two were similar to each other and different from the third. The interviewer then chose subsequent triads on the basis of past responses, following up interesting construct use, breaking down generalised terms into more specific constructs, involving the technologies in different combinations to elicit as many constructs as possible. The method permits relatively efficient, implicit and systematic data collection compared with, say, open-ended interview. It is premised on an underlying cognitive-semantic theory concerning memorial organisation and the construction of meaning through systems of similarity and difference. It strikes an interesting balance between provoking people to think, to make compari-sons and explain their criteria, and refraining from imposing the researcher's interests and preconceptions on to the interviewee. Many things can be done with the data subsequently, of either a quantitative or qualitative nature.

Further social psychological methods

These two examples serve to show some of the ways in which social psychology has moved towards more imaginative and open methods while retaining a firm grasp of issues of representativeness, the various categories of validity, reliability, awareness of the researcher's role, and so forth. One could point to many other examples, such as Potter and Wetherell's (1987) introduction of discourse analysis into social psychology, Petty *et al.*'s (1981) use of verbal elaborations of cognitive responses in the study of attitude change, Burnett's (1987) analysis of letters written to siblings as indices of sibling relationships, and Miell's use of daily diaries of everyday events regarding relationships (1987), see also Antaki (1988) on the analysis of everyday explanations.

Methodological pitfalls

There is, however, a danger that when incorporated into the study of mass communications, these methods are adopted uncritically. This creates a certain amount of redundancy as media researchers 'catch up' on the problems with these methods through empirical realisations, as well as, on some occasions, the possibility of generating quite misleading data. One example is the use of the group interview, or focus group discussion (Morgan, 1988), resurrected independently by Morley (1980) and Katz and Liebes (1986), see also Richardson and Corner (1986). Following from the argument that people's understandings are best elicited by simulations of everyday conversations rather than through individual-based methods, the audience's interpretation of the media is being studied through relatively undirected discussions held by groups of six or more people who may or may not know each other. The resultant group discourse is held up as somehow more 'natural' than individual talk. Little or no reference is made to the large social psychological literature on group dynamics (Brown, 1986). The neglect of group dynamics, like that of family dynamics criticised earlier, means that little critical awareness is given to the interrelations among the participants when analysing their discourse. This is exacerbated by the subsequent reporting of individuals' comments isolated from the context of production. Hence, phenomena are neglected which can radically restructure a group, determining what they say, such as the development of group norms, or the risky shift (in which a group becomes increasingly extreme in its beliefs, each expressing in a group context a more radical position than held when alone) or the adoption of group roles (in which individuals adopt roles such as the leader, the joker, the critic or the conservative, recognising these as vacant positions which require filling to complete the group structure).

A second example of methodological problems can be seen in the increasing interest in the role of gender in structuring people's responses to the media. Now almost replacing class as an issue of theoretical importance in audience decoding and response, researchers typically emphasise the importance of gender in their data, discriminating among men and women respondents. While motivated by 'liberal' or feminist intentions to cease treating women and men as the same, or worse, women as men (though one may argue that they thereby reproduce, certainly emphasise, any gender differences) there is a methodological point here. The current emphasis on gender in media theory mirrors that which swept social psychology in the early and mid seventies, when the then-termed 'sex differences' research was popular. Very similar research statements can be identified in current media research to those made and since heavily criticised (especially by feminists) in social psychology then: specifically those which summarise evidence as 'men think/say/desire that . . . while in contrast women think/say desire that . . .'. For example, in Silj *et al.*'s report (1988) of an Irish men's discussion group, statements offered by 'many' (unspecified) group members rapidly become identified with 'the male Irish viewer'. Such summary statements, which on secondary reporting become wholly divorced from their original, possibly qualified context, can be criticised for artificially polarising the genders. This polarisation is often based on slight differences in average responses, where in fact a considerable overlap in men's and women's responses may exist. Any overlap is typically ignored, any average difference is assumed to be of significant magnitude and the difference between the genders is assumed to be greater than that within them.

The need for or expectation of a 'finding' leads the researcher to neglect such considerations and possibly then to recreate gender differences. All these problems are exacerbated by the tendency of qualitative research to use small samples and to report selectively from their data, discussing items of interest but not presenting the range of the data or the relative frequencies of these items of interest (namely, gender differences). Thus in terms of the development of a particular approach, say a focus on gender, media research is still following and may yet learn from the history of this focus within social psychology.

Multidimensional scaling and semantic representations

Finally, let me introduce one further methodology which also attempts to represent implicit and spontaneous knowledge structures used in everyday interpretation. The method of multidimensional scaling will be discussed here in some depth as it is the method used extensively in the following chapter to generate empirical data on viewers' interpretations of television characters.

The study of semantic representations, as revealed through multidimensional scaling, draws upon what we might term the 'spatial metaphor' of meaning. This is premised upon two ideas: meaning lies in the differences between semantic units; and semantic relations are fruitfully conceptualised by analogy to physical relations. Both semiotics and the psychology of social knowledge hold that meaning lies in the similarities and differences between signs, rather than in the relations between signs and their corresponding real-world referents. The spatial metaphor exploits this concern with structural interrelations between signs, and centres on oppositions between concepts as key forms of structure, on continua or dimensions along which meanings vary, and on the belief in common underlying structure beneath apparent diversity.

Thus, to make sense of otherwise disorganised sets of objects, we group things together, recognise opposites, match and compare things on different dimensions, and so forth. The Gestalt theorists noted how proximity gave the subjective impression of similarity, how we spontaneously organise objects into coherent structures, and argued that principles of similarity and difference are basic to psychological meaning (Kohler, 1930). 'What it means to "make order": usually it means to make the factor of proximity coincide with the factor of similarity; we tend to put similar things together' (Heider, 1979, p. 21).

Social cognition and semiotics study these similar semantic phenomena in very different ways. Semioticians use conceptual analysis to reveal the underlying structures while psychologists use statistical techniques, typically multidimensional scaling or factor analysis, to reveal the common structures underlying a variety of domains of representation. For example, Dyer, Geraghty, Jordan, Lovell, Paterson and Stewart (1981), in their analysis of the programme *Coronation Street,* say that 'our method of analysis examines the oppositions operative in the serial. This approach, which owes much to Levi-Strauss (1972), seeks to uncover the concealed structures of the text within its cultural framework' (p. 84). Similarly, in drawing parallels between the Royal Family and the Ewings of *Dallas,* Coward writes: 'These conflicts and problems are expressed through a series of oppositions in the narrative. It is the function of the characters to carry one or other of the terms in the opposition' (1984, p. 165). On the other hand, Osgood, Suci and Tannenbaum (1957) in psychology use the semantic differential (a bipolar continuum of measurement) to study the semantics of personality attributes, among other things: the semantic differential is proposed as an index of certain aspects of *meaning,* particularly connotative aspects' (p. 273).

Multidimensional scaling (Kruskal and Wish, 1978; Schiffman, Reynolds and Young, 1981) analyses semantic relations by drawing an analogy between conceptual and physical proximity. It transforms distances or proximities between a set of objects into a spatial map in multidimensional space which represents the proximities in terms of Euclidean distance. In the same way that the distances between the cities in Britain are most economically and meaningfully represented on a map, conceptual relations of similarity or difference between objects of psychological interest (e.g. people, emotions, traits) can be represented as a spatial map of semantic knowledge. The map, or semantic representation, can be described in terms of orthogonal linear dimensions (e.g. for cities, the dimensions are North/South and East/West; for animal names, they are size and ferocity,

Henley, 1969). These dimensions have basic cognitive significance for the domain. All objects in the domain have co-ordinate values on each dimension, and the relations between the objects can be calculated in Euclidean distance. Additional properties of a multidimensional scaling space, as with a map, are: indication of densely or sparsely populated areas; indication of structural relations between objects other than dimensional ones (e.g. clustering, circumplex); and the possibility of testing hypotheses concerning number, salience, and identity of dimensions for knowledge organisation.

The advantages of multidimensional scaling as a model of social knowledge are: the economical summary of much information; it reveals hidden structure in the data not easily discernible from the proximities matrix; it provides quantitative, descriptive data for further analysis; the model is fitted to the data rather than forcing data to fit a pre-existing model; meaningful data reduction; it produces a usable model which can be 'read' for a variety of purposes; it produces a representation open to various processing theories; it may be used both as a discovery method or for hypothesis testing.

Most important, multidimensional scaling is a technique which adopts the implicit spatial metaphor with which we commonly discuss semantic relationships. These are otherwise difficult to discuss in everyday discourse and thus difficult for a researcher to discover. In recent years, multidimensional scaling has been used in social psychology, cognitive psychology, and market research, Shoben (1983) discusses many examples of the use of multidimensional scaling in cognition, both in discovering people's representations of different domains and in showing the use of these representations as knowledge structures guiding cognitive processing. In social psychology, Jones (1983) argues thus:

> A common assumption of social psychological theories is that interpersonal behaviour is mediated by structured cognitive representations of self and others . . . [and] that both individual adjustment and group effectiveness depend on some degree of consensus and stability in conceptions of these domains (p. 451).

Forgas (1979) argues for scaling as a discovery method in social psychology, for its many advantages of sensitivity, implicitness, and meaningfulness make it 'an excellent alternative to the qualitative journalistic, descriptive methodologies currently being advocated by some critics' (p. 254). The relation between multidimensional scaling, the spatial metaphor and the role of social knowledge in person perception can be seen thus:

> In making these [multidimensional scaling] judgments, the judge may consider the entire complex of demographic, behavioural, and personality cues that he or she deems relevant for judging pairs of individuals. For each pair judged, it is assumed that a social comparison process is evoked, essentially similar to the process typically evoked in actual social situations . . . the observed set of interpersonal similarity relations generated by a particular judge contains a wealth of relevant information about that judge's construal of self and significant others (Jones, 1983, p. 435).

5

Viewers' Representations of Television Characters

The Study of Viewers' Representations

The ways in which audiences make sense of television involve a set of processes of meaning negotiation which are neither simple nor obvious. The resulting representation constructed of a television programme reveals the person's experience of that programme and also mediates the consequences of viewing in relation to other cognitions, beliefs or actions. In a reciprocal fashion, prior cognitions, knowledge and beliefs contribute to the interpretive role of the reader. This is a two-sided dynamic in which the role of text, like that of the audience, is complex and non-obvious. While one may analyse both texts and readers separately, empirical study is required to discover what happens when they come together.

As argued previously, the study of this negotiation process, in which neither the text nor the reader must be allowed to 'disappear', has implications beyond the discovery of the sense readers make of texts. Such a study reveals the relation between empirical readings and both literary analyses of the text and sociocognitive knowledge. It may also exemplify the advantages of pursuing convergences between traditional mass communications and cultural studies, and also between media studies in general and social psychology. In this way, one may explore the concepts of the role of the reader, the compatibility between reception theory and schema theory, the importance of structural features of texts such as thematic oppositions in guiding interpretation, and so forth.

The context of the research

There are, of course, many ways to study the negotiation between text and reader, as discussed earlier, although most have been relatively unexplored. In this chapter, I will adopt a new approach which offers a variety of advantages. The research to be presented studies the representations which result from and mediate people's interpretations, rather than the process of interpretation itself. To study representations which are both relatively stable and naturalistically obtained, a domain is used with which people have become familiar as part of their daily routine over many years. An excellent example of such a domain is the characters in soap opera. As discussed in Chapter 4, multidimensional scaling offers an implicit and spontaneous method for uncovering the thematic structure of people's representations. The method fits common discourse about representations and interpretation through the spatial metaphor. Thus its results can be related to both literary analyses of texts, via oppositions and themes, and to theories of people's social knowledge of others (fictional or factual), via dimensions (see Chapter 4). Thus people's representations of television characters may be readily related to their dual determinants, the structure of the text and the readers' social knowledge.

The present research contrasts with much other multidimensional scaling research, such as that of Reeves and Greenberg (1977), Forgas (1985), Bisanz *et al.* (1978) and Henley (1969). These tend to study representations of a set of objects not commonly perceived together. For example, in studying a few characters from each of a variety of programmes, Reeves *et al.* created conditions which would mask any role for programme-based determinants of viewers' representations. To some extent, each programme offers the viewer a different world which is internally coherent: this is especially true for soap opera. The present research preserves that coherence by studying the representation of many characters within a single programme. It thus follows structuralist principles (Hawkes, 1977) which first identify the underlying systematic interrelations between elements (characters) in a set (programme). Only at a later stage of research, relationships between these structures may be sought. The mistake is to look for one-to-one relations between elements within different structures without understanding the role each plays within its own structure.

Outline of the research programme

The aim of this chapter is to uncover the structure of the complex representations which people build up through their experience with a given domain, using the method of multidimensional scaling discussed in Chapter 4. These representations provide an integrated summary of past experience, guidance for inference from the known to the unknown, and a resource for the constructive interpretation of future experiences. The study of viewers' representations may provide a 'missing link' when looking for causal relations between programmes and effects: they reveal what the viewers find salient, meaningful, and useful. In particular, one can ask whether viewers' representations reflect primarily the programme structure or the schema-driven interpretative strategies of viewers. Representations of television programmes may be predominantly domain-specific, reflecting the structure of the programme itself (Gliner *et al.*, 1983; LaPorte and Voss, 1979). Alternatively, they may be schema-driven, reflecting the viewer's more general and abstract social knowledge of real-life events and people (Ashmore and Del Boca, 1979; Drabman,

Robertson, Patterson, Jarvie, Hammer and Cordua, 1981; Fiske and Taylor, 1984; Forgas, 1985; Osgood, Suci, and Tannenbaum, 1957). This chapter seeks to establish the nature of viewers' representations of the characters in *Dallas, Coronation Street,* and *EastEnders.* Predictions made by theories of social perception are compared with cultural studies' research on programme structure so as to examine the relative importance and roles of viewer and programme determinants as reflected in the representations.

Characters were selected as the domain of representation for both theoretical and methodological reasons. Theoretically, the characters in a programme are held to mediate a range of television effects, through the processes of imitation, identification, role modelling and parasocial interaction. Especially for soap operas, the viewers become well acquainted with the relatively constant set of characters and feel involved and interested in them. Characters can be seen to carry the narrative, such that narrative or genre themes will be reflected in the construction and representation of the characters. Finally, one could argue that the openness of soap opera, where the role or the reader is maximised, is located especially in the characters. Allen (1985) argues that in soap opera, the range of choices potentially available for any particular aspect of the programme (paradigmatic complexity—typically expressed through character portrayal) is greater than the range of choices available for narrative sequencing (syntagmatic complexity), which thus tends to be more predictable and straightforward. As the characters in soap opera offer multiple possibilities, and as the viewers must be aware of the paradigm of possibilities from which any one choice is made, considerable demands are placed on their interpretative efforts.

The study of characters maps neatly on to person perception research which both facilitates the relation between programme interpretation (or characters) and social knowledge (of people). Person perception research has made considerable use of multidimensional scaling because people, like characters, form naturally distinct units which can be meaningfully grouped and compared.

Social psychological theories of peson perception were introduced in Chapter 4 as potential theories of the resources of the reader or viewer. They will be used in the present research for this purpose, to allow specification of that with which viewers make sense of programmes. The social psychological theories of person perception investigated in the present research were Stereotyping or Gender Schema theories and Implicit Personality Theory. Parallels between the representation of television characters and real-life people allow the extension of person perception theories. For people's everyday social experience of others is to some extent mirrored in the way that regular soap opera viewers immerse themselves in a particular social *milieu* for many years and build up a complex web of background knowledge, emotional reactions, and personal judgements (Cantor and Pingree, 1983; Livingstone, 1988a). How far, then, do theories of real-life person perception extend to explain the perception of television characters?

These theories will be contrasted with a literary critical view of the soap operas, to investigate the extent to which viewers' representations constitute a veridical representation of the programme. Recent research has analysed soap opera from a literary or semiotic point of view (Allen, 1985; Ang, 1985; Arlen, 1981; Berger, 1981; Dyer, Geraghty, Jordan, Lovell, Paterson, and Stewart, 1981; Mander, 1983). One important technique adopted is to identify the central binary oppositions around which the text is structured. This allows researchers to reduce the diversity of the programmes to a manageable number of issues. These are then related both to more general social issues and also to the narrative structure of the programme. Soap operas are concerned to treat moral and social issues so as to engage the viewers' interest. As numerous recent researchers have noted, soap opera is concerned with cultural and social issues of fundamental concern to people, such as kinship relations, reproduction, gender, the role of the community, and so forth (Allen, 1985; Hobson, 1982; Seiter, 1981). Characters are seen as representing the poles of the various oppositions, allowing the pattern of social interactions in the narrative to be analysed in terms of the manipulation, transformation, alignment of interaction of the central oppositions. In essence, the considerable involvement of viewers with this genre together with the conventions and history of the genre (Allen, 1985; Hobson, 1982) suggests that soap opera provides a considerable role for the viewer to be constructive and to create his or her own meanings, and yet also is of sufficient relevance for viewers to be receptive to the often non-normative messages of the programmes. The regularity and timescale over which viewers become involved with soap operas certainly ensures considerable naturally acquired knowledge whose structure can be investigated.

In sum, the aim of this chapter and the two which follow is to present a body of empirical research which (1) establishes the readings or representations which viewers construct of television characters; (2) examines the relation between representation, text and social knowledge; (3) explores the variety of secondary hypotheses concerning the role of the reader, the applicability of person perception theories, the role of text structure, the relevance of gender themes, and so forth; and (4) argues for the values of empirical research in the debate about audiences and interpretation.

An Analysis of Three Soap Operas

As discussed in Chapter 3, social psychologists frequently give little consideration to the structure of the object domain whose representation is being studied. Yet clearly this structure may affect the resultant representation. Nor should the domain be reduced to an experimentally controllable one. We will now consider the nature and complexity of the three popular programmes to be studied here, *Dallas, Coronation Street,* and *EastEnders.* While the notion of 'true readings' is a complex and problematic one, we need to assume some description of the programmes prior to studying viewers' representations of them. This description can take the form of identifying potential readings and probable representational themes based in the programmes themselves. I will assume here that literary critical or textual readings are more analytic, systematic, comparative and unmotivated than viewers' readings. Thus any discrepancies between the two types of reading may reveal predominantly the constructive activities of the viewer. One purpose of the present chapter is to make explicit the distinction between structural analyses and the viewers' own interpretations (rather than presume that the latter are merely impoverished versions of the former) by beginning to investigate empirically both viewers' interpretations and their relationship to programme structure.

DALLAS

Dallas is a very popular prime-time American 'soap opera'. It is not a true soap opera in the sense of the American daytime soaps, for it has a higher budget, is produced as a series (a finite set of episodes) rather than as a continuous serial, draws upon the conventions of melodrama as well as soap opera and is geared to a night-time audience (Ang, 1985). Nonetheless, *Dallas* is popularly treated as a soap opera and generates viewers' involvement in a similar fashion. The programme concerns the daily activities of a Texan oil community, focusing on two rival wealthy families, the Ewings and the Barnes. Plots centre on the oil business and on family issues. The programme began in the mid seventies, and has since spread around the world with great success, including Britain, where the audiences average 8–10 million.

Literary analysis of *Dallas* (Arlen, 1981, Liebes and Katz, 1988; Mander, 1983; Silj *et al.*, 1988) suggests that *Dallas* is structured around two major themes. The viewers' interest is derived from the conflict between and ambiguity in these themes as they are repeatedly enacted through various characters and plots. The first theme is that of morality, closely related to the unifying symbol of the family (implying loyalty, honesty, and durability). The second theme is the morally corrupting power of organisations, business and money, which dictate that the individual can only survive in the collective. The conflict and ambivalence between these two themes is epitomised in the character of J.R. Ewing, the arch 'baddie' of the business world who nonetheless can always justify his immoral deeds as being necessary to the smooth running of the family business, Ewing Oil. Hence, *Dallas* is concerned with 'the apparent contradiction between the success of ruthless corporate room tactics and values, usually at the hands of J.R., and the human values of family life' (Mander, 1983, p. 46). The moral and immoral are not, however, evenly balanced: 'while *Dallas* does affirm the immorality of crime, the affirmation of conventional morality and societal values is relatively shaky' (Mander, 1983, p. 45).

Ang (1985) showed that viewers perceived the characters in terms of melodramatic roles. She analysed some of the messages latent in the characters' actions, seeing them as consistent with these perceived dramatic roles. For example: 'J.R.'s actions tend to strengthen the tragic structure of feeling. He demonstrates that power can only by coupled with badness and immorality, while those who want to live a "good" life are constantly bereft of power and doomed to suffer' (p. 77). This concurs with Mander and Arlen, although Ang perceives less ambiguity in the opposition of morality and power.

Through focus group interviews during and after viewing *Dallas,* Katz and Liebes (1986) have investigated some of the ways in which programme meanings constructed by viewers differ from those implicitly assumed by content analytic and literary critical researchers. Viewers edit the stories into more linear sequences; they invoke clear, unambiguous moral frameworks for actions (this contrasts with the literary analyses of Mander, 1983, and Arlen, 1981); they negotiate between their own cultural values and those of the programme, especially when their own culture is very different from that of the programme; they may relate events in the programme to events in their own lives, retaining more or less critical distance from the programme; and so forth.

CORONATION STREET

Coronation Street has been the most consistently popular television programme in Britain since its inception in 1960 (average viewing figures are one-quarter to one-third of the population). *Coronation Street* is set in a small, urban, working class street in Northern England. It concerns the everyday events concerning a community of some twenty long-standing, interrelated characters, showing their quarrels, jealousies, hopes, habits, and romances. Even more than with *Dallas,* and more true to the soap opera genre, events unfold slowly, are complex in their implications and histories, are never fully resolved, and centre more on dialogue, especially gossip, than on action. No single perspective is prioritised and there are no heroes, but rather a multiplicity of perspectives personified in the different characters (see, for example, the narrative analysed in Chapter 3). The programme is appreciated by viewers for its warmth, wit, honesty, and relevance (Livingstone, 1988a).

Coronation Street is rooted in the social realist tradition of the late 1950s in Britain. Dyer (1981) argues that *Coronation Street* was and still is true to the four main elements in Hoggart's influential characterisation of social realist popular culture in *The Uses of Literacy* (1957). The first element concerns a focus on everyday, ordinary and mundane events and interactions in real time which are framed by conventional common sense—the normative assumptions, explanations and myths of the community portrayed. Secondly, there is an absence of actual work, despite continuous references to work and the working class and a focus on domestic lifestyles and interpersonal value-systems. This facilitates the third parallel, a heavy focus on women: women are portrayed as strong, central, and the pivot of the working class community. Finally, the programme is imbued with nostalgia for the warmth, simplicity, and charm of a world which, the genre suggests, did once exist but does so no longer.

In their analysis of the programme, Paterson and Stewart (1981, p. 84; see also Lovell, 1981) conclude that 'it is possible to see the major oppositions of *Coronation Street* as Inside:Outside and Male:Female'. Particular narratives may also be structured around specific additional oppositions which are related to these major oppositions, such as Work:No-Work. Generally, narratives are set within a class framework, so that Inside:Outside is frequently aligned with Working Class:Middle Class. Social class is a central theme in British culture and has been incorporated into British soap opera as one of its dominant features. Thus, British soap opera centres on specific, traditional working class communities and tends to represent the middle classes as disruptive, modern, and insensitive to the feelings and concerns of ordinary, working class people.

Given *Coronation Street*'s claim to realism and the parallels which viewers themselves perceive between their lives and those portrayed (Livingstone, 1988a), one might expect viewers to differ from this textual analysis by interpreting the characters in *Coronation Street* according to their knowledge of people in general. As the present studies will investigate, analyses of programmes as cultural products may not reveal the role of such artefacts in everyday life.

Coronation Street differs from *Dallas* in certain key ways. Because of its prime-time position, *Dallas* has a faster, more action-oriented pace than *Coronation Street*, and presents a far more glamorous image than the mundane *Coronation Street*. Each draws both on soap opera conventions and other conventions—in the case of *Dallas*, from melodrama, in the case of *Coronation Street*, from social realism. There is also a gender difference, insofar as the men in *Dallas* take a more prominent position, vying with the women for primacy, whereas *Coronation Street* offers a more feminine atmosphere. Nonetheless, both are similar in the adherence to the soap opera genre: each centres on the family and romance, each offers a relatively feminised style (Fiske, 1987) with an emphasis on discourse and detail, each is relatively open textually and each supports parasocial interaction rather than hero identification.

The differences between *Dallas* and *Coronation Street* are open to two competing explanations. Either all programmes differ in their central themes or British programmes differ from American programmes, although they are similar within themselves. While ideally one should study many programmes, the study of viewers' representation of characters in a second British soap opera should help to clarify the issue. If, for example, *EastEnders* is represented on similar themes to *Coronation Street,* a British/American difference would be indicated. If the two British programmes are also represented differently, it would seem that viewers' representations are sensitive to programme differences and that viewers do not abstract the commonalities across programmes.

EASTENDERS

EastEnders is far more like *Coronation Street* than *Dallas,* except that it attempts to be more up to date, more socially conscious and issue oriented, more action-packed and faster paced, and to contain more younger characters and modern issues than *Coronation Street. EastEnders* is currently the most consistently popular programme on television in Britain, averaging audiences of some twenty million viewers per episode. This soap opera, which began in February 1985, concerns the everyday lives of a working class community in London's East End. It contains characters who encompass a range of ages, ethnic backgrounds and occupations (see Buckingham, 1987, for an analysis of the programme). Like *Coronation Street,* it conforms to the genre conventions for British soap opera in the social realism tradition (Dyer *et al.,* 1981), containing strong women, a nostalgic respect for working class community life, and a serious attempt to deal responsibly with contemporary social issues in a realistic fashion. Again, like *Coronation Street, EastEnders* differs from the American prime-time soap operas in the type of community portrayed and in attempting to mirror the everyday lives of the viewers.

Studies of Viewers' Representations of Characters in Three Soap Operas

Design and procedure

The studies concerned viewers' representations of the characters in these three soap operas, where each was studied separately. The data were collected so as to be entered into multidimensional scaling analysis. This analysis was particularly appropriate, because an exploratory rather than a hypothesis-testing procedure was preferred so as to determine which underlying dimensions of character representation emerge spontaneously from viewers' judgements. People judge the similarities between the characters, and the analysis makes explicit the criteria implicitly underlying their judgements. People's judgements are not affected or constrained either by the theoretical assumptions of the researcher or by the task of making their underlying criteria explicit.

There are two widely-used methods of obtaining implicit similarity data for multidimensional scaling analysis (Jones, 1983): pair-wise similarity judgements and free sorting of objects or characters into similar groups. A high degree of similarity between the representations produced by the two methods provides evidence of a robust representation (Kruskal and Wish, 1978). The free sorting of characters into as many groups as they wish is an easier task for viewers, being both more enjoyable and less arduous. The judgements are probably more implicit and spontaneous as a result. The sorting method is preferable for research with large numbers of stimuli and where the avoidance of language is preferred, as with children or different cultures. However, this method produces somewhat less exhaustive data, because in their judgements, viewers may not mentally compare every pair of characters for similarity. Both methods were used for the study of *Dallas*, while for *Coronation Street* and *EastEnders*, only the sorting method was used.

The most basic and straightforward method of scaling was used to analyse these data, the one which makes the fewest assumptions and which is most naturally or readily applicable to psychological representations. This is the classical, unweighted, symmetric, single matrix multidimensional scaling model (see Schiffman *et al.*, 1981, for a taxonomy of common scaling techniques). The data are assumed to contain an underlying structure. If they do not, the solution will contain excessive error, as measured by the stress value. The resultant space is constant under the basic transformations of rotation, reflection, and translation. Most procedures produce a metric, Euclidean space, whether from metric of non-metric proximities data. Unlike factor analysis, the spaces between objects are meaningful.

Viewer samples

In each of the studies to be described below, the samples of viewers were obtained from the Oxford University subject panel. This is a panel of ordinary Oxford residents who volunteer to participate in psychological research and they are paid nominally for their time. They contain few students, being mainly white collar workers (such as secretaries, clerks, shop assistants), those free in the daytime (homemakers, unemployed, retired) and professionals (teachers, nurses). They are of a wide range of ages, from 18 to 80. In these samples, it proved hard to find men who would participate, even though large numbers of men watch soap operas. Consequently, despite considerable efforts, the samples contain around two-thirds women and one-third men. All the participants in this research were regular and long-term viewers of the soap opera under study: they watched the programme for most or all of its episodes each week and have done so for some years (in the case of *Coronation Street*, this could be as many as twenty years or more). For each study described below, further details on samples, procedure, and statistical results can be found in Livingstone (1987a). In addition, the *Dallas* research has also been published in Livingstone (1987b, 1988b) and the *Coronation Street* research in Livingstone (1989a, 1988b).

A study of viewers' representation of DALLAS characters

The thirteen central characters in *Dallas* (December to February 1984–5) were J. R. Ewing, Bobby Ewing, Pam Ewing, Jenna Wade, Sue Ellen Ewing, Miss Ellie Ewing, Ray Krebbs, Donna Krebbs, Lucy Cooper-Ewing, Cliff Barnes, Katherine Wentworth, Clayton Farlow, and Sly (J.R.'s secretary). A questionnaire was constructed which presented every pair-wise combination of these characters (method 1 above). For each pair, the similarity of one pair member to the other was rated by viewers using a five-point rating scale defined by the expressions 'Not at all similar' and 'Very similar'. The viewers were forty regular *Dallas* viewers, twenty-three women and seventeen men, half British and half Canadian.

The raw pair-wise similarities data were averaged over viewers and the mean similarity score for each character pair was entered into MRSCAL (Roskam, 1981), a classical multidimensional scaling program for metric data. Over all the pair-wise comparisons, the standard deviations varied from 0.423 to 1.248, indicating that the mean similarity scores were reasonably representative of the original data. The stress or error in the solution was satisfactorily low, with an 'elbow' (an indication of the minimum dimensionality for which the data can be best represented) at two dimensions (Kruskal and Wish, 1978; Schiffman *et al.*, 1981). The coefficient of alienation (an indication of the goodness of fit of the model to the data, or error) was 0.136 (which is conventionally considered satisfactory). To test the reproducibility of the semantic space, a replication of this study was carried out using both a separate viewer sample ($n=45$) and a different method of data collection, free sorting. The resultant representation was found to be highly significantly correlated with that obtained above and thus the replication was satisfactory. The representation can be seen in Fig. 1.

This representation shows the interrelations which viewers perceive to hold between the characters in the programme. Characters who are far apart in the space (such as J.R. and Bobby) are considered by viewers to be far apart conceptually, in terms of their personalities. Characters who are close together in the space (such as Bobby and Miss Ellie) are seen as similar by the viewers. Thus the spatial distances between characters represent conceptual distances. The dimensions of the space serve to discriminate among the characters, revealing the criteria of judgement implicitly used by the viewers when making their similarity judgements.

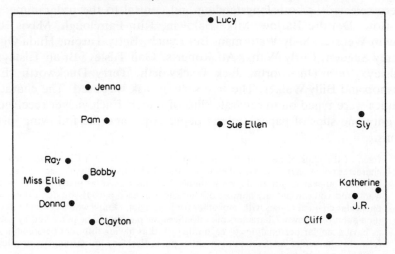

FIGURE 1   Viewers' representation of the characters in *Dallas*
(Dimension 1=horizontal; dimension 2=vertical).

The most salient feature of the character space is the strong first
dimension, which clearly separates the characters into two distinct clusters.
These correspond to the morally good or honest characters ('goodies') and
the morally corrupt characters ('baddies'). Only two characters (Sue Ellen
and Lucy) are therefore perceived by viewers as morally ambiguous. That
power is seen to corrupt is indicated by Sly's position: in her recent role,
she joined both Cliff's and J.R.'s corrupt schemes in order to help her
brother. Her basically moral aim appears less salient than her immoral
acts.

The second dimension discriminates between the characteristics within each
of the two clusters. It separates most of the women from all the men,
although the three most serious and professional of the women (Donna,
Miss Ellie, and Katherine) are categorised with the men. This suggests that
the salient feature of most of the women, that which discriminates them
from the men, is their frivolous and pleasure- or glamour-seeking nature.
The male characters are perceived as primarily business-oriented. On this
dimension, Ray occupies the ambiguous position. Based on the above
considerations, the two emergent dimensions can be labelled *morality* and
pleasure/business oriented. These two dimensions capture those implicit
relations and contrasts between the characters which are most salient to
viewers.

A study of viewers' representation of CORONATION STREET characters

Twenty-one characters in *Coronation Street*, eleven women and ten men, were selected as both longstanding and central to the programme: Ken Barlow, Deirdre Barlow, Mike Baldwin, Rita Fairclough, Mavis Riley, Kevin Webster, Sally Waterman, Bet Lynch, Betty Turpin, Hilda Ogden, Percy Sugden, Curly Watts, Alf Roberts, Gail Tilsley, Brian Tilsley, Ivy Tilsley, Vera Duckworth, Jack Duckworth, Terry Duckworth, Emily Bishop and Billy Walker. The free sorting task was used. The characters' names were typed on to separate slips of paper. Each viewer received the twenty-one slips of paper, several paper clips, and the following instructions.

> Each of the slips of paper in this envelope has the name of a *Coronation Street* character typed on it. You are asked to sort the 21 characters into piles according to how they appear to you in the programme. You may make as many piles as you want, and you can put any number of characters in each pile. If you don't think a particular character 'goes with' any other (or if you don't know who a character is), then put it on its own. Characters put into the same pile should be perceived by you as having similar personalities to each other, and as having different personalities from the characters you have put into other piles. Feel free to rearrange your piles until you are satisfied.

There were fifty-eight viewers (forty-seven women, eleven men).

Viewers' character sortings were used to construct a lower triangular data matrix with one cell for each character pair. Each cell contained the number of viewers who placed that particular pair of characters together. This matrix was entered into the MRSCAL program for metric classical multidimensional scaling (Roskam, 1981). The elbows lay at two and at three dimensions. As the stress was good for the three-dimensional solution but poor for the two-dimensional one, the three dimensional solution (coefficient of alienation = 0.1419) was selected for interpretation (see Figs. 2 and 3, to be interpreted together).

On visual inspection of the character representation based on the whole sample, several points can be made. Firstly, the characters are evenly spread throughout the space. This indicates that viewers see the characters in a multidimensional fashion, not in terms of a few discrete clusters. Consequently, most or all possible thematic positions are occupied by the characters, unlike for the *Dallas* representation, where the characters were more clustered, leaving certain areas of the space vacant. This facilitates the construction of narratives, because for each combination of dimensional or oppositional poles, there is likely to be one character who is seen to typify that particular combination of attributes.

Secondly, viewers appear to distinguish firmly between the male and female characters. The characters divide by sex in the space on either side of the top left/bottom right diagonal of the first two dimensions (Fig. 2). There are no particular groupings by age. From a knowledge of the characters, it seems reasonable to interpret the top right/bottom left diagonal as separating the more staid an responsible characters from the more roguish characters. Dimension 3 (Fig. 3) divides those characters

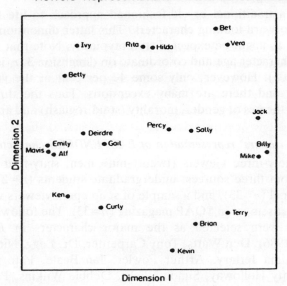

FIGURE 2   Viewers' representation of the characters in *Coronation Street*
(Dimension 1=horizontal; dimension 2=vertical).

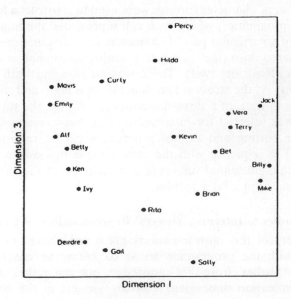

FIGURE 3   Viewers' representation of the characters in *Coronation Street*
(Dimension 1=horizontal; dimension 3=vertical).

who take a traditional or old-fashioned approach to life from the more modern, forward-looking characters. This latter dimension maps roughly on to age, as might be expected stereotypically. Note that the correlation between character age and co-ordinate on dimension 3, r, is -0.634, d.f.= 20, $p=0.005$). However, only some 40 per cent of the variance is thus explained, and there are many exceptions. Thus the three dimensions reflect the themes of gender, morality (staid:roguish) and approach to life.

A study of viewers' representation of EASTENDERS characters

The ninety-three viewers (twenty-nine men, sixty-four women) were derived from three sources: undergraduate students ($n=27$), the Oxford subject panel ($n=33$), and a sample of soap opera viewers who responded to an advertisement in SOAP magazine ($n=33$). The following twenty-five characters were selected as the major characters in *EastEnders* (in Summer, 1986): Den Watts, Tony Carpenter, Dr. Legg, Nick Cotton, Lou Beale, Naima Jeffery, Arthur Fowler, Ian Beale, Pete Beale, Sharon Watts, Lofty Holloway, Simon Wicks, Debbie Wilkins, Pauline Fowler, Ali Osman, Andy O'Brian, Michelle Fowler, Kathy Beale, Sue Osman, Angie Watts, Kelvin Carpenter, Dot Cotton, Ethel Skinner, Saeed Jeffrey, and Mary Smith. The free sorting method was used to discover viewers' representations of the characters, with the same procedure and instructions as for the *Coronation Street* study above.

The viewers' character sortings were used to construct a lower-triangular matrix of proximities, where each cell represented the number of viewers who sorted a particular pair of characters into the same group. These data were entered into the nonmetric multidimensional scaling program, MINISSA (Roskam, 1981). There was an elbow at both two and three dimensions. As the stress at two dimensions is high, and there are enough characters to warrant a three-dimensional solution, the three dimensional solution was selected for interpretation (D-hat stress = 0.1630). In this study, the sorting and ratings procedures (to be reported later) were conducted in sequence with the same sample of viewers. The representation is thus presented following a description of the ratings procedure (Figs. 7 and 8) in a later section.

Studies to Interpret Viewers' Representations of Characters

To interpret the representations presented above, one needs to be familiar with the programme so as to know the characters well. As mentioned earlier, from this knowledge, one can gather the meanings of the discrimination dimensions used by viewers in the similarity judgements. However, it is preferable to test this interpretation empirically. Further, we wish to test the relevance of textual analyses and social knowledge structures to these character representations, so as to infer their determining role in constructing the representations. These three sets of interpretations or themes were, for the design adopted, first translated into semantic differential scales which could be readily related to the character representations. The following studies report how viewers' ratings of the characters on these scales relate empirically to the character representations obtained above. The semantic differentials used are shown in Table 1. Although reported together, each of the three programmes was studied separately.

TABLE 1.

Scales derived from implicit personality theory
Theme: evaluation (intellectual and social)
              Scales: intelligent:unintelligent   DCE
                          rational:irrational   DC
                          sociable:unsociable   DC
                          warm:cold   DCE
                          likeable:not likeable   E
Theme: activity
              Scales: active:passive   DCE
                          excitable:calm   DC
Theme: potency
              Scales: dominant:submissive   DCE
                          hard:soft   DCE

Scales derived from gender schema theory
Theme: gender
              Scales: masculine:not masculine   DCE
                          feminine:not feminine   DCE

Scales derived from literary analyses of the programme
Theme: morality and family
              Scales: moral:immoral   DCE
                          values family:does not value family   D E
Theme: community and class
              Scales: working class:middle class   CE
                          central:peripheral to the community   CE

Scales derived from the researcher's interpretation of the space
Theme: staid:roguish
              Scales: roguish:not roguish   C
                          staid:not staid   C
Theme: approach to life
              Scales: modern:traditional approach to life   CE
                          mature:immature   C
                          sexy:not sexy   CE
Theme: pleasure:business-orientation
              Scales: pleasure-oriented:business-oriented   D
Theme: complicated personality
              Scales: complicated:not complicated   E

Note: DCE = asked of viewers for *Dallas* (D), *Coronation Street* (C) and *EastEnders* (E).

Design and procedure

The properties to be rated were presented to subjects in the form of a grid, with the columns labelled with the names of the characters, and with the rows labelled with the rating scales, as given in Table 1. For each rating scale, one pole corresponded to a '1' (for example, 'warm') and the other corresponded to a '7' (for example, 'cold'). Viewers were instructed to rate their impression of each characters in general as they appear in the programme on each scale. For each study, the viewer sample consisted of regular viewers of the programme judged, of a range of ages and occupations (*Dallas:* thirteen women and seven men; *Coronation Street:* fifteen women and six men; *EastEnders:* forty-seven women and twenty-four men).

For each of the character sets, average property ratings were calculated for each character by collapsing over viewers. The reliability of this averaging procedure was checked by calculating Cronbach's alpha for each property rating over viewers. These were mostly 0.90 or above, and so the means were deemed representative of the ratings. This averaged data was then entered into the PROFIT program (Roskam, 1981), together with the co-ordinates for the relevant character representation.

PROFIT (Chang and Carroll, 1968) is a method of fitting externally rated properties for a set of stimuli to a multidimensional scaling space for those same stimuli through the use of multiple linear regression. In PROFIT, each property is tested independently of the others, with the property serving as the predicted variable for the multiple predictors of dimension co-ordinates. Thus the dimensions of the space are regressed on to the property ratings, thus ensuring that the independent variables or dimensions are independent determinants of the dependent variable or property ratings. If the regression is significant, then the property can be said to 'fit' the space. If the space was constructed through an implicit method, such as similarity judgements or a sorting task, then PROFIT can be used to relate the implicit or emergent dimensions to the explicit or theoretically derived properties. It outputs each significant property in the form of a vector (the regression line) projected on to the space whose direction describes the direction in which the property increases through the space, and thus the direction in which characters increasingly represent that particular property. Unlike the common alternative of correlating properties with dimensions, PROFIT does not constrain the properties to be mutually orthogonal. Kruskal and Wish (1978) point out that oblique axes may provide a better characterisation of the 'real world', even though orthogonal dimensions provide a simpler description.

Results

The PROFIT procedure tells us three things: the relevant or irrelevant properties from the viewpoint of the character representation (as determined by significance testing); the relations between the properties and the characters in the space; and the relations between the properties themselves. Table 2 shows the degree of fit between the rated properties and the character spaces for each programme studied, and whether or not this goodness of fit is significant. Kruskal and Wish (1978) recommend interpretation only those properties whose R-squared is significant beyond the 0.01 level. This table shows that intellectual evaluation (intelligence

TABLE 2. *Comparison of the properties which significantly fit the character representations over three programmes*

Property	DALLAS	CORONATION STREET	EASTENDERS
Intelligent	n.s.	n.s.	n.s.
Rational	n.s.	n.s.	– – –
Sociable	n.s.	**	– – –
Warm	***	*	***
Likeable	– – –	– – –	**
Dominant	***	**	n.s.
Hard	***	***	**
Values Power	**	– – –	– – –
Active	*	n.s.	n.s.
Excitable	n.s.	n.s.	– – –
Temperamental	– – –	– – –	***
Masculine	n.s.	***	***
Feminine	n.s.	***	***
Moral	***	***	***
Family Values	*	– – –	***
Roguish	– – –	***	– – –
Staid	– – –	***	– – –
Central	– – –	*	*
Class	– – –	n.s.	n.s.
Sexy	– – –	***	n.s.
Approach to life	– – –	***	***
Mature	– – –	*	– – –
Business/pleasure oriented	*	– – –	– – –
Complicated	– – –	– – –	***

*	significant property, p<0.05
**	significant property, p<0.01
***	significant property, p<0.001
n.s.	non-significant property
– – –	property not tested for this programme

and rationality) and activity (active, excitable, although not temperamental) are irrelevant to all three character representations and social class
(working class/middle class) is irrelevant when tested against the British
programmes. Conversely, social evaluation (sociable, warm, likeable),
potency (dominant, hard, values power), morality, and approach to life are
generally important to representations of all three programmes studied.
Notable differences between the programmes were found for the properties of gender, family values and sexy. Certain discrepancies are
apparent which indicate specific relationships between properties and
programmes, rather than general themes. For example, although hard and
dominant are considered equivalent in Implicit Personality Theory, hard
but not dominant was significant for *EastEnders* and similarly, supposedly
identical properties like warm and sociable was differently represented in
the *Dallas* space, with only warm being a significant theme in *Dallas*).

Interpreting viewers' representation of DALLAS characters

As can be seen from Table 2, eight of the fourteen candidate properties
were found to fit the space significantly. This means that, for these eight
properties, a regression line could be drawn through the character space
for *Dallas,* with minimal error. In this analysis, the co-ordinates of the
characters on the dimensions are the independent, predictor variables, and
the values of the rated property for each character are the dependent,
predicted variable. The properties *warm, moral, dominant, values organisational power,* and *hard* all fitted the space very well ($p<0.01$). The
properties *active, pleasure/business-oriented* and *believes in traditional
family values* fitted the space moderately well ($p<0.05$).

The properties projected on to the two dimensions of the space can be
seen in Fig. 4. Each property line (or vector) describes a linear increase in
characters' ratings on that property. The vectors have been drawn on to the
space in one direction only for clarity. Thus one must imagine that each
property, for example moral:immoral, extends in opposite directions. For
example, in the case of morality, as one moves through the space to the
left, the characters are perceived by viewers as increasing in morality (thus
Miss Ellie is more moral than Sue Ellen) and as one moves to the right, the
characters become increasingly immoral (thus J.R. is more immoral than
Lucy or Bobby).

The first dimension of the space corresponds extremely well to the *moral*
property, while the second dimension corresponds to the cluster of
properties labelled *dominant, values organisational power, hard, active,*
and *pleasure/business-oriented. Warm* and *believes in traditional family
values* lie at an oblique angle to the other two dimensions, but are
associated with *morality* and opposite to the *dominant/power/hard* cluster.
Thus, for example, viewers consider that J.R. is dominant, active, hard,
values organisation power, business oriented, cold, immoral and yet

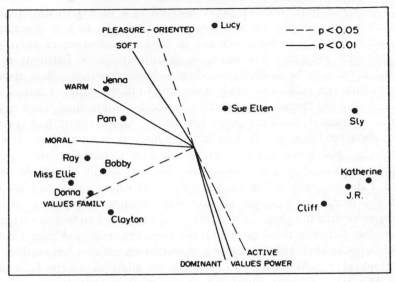

FIGURE 4   Viewers' representation of the characters in *Dallas,* showing
significant properties as vectors (Dimension 1=horizontal;
dimension 2=vertical).

believes somewhat in family values. In contrast, Clayton, like Miss Ellie,
Ray, Donna and Bobby is seen as moral, family-oriented and fairly warm,
and yet also is more dominant, active and business oriented than Ray or
Bobby. While other properties might also have fitted the space, had they
been tested, they must be semantically associated with those found to fit
the space, and so major areas of meaning have not been lost. The intuitive
interpretation of the representation offered above, centering on themes of
morality and power, was supported by this second study. The determining
roles of social knowledge and textual themes will be discussed later in this
chapter.

Dallas is thus perceived as presenting the contrast between a (mainly
female) world of pleasure, weakness and femininity and a (mainly male)
world of organisational power and hard-headed business. The former,
hedonistic world is not conceived as either more or less moral than the
latter, business world, for *morality* is orthogonal to the *potency* cluster.
With power split equally between the 'goodies' and the 'baddies' the fight
between good and bad will be equal and endless.

One might have expected that, say, morality would be associated with
business and immorality with pleasure, or that immorality would be
associated with dominance (Ang, 1985). The fact that these themes are
orthogonal allows for a greater variety of narratives, for characters may

occupy any of four, not two poles, as well as a variety of intermediate positions. One begins to see how narratives are tied to themes of characterisation, for characters are in part a reification of their past narrative involvements. For example, in different plots, harmony in the Ewing home may be divided according to business issues, while at other times characters realign to divide according to moral issues. Conflict may occur within one theme: Jenna and Pam, who are interestingly seen as very similar characters, both competed for Bobby, and yet both had reservations about his business role. Conflict may also occur across themes: while J.R., Cliff and Katherine compete in business immorality, they are all uneasily anchored in moral domesticity by their family ties (Bobby/Miss Ellie, Pam, and Bobby/Pam respectively). Sue Ellen, linked to both J.R. and the moral Ewings, yet at ease with neither, occupies a halfway position, denied the pleasurable position of Lucy, and constitutes a source of conflict between those on whom she depends, J.R. and Miss Ellie. It would appear that while many two-character narrative combinations are harmonious (e.g. Miss Ellie and Clayton), the addition of a third character (e.g. Miss Ellie, Clayton, and J.R.) creates conflict along the dimension of difference.

It is interesting that the character representation provided a greater variety of female positions. The men were seen simply as either moral and powerful or immoral and powerful. However, the women occupied all four possible combinations permitted by these two oppositional themes: Donna is perceived as moral and powerful, Jenna is moral but weak, Katherine is immoral and powerful, while Sly is both immoral and weak. Further, it was only female characters who occupied intermediate positions: Sue Ellen was seen as intermediate for both morality and potency, and Lucy was neither moral nor immoral, but clearly weak. However, the programme seems to be changing in relation to gender, and the overrepresentation of women. In the series following Pam's 'dream', the programme changed such that Bobby 'returned', but Katherine remained away, although Angelica, her apparent substitute, did not stay in her place, the programme has retained Jack in addition to Bobby, and has not returned Lucy. The programme is thus increasing its number of, and focus upon, male characters. This is most notable in the apparent (albeit temporary) return of the patriarchal head of the family, Jock Ewing. It appears that *Dallas* is moving further away from the focus upon women and feminine or domestic concerns typical of soap opera proper (Cantor and Pingree, 1983) and further towards its roots in melodrama, as identified by Mander (1983). This reflects its attempt to compete commercially with prime-time, action-adventure programmes such as *Miami Vice*. In principle, empirical analyses of viewers' character representations and their identification of major themes would allow the tracing of constancies and developments in television programmes. This would facilitate the charting of the ways programmes reflect and direct social concerns.

Interpreting viewers' representation of CORONATION STREET characters

Ten of the eighteen properties were highly significant ($p < 0.01$) and three were moderately significant ($p < 0.05$) in the multiple regression analysis (as used in the *Dallas* study earlier) which tested the fit between the character representation for *Coronation Street* and the ratings of characters on the different properties. Thus the properties of sociable, hard, dominant, feminine, masculine, approach to life, sexy, roguish, staid and moral were all highly relevant to the character representation, while warmth, centrality, and maturity were moderately relevant. The characters are seen by viewers to vary according to these properties, and this variation helps to explain the perceived patterning of the characters in the character space.

The character representation, together with all significant properties projected on to it, is shown in Figs. 5 and 6. Each property should be interpreted as a vector extending in both directions, although for clarity only positive directions are shown. Each face of the three-dimensional cube should be interpreted in relation to the other, with vector length indicating the degree to which a vector fits one face relative to another. From an examination of Figs. 5 and 6, showing the character representations with their explanatory properties superimposed, it is clear that viewers focus upon three distinct, but partially interrelated themes or dimensions. These are morality/power, gender, and approach to life.

The first theme aligns morality, which should be interpreted in the low-key sense of staid versus roguish, with potency or power, in such a way that the moral pole is clearly seen as soft and submissive (e.g. Mavis, Alf), while the immoral pole is more hard and dominant (e.g. Jack, Billy). As the morality vector is distinct from that of gender, although not quite orthogonal, this theme can be interpreted as being fairly independent of gender.

The theme of gender has a matriarchal flavour. It relates femininity, not to passivity, irrationality, or submissiveness, as would be expected from the traditional conception of femininity, but instead to maturity, warmth, centrality to the community, and to a lesser extent, sociability (e.g. Ivy, Betty). On the other hand, masculinity is strongly related to immaturity, coldness, and a peripheral role in the community (e.g. Terry, Brian). There is some area of overlap between masculinity and femininity (e.g. Curly, Vera), but no examples of cross-gendered characters. The absence of 'masculine' women paticularly would seem surprising for soap opera but for the fact that the perceived femininity has already an alternative, more powerful and matriarchal meaning.

The third theme concerns the characters' approach to life. Traditional (e.g. Hilda, Percy) and modern approaches to life (e.g. Sally, Brian) are opposed and, interestingly, aligned with perceived sexiness. This suggests that many narratives are construed in terms of a conflict between

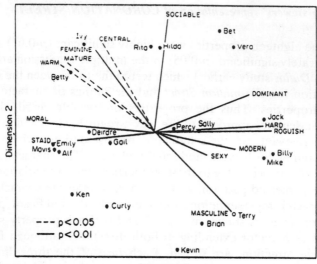

FIGURE 5 Viewers' representation of the characters in *Coronation Street*,
showing significant properties as vectors (Dimension 1=horizontal;
dimension 2=vertical).

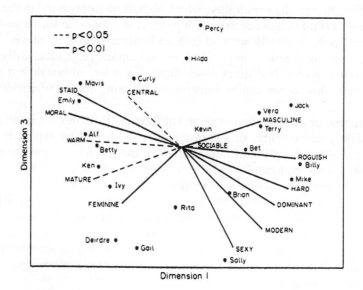

FIGURE 6 Viewers' representation of the characters in *Coronation Street*,
showing significant properties as vectors (Dimension 1=horizontal;
dimension 3=vertical).

traditional, nostalgic, domestic stability with the exciting and seductive challenges of a new and rapidly changing way of life.

This representation relates to the interpretation made of the representation in Figs. 2 and 3 as follows. The emphasis placed on gender is supported by the property fitting procedure, and this theme has gained in meaningfulness through its relations with other properties. Thus it is now apparent that a matriarchal rather than traditional conception of gender is used by viewers. The theme of roguish:staid was also supported, but again has gained in meaningfulness, this time through its association with the theme of morality. Thus, staid characters are seen positively as moral characters in contrast to the relative immorality of the roguish characters. Finally, the predicted dimension of traditional:modern in approach to life was strongly supported, and was found to be related to perceived sexiness of the characters. Thus, the interpretation of the space based on the researcher's own knowledge of the programme was supported. However, the property fitting procedure served to both validate and enrich this interpretation.

Interpreting viewers' representations of EASTENDERS characters

Eleven of the sixteen properties significantly fitted the implicit character representation for *EastEnders*, and so can be used to interpret it. These properties were warm, hard, masculine, feminine, complicated, likeable, temperamental, values the family, approach to life (modern/traditional), and moral. Centrality was moderately significant. Thus, while viewers may perceive character variation in the insignificant properties, e.g. intelligence, these properties are not the themes which underlie the implicit representation of characters. Incidentally, it was possible that certain properties did not fit the representation because there was insufficient perceived variation in that property over characters. To check this artefactual explanation the R-squared values were correlated against the property standard deviations for the same property (measured over characters not subjects). This correlation was 0.22, d.f. = 23, n.s., which means that whether a property fits the representation is not dependent on the variance perceived in that property.

Viewers represented the twenty-five main characters from *EastEnders* in three dimensions, with characters evenly spread throughout the space (see Figs. 7 and 8).

Bearing in mind that the length of a vector in two dimensions indicates the contribution of the vector to that face of the cubic representation, the three significant properties of complicated, modern and central appear characteristic of the third dimension. The first two dimensions together characterise the main face of the representation (Fig. 7). The properties which describe this face form two clusters. The first was labelled *morality/ potency* and the second, *gender*. The moral characters (for example,

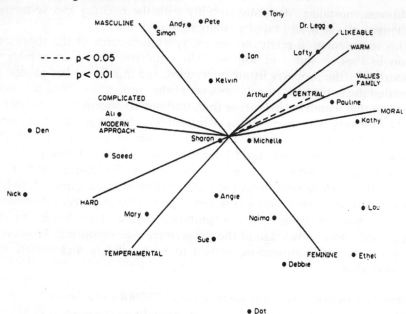

FIGURE 7   Viewers' representation of the characters in *EastEnders,* showing significant properties as vectors (Dimension 1=horizontal; dimension 2=vertical).

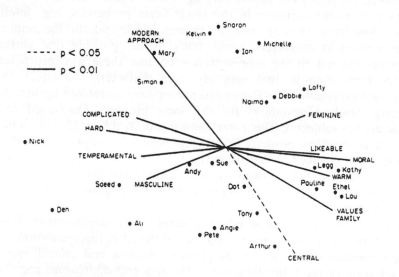

FIGURE 8   Viewers' representation of the characters in *EastEnders,* showing significant properties as vectors (Dimension 1=horizontal; dimension 3=vertical).

Pauline and Kathy) are family-oriented, warm, likeable and steady, in opposition to the immoral, unpopular and temperamental characters (for example, Nick and Ali). All of the male characters occupy the upper left part of the space (where Simon, Andy and Pete compete for the most masculine image), while the female characters are concentrated in the lower right part (exemplified best by Debbie, Naima and Ethel).

Although the property of dominance was insignificant, hard/soft lies in opposition to that of morality, so that moral characters are represented as soft (for example, Arthur and Pauline) and immoral characters as hard (for example, Den and Mary). The alignments between these dimensions suggest that for *EastEnders* viewers, certain inferences and expectations are valid or appropriate. For example, if a moral character is portrayed in an argument with an immoral character, viewers may assume that the good one is more likely to be defending a family issue, be emotionally predictable, and lose the argument than the immoral character.

Masculinity and femininity are perceived as clear opposites, with no androgynous position, and as independent of moral/potent and approach life/centrality. Gender did not correlate with properties traditionally associated with gender, such as intelligence, activity, potency, and warmth. For example, Debbie is seen as especially feminine, and thus very different from the man she lives with, Andy, who is seen as highly masculine. Yet, this does not mean viewers particularly associate Debbie with less power or intelligence than Andy, and nor is Andy seen as differing notably from Debbie in his approach to life or his morality.

The third theme, approach to life/centrality affirms the importance of traditional family and community values to the soap opera world: modern characters (for example, Ian and Kelvin) are considered less central, looking out towards change rather than in towards the 'good old ways' (as, for example, Dot and Ethel). This theme is realised through the characters' ages, as only young characters (late teens and early twenties) occupy the 'modern' pole. The remaining characters (aged 30 to 80) constitute the central core of the community—the parent and grandparent generations—and in them are invested the traditional values.

Certain properties were insignificant, including the Implicit Personality Theory properties of intelligent, active and dominant, as well as the additional properties of sexy and class. *EastEnders* contains some strongly middle-class characters (Debbie, Dr. Legg) and several who are of working class origins but who own their own business (Pete, Kath, Ali, Sue, Den, Angie, Saeed, Naima), in addition to those in traditional working class occupations (Arthur, Pauline, Lou, Ethel, Dot, Nick, Lofty, Andy).

As in *Coronation Street*, class was not a feature of the representation, suggesting that viewers are neglecting certain aspects of the programme in favour of others: they are selective in their readings of the programmes. Morality and potency were again important, and gender is central to the

British soap operas. Certain dimensions are beginning to emerge as central to the genre of soap opera, such as values family, modern/traditional approach to life, centrality to the community and morality as a specific instantiation of evaluation.

The likeable characters should be understood as especially family-oriented and moral, in contrast with the disliked characters who are, interestingly, seen by viewers as distinctly temperamental and compli-cated. While this lack of predictability and safety in certain characters is clearly essential to move the narrative along and to retain interest, viewers dislike, and maybe find it hard to identify with, such characters. The dimension of gender is not easily related to any other property studied, unlike for the *Coronation Street* study, although the fact that it cannot be related to stereotypic conceptions of gender is informative. The *East-Enders* representation resembles that of *Coronation Street*, however, in that in both viewers clearly consider that the heart of the programmes lies in the traditional or old-fashioned characters, for they are seen to form the centre of the communities while the younger, more modern characters lie on the periphery.

Comparisons Among the Character Representations

The representations obtained for *Coronation Street* and *EastEnders* characters differ from those obtained for *Dallas* characters in several respects. Firstly, although the themes of potency and morality were important in representations of the characters in both programmes, they were differently related: in *Dallas,* morality and potency were independent of each other; in *Coronation Street* and *EastEnders* they were opposed. Thus viewers of all programmes see these themes as central, but different inferential relations held between them. Secondly, the theme of gender was present in a conventional or traditional form in the *Dallas* represen-tation, although certain counterstereotypic women were recognised. This contrasts with the gender theme in the British soap operas, in which a strong but nontraditional or matriarchal conception of gender was observed. For British soap opera characters, no inferential relations are perceived to hold between the themes of gender and potency. Finally, there are certain similarities in representations of the three programmes: each representation centred on themes of morality, potency, and gender; and each neglected themes of intellectual evaluation and activity. The similarities and contrasts in viewers' representations of the characters in these three soap operas are summarised in Table 3, where any two themes which are within twenty degrees of each other in the character represen-tation are considered connotatively similar, indexing the same underlying opposition.

TABLE 3. *Main oppositions perceived in the three programmes*

DALLAS

(1)	Potency (Dynamism)	dominant	submissive
		hard	soft
		values power	does not value power
		active	passive
		business-oriented	pleasure-oriented
(2)	Morality	moral	immoral
		warm	cold
(3)	Family values	values family	does not value family

CORONATION STREET

(1)	Moral (Weakness)	moral	immoral
		soft	hard
		submissive	dominant
		staid	not staid
(2)	Gender (Matriarchal)	masculine	not masculine
		not feminine	feminine
		immature	mature
		cold	warm
(3)	Roguish	roguish	not roguish
(4)	Sociable	sociable	unsociable
(5)	Central	central	peripheral
(6)	Sexual values	modern	traditional
		sexy	not sexy

EASTENDERS

(1)	Just like us	likeable	not likeable
		warm	cold
		soft	hard
		steady	temperamental
		straighforward	complicated
(2)	Gender	masculine	not masculine
		not feminine	feminine
(3)	Community	modern	traditional
		peripheral	central
(4)	Morality	moral	immoral
(5)	Family values	values family	does not value family

The studies in this chapter together reveal the structured nature of regular viewers' knowledge of *Dallas, Coronation Street* and *EastEnders* characters. This knowledge, which is built up over years of viewing, appears to bear a complex relation to both the everyday social knowledge of the viewers and the thematic nature of the programme being represented. How far does it represent an abstraction from the key oppositions in the programme (or text) and how far does it represent a construction of textual meaning which is guided by more general social knowledge?

Implications for Person Perception Theories

It will be remembered that person perception theories (Implicit Personality Theory and Gender Schema Theory) were drawn into this research as they constituted theories of social knowledge which could specify the resources available to viewers to guide them in their meaningful representations of television characters. I argued earlier that, to the extent that viewers represented the characters in accordance with their abstract and generalised social knowledge about others, we could infer that this knowledge has a constructive role to play in making sense of television. Person perception theories predict both the nature of the organising themes or dimensions underlying representations and the relations between these themes. Having studied viewers' representations of the characters in three different programmes, we are now in a position to consider the character representations in relation to person perception theories.

Implicit Personality Theory

The theoretical predictions of Implicit Personality Theory were partially borne out by the importance of such properties as *warm, dominant* and *active*. Osgood *et al.* (1957) argue that the theme of evaluation, here indexed by *sociable, warm, intelligent,* and *rational,* is twice as important as that of activity and potency. The present data do not support this claim, and certainly they do not encourage Forgas's (1985) hope that all domains can be unified through their semantic dependence upon Osgood's original three dimensions. Sociability was not correlated with warmth, and intellectual evaluation was irrelevant. Implicit Personality Theory not only specifies particular semantic fundamentals, it also specifies their mutual relations, namely orthogonality. In relation to the interrelations between the dimensions some of the results are contrary to predictions: morality and sociability tend to be orthogonal when they 'should' be positively correlated; morality and potency are strongly negatively correlated in both British programmes, not orthogonal. Potency and social evaluation are orthogonal, as expected, only in *Dallas;* in *EastEnders,* hard and likeable are opposed. Insofar as activity is relevant as a dimension, it creates a dynamism dimension (namely activity aligned with potency, Osgood *et al.*, 1957). In *Dallas*, active, dominant and hard are aligned; in *EastEnders*, temperamental and hard are aligned. However, in *EastEnders* the dynamism dimension is also aligned with most of the evaluative properties, creating a general 'just like us' or uncertainty:familiarity dimension.

It appears that several themes were relatively unimportant to viewers' representations (see Table 2). These were intellectual evaluation (intelligence and rationality) and activity (active and excitable). Further, some themes were not as coherent as they 'should' have been (e.g. sociable and warm should have been highly correlated to represent the theme of social evaluation). Yet both social evaluation (sociable and warm) and potency (dominant and hard) were important, as predicted. Thus Osgood *et al.*'s dimensions were only partially relevant to the representations of television characters.

In general, properties are correlated as predicted by implicit personality theory (e.g. dominant/hard, likeable/warm). They index meaningful, underlying dimensions related, if not identical, to evaluation, potency, and evaluation. However, properties which should index the same underlying dimension according to implicit personality theory, are not always highly correlated (e.g. sociable and warm in *Coronation Street*). Conversely, properties which index orthogonal properties according to implicit personality theory may be highly correlated (e.g. warm and hard in *EastEnders*). Certain dimensions neglected by psychology (e.g. sexy, see Ashmore *et al.*, 1986) or approach to life (traditional/modern) and moral are central to the character representations, suggesting that person perception theories have overly restricted the range of themes which people may use to represent others. This latter point is supported below by the use of text-related themes by viewers.

Gender Schema Theory

Gender Schema Theories suggest that gender would provide a basic theme for organising viewers' representation of characters. However, for the study of *Dallas*, neither masculinity nor femininity fitted the implicit representation. So, although it is only women in *Dallas* who occupy the weaker and softer half of the space, viewers do not perceive the characters in terms of the properties, *masculinity* and *femininity*. This unexpected result may be explained by suggesting that *Dallas* is seen to include mainly stereotypic women (e.g. Lucy) and men (e.g. J.R.), as soap operas are commonly held to do, but it also includes a few counter-stereotypic female characters (e.g. Donna) which prevented the emergence of a general gender dimension. The role of gender differs across representations of the three programmes: the *Dallas* representation appears to contain a gender dimension which is strongly undermined by the existence of three counter-stereotypic women; in *Coronation Street* and *EastEnders,* gender is important and independent of all other themes, and in *Coronation Street* particularly, it carries matriarchal rather than traditional connotations. Thus one cannot infer with any certainty about characters' morality or sociability by knowing their gender.

The importance of the themes of masculine and feminine supports the strong emphasis placed upon gender by person perception theorists (Ashmore and Del Boca, 1986; Bem, 1981). Yet masculine and feminine are strongly negatively correlated. This fits with traditional assumptions that, for example, the more masculine one is, the less feminine one must also be. It also fits with the finding reported in Brown (1986) that if asked to describe themselves directly in terms of masculinity and femininity, respondents use these terms oppositionally. The possibility of androgynous (i.e. equally masculine and feminine) perceptions of characters is thus precluded: contrary to Bem's work on androgyny, viewers do not perceive these two themes as mutually compatible, independent themes, but as oppositional. As pointed out above, the meaning of this gender dimension, however, is not as predicted by gender schema theories. The gender dimension found in the character representations is not related to either intellectual evaluation or activity, both non-salient themes, nor with potency (with the exception of *Dallas*), a highly salient and yet orthogonal theme to gender. This contrasts with Ashmore and Tumia's (1980) finding of an association between weak/strong and feminine/masculine, and suggests that viewers are not generally using standard, abstract gender stereotypic knowledge in order to construct their understanding of characters. Women in soap operas are not seen as irrational, unintelligent, or powerless, as traditional conceptualisations of femininity would suggest.

Implications for Textual Analyses

Thus the role of social knowledge operates in part to override the themes foregrounded in the programme structure. This may be observed in the clarity of the moral and immoral clusters, in the independence rather than opposition of the themes of morality/family and power/business, and in the relevance of such themes as warmth and activity. On the other hand, the structure of the representations also suggests that viewers are receptive towards or influenced by the programme structure, which thereby overrides their own stereotypic frameworks. The importance of morality similarly suggests viewers' receptiveness to the mythic functions of soap opera as a forum for cultural debate (Allen, 1985; Newcomb and Hirsch, 1984). Viewers are clearly aware that the characters occupy different moral stances and find the moral narratives or messages central to the programme as an appropriate way of conceiving of the characters more generally.

To take the case of the *Dallas* representation, we can conclude that Mander's (1983) literary interpretation of *Dallas* is largely supported by the present results. The major theme of morality emerged, and was related to the importance of traditional family values, although not opposed to the importance of business. The focus upon moral ambivalence, as proposed by both Mander (1983) and Arlen (1981), did not emerge, however. For example, J.R. is clearly set against the rest of his family as the unambiguous force of evil, and is not located within a moral conflict between family and organisation. These results agree with Liebes (1984) in suggesting that viewers are less sensitive to the ambiguity of good and evil, and more to their clear opposition. In this respect, the morality dimension appears more akin to Osgood *et al.*'s (1957) evaluative dimension: having identified the centrality of morality as a theme in the programme, it seems likely that viewers' use this more universal framework to disambiguate the presentation, clarifying and polarising the characters so as to evenly balance the moral against the immoral. This casts a more optimistic light upon the programme than is suggested by Mander.

The concept of morality, so central to all three character representations, is not simply an instance of the general evaluative dimension: the traits used to operationalise the negative pole of that dimension (e.g. unpopular, irritable, boring, unintelligent, see Ashmore and Tumia, 1980) are conceptually distinct from that of immorality, and do not describe the immoral characters. Specifically, in *Dallas,* morality is related to warmth but less so to valuing the family; in *Coronation Street* it is not very related to warm or mature and is orthogonal to sociable; in *EastEnders* it is correlated with, but conceptually distinct from, the evaluative dimension (likeable, warm, etc.), and with family values. This supports the specific emphasis on morality (because of its relation to myth and social prescriptions) within cultural studies, and argues against its reduction to general evaluation. One might suggest that viewers focus on what the characters do with their positive attributes (thereby linking representation of character to that of narrative): the 'baddies' use them for exploitation and deceit; the 'goodies' use them for righting wrongs and helping others. A focus on morality implies judgement of the characters' actions and also an appreciation of the narrative implications of assigning characters to a moral category. The relation in the present results between morality and the theme of valuing the family fits with one of the few pieces of research attempting to correlate viewers' beliefs with exposure to soap opera. Pingree *et al.* (1979) found that soap opera viewing was positively correlated with a belief in traditional family values. It is noteworthy that the role of traditional family values emerged as a salient theme for viewers in their interpretation of *Dallas*.

Turning to the semiotic analysis of the British soap operas, specifically *Coronation Street,* as a predictor of character representation, it seems that the concept of Insider:Outsider (or central:peripheral to the community) was important to viewers, as suggested by Dyer *et al.* (1981). However, it was not related to Working class:Middle class, as they had argued, but instead was more related to gender, at least for *Coronation Street*. It is men who are seen to threaten the stability and security of a primarily female and domestic community, not the middle classes who threaten to disrupt a working class way of life. Further analysis is required to determine if such a view is also present in the text, although missed by Dyer *et al.*, or whether it is of the viewers' own construction.

The centrality of gender in a matriarchial rather than traditional form in the character representation can be explained in terms of Dyer *et al.*'s analysis, suggesting that viewers are receptive to *Coronation Street*'s and possibly *EastEnders*'s non-traditional conception of gender and that they incorporate this into their understanding of the characters, in preference to their more abstract social knowledge about gender. As Modleski (1982) has argued, women's pleasure in soap opera derives in part from the centrality of images of the powerful mother and also from the dominant role of the villainess, an expression of that part of themselves which women must usually suppress.

Why was class absent from the viewers' representations of the British soap operas? If we examine the mean ratings given to each character in *Coronation Street*, it is clear that viewers certainly perceive variation among characters, from Emily, the most middle class, to Jack, the most working class. Use of the scale was heavily skewed: Emily, Mike, Alf, Ken, Mavis, and Sally were perceived as intermediate in class; Percy, Curly, Gail, Billy, Deirdre, Rita, and Betty were perceived as fairly working class; and Ivy, Brian, Jack, Terry, Kevin, Vera, Hilda, and Bet were perceived as truly working class (see Livingstone, 1987a, for details). It is not, therefore, that viewers cannot identify the characters in terms of their social class. It is instead that they do not, when asked for their spontaneous and implicit character perceptions. Further, class is not semantically related to the themes which are used to represent characters (otherwise, it would have been correlated with these themes, and thus also significantly fit the space). It seems unlikely that the viewers regard class as important but too obvious to use as a discriminator of characters (for the same would surely apply to gender) or that viewers perceive the role of class and yet deny its importance (this explanation is undermined by the implicit nature of the sorting task) or, finally, that they perceive the role of class but do not use it as a discriminator of personality (for strictly speaking, the property of role in the community is also not a feature of personality: the term personality as used in the sorting instructions was clearly taken by viewers simply to indicate a focus on the nature of the person rather than, for example, their hair colour or occupation). It may be that class does not play the structuring role in the programme that has been suggested by text analysts: this point will be pursued in Chapter 6. In general, it seems that viewers do not passively receive the programme as presented, but that they make their own sense of it through selective and constructive cognitions, neglecting the role of class in favour of themes of more interest or relevance to them, such as gender.

Certain genre-related properties (e.g. modern or traditional approach to life) correlated with different properties in different programmes: with sexy in *Coronation Street;* with centrality in *EastEnders*. Thus in *Coronation Street,* the modern characters are sexy but not necessarily peripheral, while in *EastEnders,* the modern characters (who are also younger) are more peripheral, but not necessarily more sexy. They may also serve to qualify the meaning of other dimensions (e.g. alignment of maturity with gender in *Coronation Street*).

Narrative differences between the programmes can also account for differences in the representations. For example, 'family values' is closer to morality in *EastEnders* than in *Dallas*. In *Dallas,* moral ambiguities arise from the immoral characters acting immorally mainly for the sake of the family (e.g. J.R. and Cliff), whereas in *EastEnders,* the immoral characters tend to have unstable, incomplete or unhappy families (e.g. Den and Nick), so that family values and morality are not in conflict.

The representations can be seen as providing a number of functions for media researchers, allowing them to go beyond the simple assumption that viewers make sense of programmes just as researchers do. For example, representing viewers' knowledge of characters may provide a resource for understanding why certain correlation studies succeed or fail, for measured effects depend on interpretation. It may also provide a basis for designing future media research (using paradigms of cultivation, identification, or comprehension) grounded in the actual nature of viewers' cognitions. Similarly, we can gain an insight into the specific nature of viewers' interpretations of a programme, the distinctions and associations they make, the themes they find salient or irrelevant, and so forth. Finally, these studies can indicate the extent to which actual interpretations of a specific domain correspond both to interpretations made of other social domains and to those interpretations which textual analysts implicitly assume that viewers make.

The Role of the Viewer in Representing Television Characters

The studies of *Coronation Street, EastEnders* and *Dallas* show that viewers are able to construct a coherent representation of the characters in television programmes. These representations indicate something of their experience and understanding of and pleasure in the programme as a whole, indicating, for example, how character representations relate to and facilitate interpretation of the narratives. The structures of the representations provided evidence for the constructive use of person knowledge as the social knowledge resources of interpretive viewers. This is exemplified by the common importance of the themes of potency, gender and social evaluation in the character representations and by the neglect of social class.

The research also revealed ways in which viewers are receptive to the structure of the programme in precedence to the dictates of abstract social knowledge (as illustrated by the importance of the themes of morality, centrality to the community, matriarchal femininity, by the neglect of certain person perception dimensions and by the modifications made of the relations predicted to hold between these dimensions). The existence of differences between the representations for the three programmes further suggests viewers' receptivity to different programme structures. Such findings argue against a heavily top-down or overly constructivist approach which holds that viewers see what they want to see, or reduce all information to a standard formula: such differences can only have arisen from an interaction between social knowledge and the nature of the texts. Thus they argue against a simple reception model. Social knowledge and text structure are both determinants of viewers' representations, and each serves to modify or buffer the influence of the other (cf. the top-down: bottom-up debate in cognitive psychology; Bobrow and Norman, 1975; Neisser, 1976). The resultant representation depends on the input of each and of the nature of the interaction or negotiation between the two.

The character representation also has implications for the study of the effects of viewing by revealing something of the 'role of the reader' or the activity of the viewer. Insofar as viewers have been shown here to be sensitive to messages concerning non-traditional images of gender and concerning the centrality of women in the community, one can predict that viewing this programme, or possibly viewing soap opera in general, will increase viewers' non-traditional conceptions of women (Pingree, 1978) and help to combat the effects of the considerable degree of traditional gender stereotyping on television (Durkin, 1985b). Conversely, the neglect by viewers of messages concerning social class suggests that viewing may not be increasing beliefs about social class distinctions, despite the apparent emphasis on such distinctions by the programme itself.

These suggestions, together with others which may be derived from the present research concerning, say, the salience of approach to life, the relation between morality and power, the unimportance of intellectual desirability, or the absence of a relation between gender and power, all these suggestions remain to be investigated. Together, they demonstrate some of the ways in which a study of viewers' interpretations reveals potentially fruitful directions for the study of media effects, whether one draws upon theories of role modelling, cultivation, or identification. The study of media effects must, it is argued, take into account the interpretive activity of the viewer, as viewers do not simply receive programmes as they are presented, not do they simply impose meanings on to the programmes in accordance with their prior knowledge. Finally, in relation to the potential convergence between traditional and critical mass communications over the study of the audience, I would suggest that the present research represents one way in which theoretical concerns developed within cultural studies can be investigated using empirical methods and can thus further research on the ways in which media effects are dependent upon viewers' interpretations of television programmes.

6

Representation and Mediation

The representations constructed by viewers of familiar television characters which were studied in the previous chapter raise a range of questions to be addressed here. These questions concern the robustness of the representations, the relations between the representations, the implications of their relations to social knowledge and to text analyses, and the conclusions to be drawn regarding the mediating role of such representations in media effects. In other words, not only do these character representations indicate the readings made by viewers of the programmes, but also they themselves must be 'read', and they can be read in the context of different questions and theoretical concerns.

The Robustness of the Character Representations

Before analysing further the implications of the character representations, we should consider how well they capture stable and reliable themes or dimensions of interpretation and representation for long-term viewers of a programme. Robustness or reliability can be assessed in several ways—over data collection methods, viewer samples, temporal duration, viewer subgroups and levels of abstraction of meaning for which the representation is valid.

Reliability of method and sample

Taking the questions of method and sample together, the study of *Dallas* characters, a replication study was conducted (see Livingstone, 1987b). A virtually identical character space was produced using two different methods (pair-wise similarity judgements, in which each pair is individually compared for their perceived similarity in personality, and the sorting task, in which all the characters together are sorted freely into variable sized subgroups, according to their perceived similarity in personality). For the two studies, separate samples of viewers were used, matched approximately for age, gender, occupation and viewing experience. Hence, the character representations are replicable and thus reasonably robust. Although no replication was attempted for the semantic differential task, for each study, a reliability coefficient (Cronbach's alpha) was calculated for each rating scale. In general, these coefficients exceeded 0.9, showing that viewers were in substantial agreement over their rating of each character on each scale.

Durability of representations

The durability of the representations is called into question when major character changes are introduced in the programme. If the replacement of certain characters by others leads to changes in viewers' understanding of basic themes, then one would expect the representations to change over time. Character replacement may alter the balance of moral to immoral characters, or it may eliminate all weak characters, so that potency is no longer an issue, and introduce alternative or competing themes, such as intelligence or co-operation. On the other hand, the new characters may be purely cosmetic, providing new faces and new narrative possibilities, but no new underlying themes or thematic relations between characters.

The *Dallas* study was extended by studying representations of three new characters brought in for one series to replace three central characters in the programme. The results showed that the old characters were directly replaced by new characters in such a way that the underlying character representation, organised around morality and potency, was basically unchanged (Livingstone, 1987a). Thus, Jack Ewing replaced Bobby Ewing, Angelica de Niro replaced Katherine Wentworth and Jamie Ewing replaced not Lucy Ewing-Cooper as had been expected but Bobby Ewing in the semantic character representations. The old characters directly matched their replacements on the perceived main themes of the programme, and therefore the new characters 'took over' the oppositional similarities and contrasts with all other characters. This functional equivalence between old and new characters was supported by the main narratives of the new series: Jack took over from Bobby in his romance with Jenna and father-figure role to Jenna's daughter, Charlie; Jack also became a partner with J.R., replacing Bobby to some extent in the narratives, if not in power; and Angelica took over Katherine's role in trying to beat J.R. and use everybody else for her own manipulative ends.

Individual differences

In the study of each of the three programmes reported in Chapter 5, the samples were subdivided: according to gender and nationality (for *Dallas*) and for gender and age for the British soap operas. For *Dallas*, as this was studied by pairwise similarity judgements, subgroups were compared using INDSCAL to see if they differed in their use of the dimensions. For the British programmes, subgroups were compared by scaling the sorting data for each subgroup separately. Resulting representations were compared using canonical correlation. In all, the representations across subgroups were remarkably similar (Livingstone, 1987a), although there were slight and inconsistent differences by gender, where the men differ slightly from some of the women in the third, minor dimensions. In general, there seem to be few differences in representation for groups divided by demographic variables.

This conclusion can only be drawn with reservations because after subdivision all the samples were rather small for multidimensional scaling. One could also subdivide viewers in different ways, according to social class for instance or their identification with different characters (see Chapter 7). The similarities between the character representations produced by different subgroupings of viewers provide split-half reliability for the representations produced from all viewers together. The observed consensus is interesting because, for example, *EastEnders* aims to attract younger viewers, *Coronation Street* is thought of as appealing especially to older women, and *Dallas* captures more of a male audience. One might have expected age and sex differences in representation as a function of viewers' different interests and knowledge directing their interpretations. However, the existing differences in actual viewing patterns (see Table 1, Chapter 2) does not appear to lead to substantial interpretative differences in the major themes of character representation.

Traits and dimensions

Finally, one might ask about the level of abstraction at which the character representations are pitched: they reveal the main themes or dimensions of representation, but they do not admit of minor themes, contradictory or problematic character positioning, or more subtle shades of meaning. Are the themes presented in Chapter 5 a fair summary of more detailed knowledge of the characters? A methodological concern which relates to this question is whether the use of *a priori* semantic differentials can validly elicit supposedly implicit and unconstrained themes of the representations. Rosenberg and his colleagues (Kim and Rosenberg, 1980; Rosenberg and Sedlack, 1972) argue that semantic representations based on trait descriptions provided by the researcher may differ from those based on subject-generated traits. Research is more likely to produce results consistent with Implicit Personality Theory when the researcher provides the traits. This is unsurprising, as usually the traits are specifically chosen as exemplars of the underlying dimensions of evaluation, activity, and potency. People's representations of others can be reasonably well described and most conveniently studied using traits related to these three dimensions. However, this may not be the best way to discover spontaneous representations for a particular domain as these may be organised according to themes other than evaluation, potency and activity.

In general, the methods of the present research are not vulnerable to this criticism. The sorting task was deliberately employed to preclude imposition of the researcher's theoretical concerns on to subjects' responses. This method avoids both the use of *a priori* traits and the laborious task of deriving a character representation from free trait descriptions. Furthermore, PROFIT does not assume that the rated properties will fit the representation or constrain the properties to be orthogonal. Instead it tests for the degree and direction of fit between the implicit representation from the sorting data and the rated properties of *a priori* theoretical interest.

However, different traits from those tested may in fact have been implicitly used in the sorting task. These traits may or may not be correlated with the properties used in the rating task and PROFIT. A property which significantly fits the representation may correctly identify a dimension of the representation but only be correlated with the actual property used by subjects (for example, the morality dimension may really be a 'happy/depressed' dimension; similarly, 'potency' may be seen positively as 'strength' or negatively as 'aggression').

To examine the relation between freely used traits and rated properties, a representative subsample of viewers in the *EastEnders* study were explicitly requested to describe the basis for their character sortings by providing a description of each group that they constructed. This free description task was completed after the sorting task, in order that the sorting task was unconstrained. To ask subjects to explain the basis of their sorting is arguably as problematic as to leave the sortings unexplained, for one may invite rationalisations rather than explanations. However, it seems a waste never to ask viewers why they sorted the characters as they did. The descriptions provided by each viewer were broken down into constituent trait adjectives or phrases, each of which was considered descriptive of each character in the group to which it had been applied. The resultant adjectives or phrases were reduced by combining traits which were synonymous in meaning and by standardising grammatical form, resulting in 115 unique traits for analysis.

In general, when compared with viewers' free trait descriptions of characters, the rated properties which described characters in the representation were supported. For example, the free traits typically used to describe the characters (Tony, Legg, Pauline, Kathy, Lofty, Arthur) associated with the 'moral/weak/just like us' pole of the *EastEnders* representation were as follows: caring, hardworking, values the family, weak, helpful, reliable, have problems, confident, kind, sensible, boring, honest, unstable, frustrated, loser, determined, childlike, ordinary, likeable, try their best, traditional, moral, happy go lucky, straightforward, muddle through, and insecure. In contrast, the 'immoral/dominant/unlike us' characters (Den, Nick, Saeed, Mary) were described as selfish, uncaring, criminal, weak, devious, nasty, loser, hard, irresponsible, bad, and so forth. Thus characters located at each pole of significant properties are freely described in terms consistent with those properties and not in terms inconsistent with them.

Few inconsistent traits were used of the characters, the exceptions being 'weak' for the immoral characters and 'unstable' for the moral characters. However, approximately half of the traits in the free descriptions for the moral and immoral characters were semantically unrelated to the rated properties. These were generally common to both groups of characters and concerned assessment of the characters' maturity and competence (insecure, confused, childlike, have problems, frustrated, loser). Viewers may find this a comforting view of others, perceiving a world in which everybody has problems and no-one is very clear about their role in today's complex society or confident of their powers to succeed. Whether good or bad, strong or weak, all are seen as insecure inside.

Some traits in the free descriptions did discriminate the characters and may be summarised as traits which attribute to characters either the ability or inability to cope with inner insecurities. Viewers could be said to endorse a simple psychodynamic theory of identity formation in a complex, realistic world. This is consistent with Moscovici's work on the filtration of psychoanalytic concepts into everyday thinking (Moscovici, 1984). This implicit theory integrates the traits for each cluster thus: while everybody has problems and insecurities, those who have the inner resources to cope can be good, kind people, in contrast to those lacking such resources. 'Cope' is the operative word here: these people do not resolve their problems and become strong, they merely 'muddle through' and become solid, decent citizens. Those with a tendency to self-pity, who cannot integrate or take responsibility, instead become immoral, unpopular, cold people. Social rejection and lack of connection with others makes these individuals appear, at least superficially, tough and hardened.

The analysis of the free trait descriptions provided by viewers for discriminating among moral and immoral characters adds to the richness of our understanding of their character representation. The character representations obtained earlier, based on general themes or oppositions, represent an abstraction from a more detailed knowledge base. This abstraction relates relatively simply to the underlying detail partly because viewers tended to perceive the characters in terms of mutually consistent traits (this occurred in 84 per cent of the descriptions; Livingstone, 1987a) rather than inconsistent traits (e.g. characters are seen as both moral and honest rather than as moral and nasty). However, it should not be forgotten that viewers have this more detailed knowledge about characters on which they may draw when interpreting specific narratives or resolving apparent contradictions between portrayed traits.

A generic representation for soap opera characters?

Having considered the character representations at a lower, more detailed, level of abstraction, one can also consider them at a more general level. Do the representations for the three programmes relate to each other insofar as each is a version of a general, 'soap opera' representation which viewers have built up for the genre as a whole? Certainly viewers made use of a variety of traits in the above description task which relate more clearly to the characteristics of the genre than to traits typically derived in research on everyday person perception. For example, viewers described characters in terms of values family, confident, criminal, have problems, misfit, loser, seeking family, roots in East End, muddle through, fights prejudice. However, these traits were in the minority: in the main, the characters were described in a way indistinguishable from real people, using common trait descriptions such as caring and kind just as they do for ordinary people that they know. Nonetheless, the use of these genre-related terms reveals the role of a knowledge of genre conventions in structuring understandings of the characters. Extrapolating from the media to everyday life more generally, this raises interesting questions for theories of social knowledge about the role of what one might term genre-related conventions in social situations. For example, the emphasis on intellectual evaluation themes in the person perception literature but not in the present soap opera research reminds us that person perception research is typically conducted on students in academic settings, where such themes are specifically, and perhaps not more generally, relevant. In academic settings one might also expect free trait descriptions to involve other conventional terms (e.g. highbrow, swot, good at exams) to appear. The degree to which one can generalise from one situation to another, and the relation of specific to general characteristics remains a problem for theories of social knowledge, and is especially noticeable when one applies these theories to the media, with their clearly distinct genres.

Comparing across the three character representations, we saw several common features: the themes of morality, potency and gender (and the theme of approach to life for the British soap operas); and the absent themes of social class and intellectual evaluation. Could we say that viewers have a common, three-dimensional scheme with which to approach any specific soap opera? Such a generalisation requires qualification. Morality is central to all three programmes, yet it varies in meaning, from the staidness or roguishness of *Coronation Street* to the major clashes between good and evil in *Dallas*. Potency is also central, but in *Dallas* and *EastEnders* combines with activity to create a dynamism dimension. In the British soap operas, gender received a matriarchal flavour in viewers' representations. In *Dallas,* although non-significant, gender was clearly present in a traditional form (the men and women were discriminated by power and activity) and yet notable counter-stereotypic characters were perceived. As everyday person perception is characterised by the three dimensions of evaluation, potency and gender, the representation of soap opera characters is not so different from that of people in everyday life. It seems more parsimonious to regard each representation as an instantiation of a more general schema for person perception, which can be varied in important ways in line with the conventions and structure of specific programmes.

Social Knowledge and Character Representation

The discussion of the implications of the character representations in Chapter 5 was intended to develop the argument that studies of audience response need a theory of the viewer which could be sought within social psychology (see Chapter 4). Further, it was suggested above that theories of social perception could be modified so as to regard apparently divergent representations of people or characters as instantiations of a general schema. This implies that, as in the present case, studies of viewers' response to the media can feed back into social psychological theories of everyday life. This may help to compensate for social psychology's lack of a theory of the text, which became clear when trying to study audience response to a tangible and conventionally structured object of perception—a television programme (see Chapter 3). The implications of the character representations for theories of social perception will be considered here.

The limitations of person perception theories

Television characters often constitute 'significant others' for the viewers: they are regarded as extensions of the viewers' social network, as 'real people' (Livingstone, 1988a). As person perception theory has already been applied to political figures (Osgood *et al.*, 1957), whom subjects do not know personally, it should surely also apply to well-known television characters, such as those in soap opera. In the present research, person perception theories generally predicted the dimensions along which characters were represented. This suggests that these theorists' aim of producing an abstract and generalised representation of person knowledge may be viable. It also supports a significant role for person knowledge as a resource in character interpretation. The role of this resource was suggested more forcefully when person knowledge appeared to override textual structure in character representations.

However, person perception theories were less successful in predicting the connotations or correlates of the main dimensions and in predicting the interrelations between the dimensions themselves. The present research differs from most past research in person perception in that it studies naturally acquired, complex social knowledge for which all subjects had equivalent access to the source. It was concluded that differences between present and previous findings may not reflect problems with person perception theory *per se* so much as with its application or instantiation.

Thus the abstract knowledge structures for person perception are not directly reflected in specific character representations because the structure of the domain (the television programme) modifies, elaborates or overrides this abstract knowledge when representing the domain.

This failure of these theories to predict certain dimensions or relations between dimensions in the character representations, and most particularly, the failure to account for differences between the representations and the role of programme structure in accounting for these differences, raises a number of questions about the applicability of social perception or knowledge theories.

There are various design problems facing social perception or implicit personality theories (Livingstone and Lunt, 1989). Specifically, existing research designs tend to be one of two types. People are asked to judge either a set of other people that they know well but which are not therefore shared across the judges (e.g. Rosenberg and Sedlack, 1972) or they are presented with scenarios depicting hypothetical people or stereotypes who are known superficially but equally to all (e.g. Forgas, 1985). In other words few, if any, designs involve judgements of people who are both consensually and well known to all the judges.

These design limitations lead to several problems with the evidence typically used in support of Implicit Personality Theory. When people make judgements about others well known to them they judge people such as their father or best friend. This means that differences between judgements about fathers are possibly the result of differences in fathers rather than indications of differences in the judges' construct systems. Modelling across such idiosyncratic differences can produce a spurious representation. Alternatively if people make judgements about scenario descriptions of people or prototype labels, then one cannot be sure that the resultant representations are routinely used in everyday person perception or that they are considered as relevant for the perception of familiar people. Thirdly, the use of personality traits rather than people as the objects of judgement raises the problem of atomism or emergence: although implicit personality theorists rarely discriminate between evidence collected from trait judgements and that collected from personality judgements, the former type of evidence assumes that perceptions of persons can be understood simply as aggregates of trait descriptions. This has been the subject of much debate (Schneider *et al.*, 1979).

It should be noted that, as Implicit Personality Theory concerns the judgement of other people, the attempt to resolve the design problem by studying traits rather than people (to gain consensus through traits and ecovalidity through reference to diverse people) gives rise to further problems. It is not clear from the representation of a personality trait space how the people themselves are represented. Finally, there is a problem of contextualising the stimuli judged, whether persons or traits. Both designs suffer from the problem of selecting stimuli across the range of domains represented and thus divorcing each stimulus from its perceived context of application. Maybe, for instance, people do not think of fathers and friends together, but maintain separate representations for family and acquaintances (an equivalent to genre in the media), separations which are lost in the attempt to sample across all domains together.

This discussion relates to the key problems in social psychological method more generally, referring to the problems of relativism in stimulus meaning, the use of superficial or artificial stimuli, the problem of emergent meanings from the particular combinations of items and the problem of context of use. A solution to these limitations is to find a shared, culturally real, set of objects of person perception. It has been argued here that soap opera characters represent just such an example of well and yet consensually known objects of perception and representation.

Returning, then, to the findings of Chapter 5 regarding the applicability of person perception theories to the representation of well-known television characters, what can be said about the mixed success of these theories? The problematic application of Implicit Personality Theory to a real world, complex domain such as television characters need not be taken as lack of support for the theory. For generalised or abstract targets, the theory works reasonably well. Thus the present results can be used more constructively to complicate the theory: Implicit Personality Theory works if it is seen as identifying only one of two sets of determinants, namely those to do with the viewer. To this one must now add that the structure of the domain of application modifies, and gives a particular instantiation to, an abstract schema.

The importance of genre

If one considers different cultural genres concerned with the themes of, say, intelligence and power, it is apparent that these two basic themes may be differently related to each other. For example, in one context or genre, exemplified by the adventure epic, *The Lord of the Rings,* Intelligence is strongly positively correlated with power: the clever heroes win through over the stupid villains (epitomised by the animal-like orcs). In contrast, a popular strand of stereotyping (common in children's comics) represents intelligence through the weedy bespectacled swot, who has little power in contrast to his beefy opposite, notable for his lack of brains. The *Star Wars* films exemplify a further popular relationship, where intelligence is orthogonal to power: goodies and baddies are equally powerful (until the end) and both highly intelligent: a battle of wits.

If different cultural genres exemplify different interrelations between basic themes, why has person perception theory been concerned to specify orthogonality between dimensions? One could argue that the model is parsimonious to operate in that, faced with a wide range of cultural domains, it would be maladaptive to assume any kind of inferential relation between these basic themes. While within themes, inferences are generally reasonable (e.g. if someone is likeable, they are probably also fairly attractive, sociable and warm), the main semantic themes have been related in different ways in different contexts precisely because they are culturally important. Different genres are concerned to establish different world views. For example, the narrative structure of *The Lord of the Rings* is organised so that, while the reader begins with a readiness to perceive themes of intelligence and evaluation (and potency, activity and gender), he or she is, according to the semantic differential model, open in beliefs about their interrelation. The narrative must then work to draw in the reader, trying out different alignments and finally convincing the reader that one particular alignment is the most natural. In this narrative, two characters play critical roles in this process: Boromir, the least intelligent of several heroes, succumbs to evil forces and is killed; and Gollum, a wicked figure whose moments of intelligence and honesty serve to save his life (give him power), albeit temporarily. In this genre, power is a matter of life and death, but different genres use different conventions to establish their world view and convince the reader that, say, intelligence means power.

If one argues that people routinely keep in mind many possible alignments of basic themes, one must still explain when and why each is used. If instead one argues that people have abstract schemata which make certain aspects of the world salient (e.g. the content of basic cultural themes) and are open on others (e.g. relations between the themes, as represented through orthogonality), then the different contexts provide an explanation of when and why abstract schemata are differently instantiated, namely as a function of the domain structure. To elaborate this argument, a theory of social contexts and conventions is needed (of genre, myth, situations and so forth), and a theory of influence is needed to predict when domain structure is influential or is overridden.

On a methodological level, there are problems with the original semantic differential model, as this assumes that whatever the structure of individuals' models, these are universally applied to all domains without modification. Thus in Implicit Personality Theory research, subjects' ratings are always collapsed over the different targets. As noted above, it is assumed that the same relations hold between evaluation, potency and activity when someone thinks of people at work, their family, people they know well or politicians they have never met. Certainly if one averages over dimensional alignments for these different domains, orthogonality may result. But this would be misleading in relation to different domains of person perception. While Rosenberg (1977) attacks the practice of collapsing over subjects, losing individual differences, there is surely an equivalent argument against collapsing over target domains, as these too, may introduce additional sources of content variation. If one accepts that target domains introduce content dimensions into people's implicit personality theories, then the study of mass communications is one way of investigating the sources of these dimensions.

Causal inference

Having argued that social knowledge must be flexibly applied or instantiated in particular domains, showing receptivity to the structure of the domain being thus represented, we should back track a little to deal with the problem of causal inference. In talking of top-down and bottom-up processes, which any research on social perception and interpretation does explicitly or implicitly, we imply causal processes in which the perceiver modifies his or her knowledge or conversely, the perceiver imposes his or her schemas on to the world. The balance between these two processes was discussed earlier in relation to the more general issue of the balance in power between audience and programme, reader and text. So we should consider the nature of these claims carefully.

The first and most obvious point is that the present research has not involved experimentation: viewers were not randomly assigned to watch particular programmes, programme materials were not deliberately man-ipulated, and dependent variables independent of previous knowledge were not measured. This research was concerned to discover character representations, match these to prior social knowledge and textual structure, and provide a basis for future 'effects' studies.

However, the results provide correlational evidence from which causal inferences may be drawn. The previous chapter contains separate samples of viewers who each regularly watch one soap opera. From these, three character representations have been obtained and described. It has been assumed that the samples of viewers all have the same abstract social knowledge of other people, and that the textual structures of the three programmes are different. This permits the straightforward claim that, to the extent that the three representations are structurally similar, viewers' social knowledge is influential in determining the representations, and to the extent that they are different, programme structure is influential. Thus top-down (namely, viewers' schemata) and bottom-up (namely, textual structure) determinants of character representation are indicated. This could be modified to claim additionally, that if the representations are similar but they differ from person perception knowledge, then textual structure would appear to be influential in terms of genre rather than individual programmes.

Unfortunately, the two assumptions, of constant social knowledge and of variable texts, are problematic. First, the samples of viewers were not identical in each study. Further, each sample was self-selected as viewers of a particular programme, thus complicating causal inferences (a classic problem in mass communications research). Second, if the representations are similar, this may be due to similarities between social knowledge and programme structure, so that the structure of the representation is also 'in' each of the programmes.

The first problem is apparently practical, for a within-subject design could have been used, studying the same viewers for each of the three programmes. However, this solution itself is problematic. People who regularly watch all three soap operas may not be typical of the soap opera audience as a whole. Moreover, although they were not very different, retrospectively the three samples could have been better matched demographically. Nonetheless, the same viewers may not be psychologically the same when watching (or recalling) different programmes: they may watch each programme with different needs, in different domestic contexts, and in relation to different social knowledge and personal experience. Thus controlling for subjects is difficult.

The second problem is clearly theoretical: how can one determine whether or not the structure of a character representation mirrors that which is 'in' the text? Increasingly, researchers in cultural studies no longer believe in unique meanings within the text. While theoretically, the arguments against unique and fixed meanings are strong, some problems remain. For example, we may debate whether *Coronation Street* offers a feminist or reactionary view of women, but we do not doubt that it concerns a Northern working class community, that it is rather dated, and that it is not a nature documentary. In other words, the boundaries of textual indeterminacy have not yet been adequately addressed. A further problem is similar to that faced by uses and gratifications research, namely that the greater the role given to viewers to construct their own meanings from the text, the more one must abandon the question of cause altogether. The viewer becomes all powerful, and television merely provides the raw materials. As noted earlier, this parallels tendencies within sociocognitive research to overemphasise the constructive aspects of perception, neglecting the limits placed on this process by the structure of the real world.

The analysis of meaning

In media studies, a variety of methods have been used to analyse meanings. In the main, I have relied on literary or textual analysis to compare text structure with viewers' representations. Other researchers make more use of content analysis (Cantor and Pingree, 1983; Cassata and Skill, 1983) or discourse analysis (Lerman, 1983; Trew, 1979). Each of these methods has very real problems concerning the kinds of textual structures which they can identify and the certainty with which they can identify them. None is exhaustive, for both qualitative and quantitative methods can be more certain of what they have found, than of not having missed what is 'really' there. Yet the claim that viewers' representations contain structures absent from the text requires that this latter problem, in statistical terms, type two error, is minimised. These two approaches, literary and content analysis will be compared empirically later in this chapter, when we begin to relate perceptions of characterisation to the narrative structure of the programmes.

The problem of not really knowing what is in the text can be extended to our knowledge of viewers. For we do not know all the viewers' repertoire of social knowledge which is available when interpreting television. The issue of causality has bedevilled mass communications research throughout its history. Even the experimental approach has problems, for there are no normal, naive viewers, viewers may selectively attend to experimental materials, and we cannot conclusively know what is 'in' the experimental materials, especially once complex, connotational meanings are studied.

Yet the causality question is too important to abandon, for people spend much of their leisure time watching television. Everyone knows of anecdotes suggesting evidence for and against influence, for selective attention and for mindless absorption. Unfortunately, researchers often know more of the epistemological problems with their claims than of ways to overcome these problems. To know the initial knowledge of viewers and the content of texts, to bring these together in natural circumstances and to have adequate access to one's dependent variables, is an impossible ideal. Thus research must be pragmatic. Forgoing the experimental approach, the present research has gained the following advantages: it has studied naturally acquired knowledge of complex and lengthy television programmes, with culturally significant, although latent, meanings; it has studied programme knowledge naturally integrated with social knowledge; and it has used methods which indicate little of the researchers' concerns to viewers.

This book is located within previous research from social psychology and media studies. Although the contents of a text or people's minds cannot be directly known, there are theories about these contents. These theories mediate between the materials we work with and research conclusions. To recognise the mediating role of theory is to recognise that research conclusions are fallible because theories have the following attributes: they structure our perception of the domain under study; they have problems of operationalisation; they are usually slightly dated when applied to a new domain; and there are usually competing theories, rather than a single good theory. Consequently, the present research is fallible in that: certain questions were asked and not others; there is a heavy dependency on the semantic differential and multidimensional scaling in operationalising the research questions; there have been rapid developments in cultural studies and in social perception theory and cognitive science, making certain aspects of the selected theories slightly dated; and Implicit Personality

Theory, Gender Schema Theory, and certain literary analyses were selected instead of, say, categorical theories of person perception, personal construct theory, content analysis, or other literary analyses. Nonetheless, the theories selected in this research have considerable empirical support. To some extent, the study comparing free descriptions with property ratings (above) is checked whether theory was guiding research too much. Finally, the semantic differential was used only in relation to the more implicit character sorting method, it was not used to construct the representations themselves.

In conclusion, the present research has drawn on person perception theories and cultural studies as the theoretical frames through which the issue of causality must be approached. Bearing in mind the above arguments and caveats, it is suggested that: where the three character representations differ (jointly or individually) from theories of person perception, this may be a locus of bottom-up influence, in which textual structure (programme or genre) affects character representation. Conversely, where the character representations differ from literary readings of either the programmes represented or the genre as a whole, this may be a locus of top-down influence, in which social knowledge affects character representation.

Relating Characterisation to Narrative

The analysis of texts: the example of social class

The issue of how to determine the themes available in a programme around which viewers may negotiate their understandings of events portrayed remains a difficult one. Nonetheless, one must rely on some analysis of the text to draw conclusions about the constructive activity of the viewer in the light of the representations which they in fact construct. For example, in the study of *Coronation Street* in Chapter 5, considerable emphasis has been placed upon Dyer *et al.*'s (1981) analysis of the programme, in the absence of any alternative analyses. The most salient example of viewers neglecting an aspect of textual structure in favour of prior person knowledge was the finding in the above studies that viewers seemed to neglect the theme of social class and, consequently, the relationship between class and centrality to the community, which Dyer *et al.* regarded as particularly important. This issue of class was a theme regarded as particularly important by Dyer *et al.* (1981). It can be argued that some check is required on the validity of their analysis before conclusions are drawn: maybe class is not really a general theme in the programme, but they found certain salient but unrepresentative examples for which it was important.

It was noted above that one could conduct either interpretative or frequency based analyses of dominant themes. Yet rarely are both conducted on the same material, so that one can be directly compared to the other. So, to examine the validity of Dyer *et al.*'s emphasis on class, some quantitative index of the role of class in the programme can be obtained. To make this index readily comparable to viewers' representations of the characters, a frequency analysis of the patterns of interactions among characters was conducted (see Livingstone, 1989a for further details). This has three advantages.

Firstly, it checks the semiotic analysis of qualitatively significant interactions with a quantitative index of frequent interactions. Although contradictory results between these approaches would require a theoretical choice, a conjunction between the two would strengthen each. Secondly, the data can be used to generate a multidimensional representation of characters which is directly comparable to that of viewers' similarity judgements. Thirdly, the index of frequency is open as to the type of interaction or the reason for interaction, just as the index of perceived similarity was open to the criteria used to judge the similarity of characters. The representation can be later interpreted by projecting property ratings for characters.

Following Dyer *et al.*, it was hypothesised that class will be a major feature of character interactions in *Coronation Street*. As a consequence, the character representation constructed from interaction frequencies should differ substantially from that held by the viewers of the characters' personalities.

A study of social class in CORONATION STREET

A consecutive sample of *Coronation Street* was video-recorded for a three month period in 1984 (twenty-nine episodes of 25 minutes each). These episodes were content analysed for the frequency of interactions between the twenty-one characters. Character interactions were coded for each scene in the text, where a scene was the period between two cuts, where a cut involved a camera move to a changed location and/or a changed character combination. For each scene, the frequency of interaction—at least one verbal utterance between a character pair—was coded for each combination of characters present. The number of utterances for each character pair per unit was not coded, nor were any interactions involving non-central characters. The codings were summed to produce a lower-triangular data matrix containing the frequency of interaction between each character pair over the three months.

Five of the episodes were double coded, with a reliability index of 90 per cent. The frequency matrix was entered into a multidimensional scaling program (MRSCAL) to represent the structural interrelations between characters. Based on the 'elbow', stress values and interpretability, the two-dimensional solution was selected (see Livingstone, 1989a for further details of procedure and statistics).

The character representations based on viewers' character sorting (Figs. 2 and 3, Chapter 5) and on actual interaction frequencies between characters (Fig. 1, present chapter) were compared directly by entering the co-ordinates into a canonical correlation analysis. There were no significant correlations between the two spaces: thus, they cannot be said to be similar in their dimensions. Further, the property ratings obtained earlier for each character were regressed on to the 'interaction' space using PROFIT. Only two properties were significant, social class and intelligence. The interaction space with these two properties projected on to it is shown in Fig. 1.

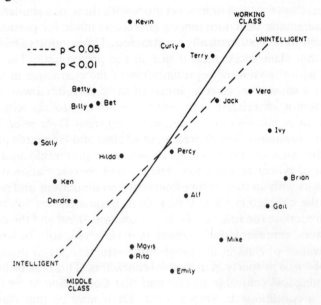

FIGURE 1   Representation of the characters in *Coronation Street* based on interaction frequencies (Dimension 1=horizontal; dimension 2=vertical).

Figure 1 reveals that character interaction frequency in *Coronation Street* is primarily organised around either work or family groups. These inter-relate through the dual membership of certain characters (as at 1985/6). 6). Reading clockwise from the top of the space: Kevin, Curly and Terry are the young lads who drink and work together; Terry, Jack and Vera are the Duckworth family; Vera and Ivy work together; Ivy, Brian and Gail are the Tilsley family; Mike is rather on his own—he works with Ivy and Emily and socialises with Brian, Alf or Rita in the pub; Emily is a close friend of Rita and Mavis, who work together; Ken and Deirdre are married; Sally works for Ken and had an affair with Billy; Billy, Bet and Betty run the pub; and Hilda and Percy occupy central positions through their links to everybody as the Street's gossips and busybodies, while Alf meets most people in his shop.

What is the role of social class in the structure of the programme? Much of the action in *Coronation Street* clearly hinges on interactions based on family and work relations. This is unsurprising and is consistent with Dyer *et al.*'s reading of the programme as centred on domesticity and work. However, there is some room for flexibility in this system through selection of friends, romances, and drinking partners. This narrative flexibility appears to be constrained by the social class position of the characters. From the statistical significance of class in the PROFIT analysis, it appears that characters socialise or interact more with those of a similar class. Thus, the paradigmatic selections among characters made for particular interactions seem to be systematically constrained. This supports Dyer *et al.*, who argued that class is a central theme in the programme. The results also conflict with the viewers' representation of the characters in Chapter 5.

Figure 1 shows that class is perceived to be correlated with intelligence. Yet it is not correlated with power, centrality to the community, or warmth, as might also have been expected from Dyer *et al.*'s alignment between *Coronation Street*'s treatment of class and Hoggart's nostalgic and subversive view of the working classes as a preferable and alternative resource of power and opinion. The present representation of characters provides us with an indication of narrative combinations and permutations among the characters by indexing their frequencies of interaction. The results underline the role of class in *Coronation Street* and the contrast with the viewers' representation suggests that viewers ignore or underestimate the relevance of class in the programme structure, even though they are aware of it as a property of individual characters. This may be because class is becoming less central in Britain and that *Coronation Street* is somewhat behind in continuing to emphasise it. Or it may be that class has been naturalised and, in accordance with the genre, personalised, so that viewers do not perceive class messages. For example, the middle class factory owner, Mike, may be seen as an unsympathetic tyrant as a function not of his class but of his personality or his masculinity.

Character, personality and narrative

What does the disjunction between character interaction and character personality imply for the structure of narrative and for viewers' readings of programmes? One may have supposed that characters' personalities are established through their proximities to each other. For example, it may have been that Curly and Terry, through being friends, come to seem similar in viewers' perceptions, or that Ken and Deirdre appear more similar because they are married. In fact, the very opposite seems to be true.

Characters perceived as similar are less likely to interact (e.g. Bet and

Vera or Ken and Curly) than are personality opposites. Interactions occur between personality opposites on the dimensions central to the programme. These interaction patterns are likely to be institutionalised in the narratives through work relationships or longstanding friendships and, of course, these latter may lead to marital, or other family relationships, which make permanent the enactment of a particular opposition. This makes sense, as it is through the enactment of the thematic oppositions, with each pole personified by a particular character, that the narratives gain interest, involve conflict, and explore culturally important oppositions. The opposition on which a particular character pair differ is likely to be the one on which their interactions are based. For example, Mavis and Rita (friends and workmates) clash over Rita's bossiness (greater dominance), Mavis' prudishness (more staid and moral) and Rita's more modern approach to life compared to Mavis' traditional, often nostalgic viewpoint. As the main aspect of their friendship is gossip over events in the community, their various differences are expressed through their commentary on the actions of others. Based on salient oppositions, this apparently trivial gossip ensures two alternative viewpoints on the actions elsewhere, establishing a range or perspectives for viewers.

This suggests some of the ways in which the textual openness of soap opera (Allen, 1985; Eco, 1979a; Seiter, 1981) may be achieved. It also reveals the importance of character knowledge to the constructive role of the reader. Allen (1985) discusses the relative importance of the paradigmatic over the syntagmatic in soap opera. He argues that the wealth of knowledge that viewers bring to interpretation about characters' personalities and histories means that each superficially simple action or stereotyped narrative gains interest paradigmatically through knowledge of the characters involved in terms of a range of relevant thematic oppositions.

Characters perceived as similar may serve as functional equivalents in interactions. For example, to illustrate a moral conflict, Jack may clash with either Ivy or Curly. This gives the scriptwriters the flexibility to select, say, Ivy (a Catholic) for a religious conflict or Curly (male) for a clash over the treatment of women and the role of courtesy. This flexibility is limited partly by the constraint of preferring within-class interactions and also by more detailed character attributes or histories established over the years (certain narratives may require married or young characters, for example). Nevertheless, it would seem that narrative interactions between the character establish thematic difference or opposition, not perceived similarity, between characters.

In relation to the interpretative role of the viewer, viewers may generate particular expectancies about narrative development, make predictions about the course of events, and readily identify the issues at stake, all on the basis of their more permanent knowledge of the characters involved.

From the relationships between characters in the scaling representation, one can see an operationalisation of the concept of paradigm: if all characters are potentially available for a particular narrative role, then the selection of a specific character gains its significance for the viewer through its relations to other, non-selected characters. The reader or viewer must follow the developing thematic contrasts or equivalences established between characters during the course of the narrative. We will see in the next chapter how narratives focus on personality conflicts rather than similarities, generating interest and a role for the viewer through the use of character information in narrative development.

7
Divergent Interpretations of Television Drama

Consensus and Divergence

Viewing can no longer be seen as the passive uptake of and response to a manifest and discrete message (Katz, 1980). Much television programming, especially soap opera, is designed to engage and involve the viewer. The more open and diverse programmes are, the better they may implicate the viewers in the construction of meaning and thus enhance their interest both cognitively and emotionally. 'We begin with the observation, based on careful textual analysis, that television is dense, rich, and complex, rather than impoverished' (Newcomb and Hirsch, 1984, p. 71). The question then becomes, how is this complexity understood by viewers? Thus far, the theoretical issues surrounding viewers' interpretations have received far more considerable attention than have empirical issues. Many discussions of audience interpretations are more speculative than investigative, and studies of the audience are in this respect just beginning.

With a more complex notion of both programmes and viewers, the need for a way of studying viewers' interpretations becomes more pressing. Fejes (1984) discusses how critical mass communications research has frequently neglected to study the audience at all, and Radway (1985) shows how current theorising about texts and viewer has now foregrounded the viewer: 'these theorists [from reader-response theory and reception aesthetics] sought ways to reassert the essential dependency of meaning upon the interaction between the reader and the text' (p. 339).

If the viewer is cognitively involved and the programme is sufficiently open, allowing multiple interpretations, leaving sufficient ambiguity, and so forth (Eco, 1979a), then we need to investigate not only the nature of viewers' interpretations, but also the extent to which these interpretations diverge from each other. Further, we must assume neither complete consensus nor complete divergence in interpretations, but instead begin to investigate the areas of consensus and divergence.

The research presented in Chapter 5 focused on people's interpretations of television characters and has generally found consensus in interpretations. Viewers of programmes involving well-known characters have been found to represent the characters according to similar themes and they

165

perceive similar relations between the characters. However, the issue of consensus should be pursued because other recent empirical research within cultural studies reveals a significant and interesting degree of divergence in interpretation of the same characters or events in soap opera (Ang, 1985; Hobson, 1982; Katz and Leibes, 1986; Morley, 1980).

There are three possible resolutions of this contradiction. These concern differences between the present and the cultural studies research in terms of methodology, in levels of textual meaning studied, and in definitions of viewer groupings. The recent empirical work on viewers' interpretations uses a different, namely qualitative, methodological approach from that of the research conducted here. Although their findings are often highly suggestive, one is left with doubts concerning the representativeness of the illustrations provided and the reliability of the findings. Nonetheless, qualitative methods have notable advantages in terms of sensitivity, richness, and complexity. Further research should now be seeking to examine divergence in interpretations more systematically and with a greater variety of methods for convergent validity.

Alternatively, it may be that while consensus exists in relatively abstract meanings, divergence may be found at a more concrete level. The multidimensional scaling studies presented in Chapter 5 index fairly general and abstract representations of characters. These representations are a summary of general programme themes, as the viewers perceive them, and provide a resource for the interpretation of particular narratives. Yet, viewers' character representations need not completely determine the interpretation of particular narratives, as at this more specific and concrete level of interpretation, many other factors (e.g. the particular interests or preferences of the viewers and the specific details and history of the narrative) may operate. Thus divergence in interpretation may still exist at this lower level of analysis. This possibility will be investigated in the first, exploratory, study presented in this chapter.

The third possible resolution of the contradiction between divergence and consensus in findings is that divergence in interpretation does exist, but not as a function of viewers' age or sex, as examined in the multidimensional scaling studies. In the second study presented in this chapter, viewers' interpretations of a narrative will be studied in some detail by dividing viewers according to their interpretations, rather than their demographic background. Any correlates of divergence, whether sociological or psychological, will be investigated independently after natural interpretative groupings of viewers, if any, have been discovered. The relatively low stress or error in the multidimensional scaling spaces obtained earlier suggests little divergence among viewers. But if this chapter reveals divergence in the instantiation of consensual, abstract character knowledge in relation to specific narratives, then determinants of divergence at this more specific level of narrative analysis may be further investigated.

A Typology of Divergence in Narrative Interpretation

In order first to gain some initial idea of the nature and extent of divergence in specific interpretations of character and narrative among viewers, a preliminary and open-ended investigation was conducted. Do viewers spontaneously diverge in their interpretations when specific narratives are examined in detail? If so, what types of divergence are exhibited and which aspects of the characters and narratives do they concern? Very little is known of these issues to date. This study is intended as an initial approach to the problem in order to gain some idea of the nature and range of interpretative divergence. Its aim is to construct an initial taxonomy of types of divergence.

This study should link the character representations to the qualitative research of cultural studies on the viewer by investigating, in addition to the divergence question, the role of the representations in interpreting specific narratives. In relation to divergence, this study takes a social psychological approach, drawing in particular on the early work of Bartlett (1932) and his more recent followers (Mandler, 1984) on the ways in which memory distortions systematically create divergences among subjects. More generally, the role of the reader/viewer can be approached by identifying whether and when social knowledge in addition to character knowledge is used to make sense of the text presented.

A study of divergent interpretations

Twenty seven women of a range of ages and occupations (not students) who were all regular and longstanding viewers of *Coronation Street* were asked to recall four narratives involving the popular and central character, Rita Fairclough. No restrictions were placed on which narratives they recalled: they were simply asked to recall any narratives which they had seen at any time in the programme's history. They were each provided with sufficient blank paper and no time limit and asked to describe freely the narratives as they remembered them, including in their accounts details of what happened, how Rita and other characters reacted or felt, and what the events might reveal about Rita's character. These instructions were given to encourage viewers to reveal their own inferences and judgements and to discourage a bland, denotative or behavioural description.

A wide range of narratives were recalled, ranging over many years, although the majority concentrated on the character's recent history. The accounts were first sorted by the narrative recalled, and then compared to see how the same narrative was recalled by different viewers. Were they consensual in their descriptions and what degree and types of divergence occurred? The results reveal something of viewers' spontaneous experience of the programme, as the memories which they recalled are presumably the most readily available and salient to them when viewing the programme and interpreting new narratives. The discussion that follows should be regarded as illustrative of the kinds of points which might be pursued in further, more systematic research.

Results

All the accounts provided by viewers were read closely by the researcher. The following discussion results from a detailed consideration of all accounts, and those presented for illustration were selected for their representativeness of a particular point. The material is organised around categories of divergence in interpretation and these categories represent abstractions formulated on reading all the accounts and attempting to summarise main themes or trends observed within the data. In the illustrations to follow, each account is reported in full (numbers indicate the viewer).

Narrative recall and character representation

Much attention focused on Rita's friendship with Mavis Riley, her co-worker in the local newsagents which Rita owns and runs. As was shown in Chapter 5, both of these women are popular, middle-aged women who are less working class than most other characters. From the multidimensional scaling character representation one can see that viewers represent Rita and Mavis as quite different in personality on the dimensions of sociability (dimension 2), morality (dimension 1), power (dimension 1), and approach to life (dimension 3). Thus Rita is seen as more dominant, modern, and sociable than Mavis, who is in turn seen as more moral, traditional, and staid. They are fairly equivalent in femininity.

This general characterisation of the characters' personalities and, more important, of the differences between their personalities, translates neatly into the themes of the narratives in which Rita and Mavis are typically involved. Narratives which centre on their relationship often concern Rita's teasing dominance or bossiness conflicting either harmoniously or more acrimoniously with Mavis's old-fashioned and rather silly weakness and shyness. Narratives thus concern the areas of personality conflict or contrast rather than those of consonance, such as their femininity or warmth.

As will be seen from the illustrations of interpretative divergence to follow, most viewers concur on these general assessments of the characters. The dominance of Rita, for example, or the traditional morality of Mavis may be thus seen as consensual social facts. Divergence then lies in what viewers 'do' with these facts, i.e. how they divergently apply this consensual and abstract knowledge to specific narratives. For example, is Rita's dominance a positive or negative attribute, or how central to Mavis's personality is her old-fashioned outlook and what are its consequences for her actions? However, narratives contain more than character portraits and divergence can also lie in the interpretation of additional aspects of the events portrayed, as will become clear.

Character evaluation and narrative focus

The first type of divergence observed concerns different interpretations of character evaluation and narrative focus. Seven viewers described the teasing relationship between Rita and Mavis, which appears to generate much narrative tension. Their foci were different, and these differences reveal underlying differences in evaluation and assessment of the two characters. They may also indicate divergent tendencies to represent different aspects of the same narrative, namely behaviours, personality, context. Thus, for example, 21 is straightforwardly critical of Rita as a domineering person. She hints that Rita may not acknowledge Mavis's contribution.

> 21 She runs the shop successfully with Mavis's help. She's domineering over Mavis.

Another viewer, 17, is also critical of Rita as someone who causes trouble for Mavis and fails to help where she might. Her account focuses more on actual events and makes no inference about the characters' personalities.

> 17 I think Rita gives Mavis a lot of trouble in the shop, especially when she was involved with the musician (?). When she was not well and she got caught with the man pulling his trousers up, Rita could have helped in that situation but didn't.

In contrast, 15 focuses on personality traits. She also diverges from 21 and 17 in being highly positive about Rita, perceiving her use of her power and strength to do good and help the weaker and rather irritating Mavis.

> 15 Employing and befriending Mavis Riley shows that Rita is a fairly warm and sensitive person with a fair amount of patience. Mavis would perhaps not be the ideal choice in many employer's eyes!

Viewer 10 also reflects a positive view of Rita, emphasising more her aims in trying to change Mavis, rather than merely tolerating or compensating for Mavis's failings.

> 10 Teasing Mavis over her friendship with the potter (name not remembered) who displayed an artistic nature + eventually moved to Yorkshire. Rita's friendliness and warmth to her friends was apparent in her teasing of Mavis, but it also highlighted her more independent streak—pushing Mavis on—to do things she usually wouldn't have considered—Supportive nature.

Viewer 09 is similar to that of 10: in both the 'giving trouble' of 17 is seen more innocently as 'teasing'. Rita is seen here more trivially—a light-hearted, rather insensitive person unlike the deeper, warmer view of 10.

> 02 Constant joking with Mavis in shop, teases her about going off with men and not doing her driving—drives Mavis mad tho' Rita only does this for fun. Sometimes appears to go too far and seems a little cruel, tho' it is obvious that she means no harm and only wishes to bring Mavis out of her shell a little. She is quick-witted—gives lively answers and has a good sense of humour—tho' sometimes sarcastic.

Viewer 09 sides with Mavis rather than Rita, though Rita is still seen positively. This viewer seems to be identifying with the victim in this relationship. In contrast, 07 sees things from Rita's perspective. She also provides the most complex account, assessing Rita's motives, needs, and personality, and placing these in the context of her life events.

09   Mavis Riley, comes up against a lot of Rita's leg pulling, she teases Mavis so much about the men folk, (she has so much fun in her) and I feel that sometimes she takes it too far as Mavis gets very embarrassed about it all.

07   After the initial shock of her husband's death etc had passed, and she got over an emotional torment of remembering, she slowly slipped back into the Rita we all know and love, teasing Mavis and sending her up all the time, trying to succeed in getting her to take driving lessons and do something 'positive' in her life, making use again of the driving instructor being a 'fella' for her to try to throw her on to again. She seems to thrive on having someone to have control over in some way, exercising her authority but staying sensitive to their feelings when danger is in sight.

Evaluation of personality traits

A second type of divergence concerns the evaluation of a personality trait. Eleven viewers recalled one specific event in the relationship between Rita and Mavis which together illustrate a further set of points. This narrative concerned Rita's attempts to get Mavis to learn to drive. Viewer 23 provides the straightforwardly positive viewpoint, while 26 is clearly negative. Both viewers acknowledge Rita's dominance over the situation, but they make radically different assessments of Rita's use of her power.

23   Her decision to get Mavis Riley to drive a car was forthright and appeared natural and easy. Even when things went wrong Rita gave confidence to Mavis holding her up until she eventually saw the fruits of her endeavours when Mavis passed her test.

26   She finds great delight in putting Mavis Riley in difficult situations making Mavis take driving lessons against her will. She seems to become stronger talking down to and taking 'the mickey' out of her.

Interestingly, only one other viewer of the eleven who remembered this narrative agreed with 26, namely 03.

Interpretations of a single event

Thirdly, viewers diverged in their interpretations of a single event. The comparison between 03 and 16 illustrates the diverse interpretations which can be placed on a single action (decorating the flat).

03   Rita badgered Mavis into learning to drive, she was devious about it by the way she had Mavis's flat decorated in exchange.

16   She persuaded Mavis to have driving lessons and told her that she would pay for them, and have her flat painted and decorated for her. This shows she can be very kind and generous.

At this point, we should note the balance between consensus and divergence in interpretations: there is a consensus among the other viewers in favour of Rita's kindness which suggests limits to divergence. One should not expect all viewers to represent narratives wholly differently.

Complexity and the use of rhetoric

Fourthly, viewers differ in the complexity of their interpretations and in their use of social rhetoric. Within this overall evaluative consensus, certain viewers offered a more complex viewpoint: 25 resolves the apparent contradiction between 23 and 26, the positive and negative views of Rita by subordinating the negative actions to the status of a means to achieve a positive aim. In this resolution, she draws upon a general social rhetoric, the cliché that one has to be cruel to be kind, with an awareness that she was doing this as indicated by her use of quotation marks. Thus the narrative is interpreted by using a cultural framework for resolving apparent contradictions.

> 25   Teaching Mavis to drive. Rita showed great determination in forcing Mavis to learn to drive mostly against her will. Even though she did force Mavis, Rita knew and understood that she has 'to be cruel to be kind' to Mavis in order that she would drive.

In different ways, 15 and 04 both also complicate the simple view of Rita's altruism: 04 notes the value to Rita of her partner being able to drive, while 15 hints at a deeper psychological bond between them that benefits Rita by compensating for her lack of children. Here too, social rhetoric serves as an explanatory resource for the interpretation of particular events, allowing the viewer to go beyond the information given.

> 04   She encouraged Mavis to take her driving test and lent her the car and paid for the driving lessons. This was to help herself out by enabling Mavis to go to the wholesalers but also to try and get Mavis out and to give her more confidence.

> 15   Rita's encouraging Mavis Riley to take driving lessons and financing them could be taken as a genuine reflection of her caring for Mavis (could almost be child substitution!), and wanting her to perhaps get more out of life and become a little more independent.

Inaccuracy in recall

Fifthly, one should not forget perhaps the most obvious source of divergence, namely that due to inaccurate comprehension or recall of a narrative. Especially when recalling long past narratives, some viewers may misunderstand what happened or misremember an event. False recall can be claimed only for the closed aspects of the text, those aspects which are sufficiently unambiguous for recall to even be assessed in terms of accuracy. Any inaccuracy is, as predicted by schema theory, integrated meaningfully into the account. For example, twelve viewers described the events following the death of Rita's husband, Len, in which it emerged that he had been having an affair at the time of his death. Most viewers recalled Rita's determination to discover who the 'other' woman was and to meet her. Two viewers recalled wrongly that the woman sought out Rita, rather than the other way around. Compare 19 and 05:

> 19   Rita Fairclough found out her husband was having an affair, he was going to meet his friend on the night he died in a car crash, he had had this liaison for quite a long time, and Rita was terribly upset. After Len died his friend came to see Rita and Rita felt so sorry for her, she couldn't bring herself to say what she felt, because this friend had no friends or family after her husband had died. Rita was a very kind and loyal person, who expects others to be like herself.

> 05   When Rita found her husband had been unfaithful, even though he was killed in an accident, she found out who the woman was and went to see her. After her initial anger at the woman she could understand how it happened.

Yet all agreed on the gist of the narrative, as story grammar researchers predict (Mandler, 1984), namely that Rita discovered the affair, met with the other woman, came to understand her, and thus came to terms with her own loss.

Critical distance

A sixth type of divergence arises from differences among viewers in the degree of critical distance with which they appear to relate to the text. For example, regarding Len's death, many viewers were very involved and moved, as it was an emotionally sensitive series of episodes. Most viewers entered the drama in their descriptions, exhibiting Liebes and Katz (1986) referential mode of viewing. For example, 15 talks of Rita as a person, as she might of someone that she knows.

> 15   Rita's reaction to the death of her husband Len was very sensitive and very real, showing that she is an emotional person which was not always apparent in other situations. She was probably quite emotionally dependent on Len, although having a fairly strong character this again was not always evident.

Compare with 09, in which the viewer appeared to stand back and admire, assessing the quality of the events as fictional construction. This viewer exhibits the critical mode of viewing, but most viewers, nonetheless, recalled events within the referential mode.

> 09   At the time of her husband's sudden death Rita Fairclough played the part of a tragic widow with feeling and dignity. She was able to show what a good actress she is.

Inferential connections

A further type of divergence relates to the connecting inferences which viewers must make in order to generate a coherent reading of the narrative. For example, the events in which Rita rented Len's building yard after his death to Bill Webster also illustrates the treatment of misremembered or misunderstood information. Did Rita rent the yard to Bill, or did she sell it to him? This apparently minor point was given particular significance by viewer 11, who interpreted the 'fact' that she has rented the yard as evidence of Rita's kindness.

> 11   After her husband died she let (as a loan) his workshop to a chap who hadn't
> enough money to buy it, so as to give him an opportunity to make good, rather than
> sell it outright and be sure of the money.

On the other hand, 13 interpreted the 'fact' that she sold the yard as evidence of her braveness and strength of character in making a fresh start for herself.

> 13   I like the way she has made a new life for herself after Len's death, like making
> the decision to sell the wood yard and business to another man and lending him the
> money to start his own business off with.

Attribution of motivation

A related type of divergence concerns differences in the attribution of motivation to particular characters. In some cases, viewers agree on the events which occurred, but disagree on the motivations which they attribute to the actors. Both 18 and 14 noted Rita's decision and actions surrounding their fostering of Sharon, but 18 saw her actions as self-motivated, and therefore saw her discussions with Len as persuasion, while 14 saw her actions as generously motivated to help Len, so that no discussions were seen as important.

> 18   Won Len over when she wanted to foster children and grew very fond of girl
> they had, although she was very independent herself.

> 14   When Rita knew a child would add to Len's happiness, she took in a young
> teenage lodger, who became a great favourite of them both, and ended up working
> for Len in the work-shop. They were both very upset when the time came for her
> to leave them.

Involvement

The ninth and final type of divergence observed in these data was due to different degrees of involvement of viewers with the events portrayed: this could be considered the opposite of the point about critical distance above. For example, most viewers saw the fostering as something which Rita wished for herself, although Len was seen as happy with the arrangement, if he was mentioned at all. The account given by 07 provides another testament to viewers' involvement with the events and characters, to their reference to general social knowledge in interpreting events (women's need for children), to their willingness to fill out the events with their own inferences, and to their belief that the characters grow and change as do real people, unlike cardboard or stereotyped fictions.

> 07   Her love for children came out again when a girl from a problem home was put
> in her and Len's care when they applied for adoption. It's understandable her
> maternal feeling for a baby to cuddle were there, but age was her greatest handicap
> which hurt her. This lady showed deep change at this stage compared to when she
> first appeared. I feel it helped the relationship with her husband too because he too
> loved Sharon and they both helped to teach an unruly girl what love was and that
> they trusted her even if nobody else did.

Summary

This study of viewers' interpretations of narratives which they viewed under natural conditions illustrates the following points. The interpretation of character and of narrative is inextricably related, for viewers use their knowledge of characters to create coherent and consistent meanings for the events they perceive. Viewers diverge in their interpretations in a variety of ways: (a) evaluation of a character as generally positive or negative; (b) narrative focus in the account given (e.g. personality, behaviours); (c) complexity of the interpretation; (d) character whose perspective is taken in observing events. Further, is rather more consensus than divergence in interpretation across viewers: consensus is revealed in assessments of the characters' personalities (as in the character representations) and in majority endorsement of certain interpretations over others.

Viewers are willing to draw their own inferences about the significance of events observed. These inferences concerning motivations, feelings, or intentions serve to fill out the interpretations. Often they draw upon more general mythic or culturally consensual knowledge frames concerning, for instance, rhetoric about maternal feelings, the nature of relationships, or ways of helping or influencing others. Viewers may misremember certain aspects of a narrative, but all interpretations are nonetheless made coherent and contain the gist of the events which occurred.

Finally, the interpretation of narrative connects with the representation of character. Narratives are interpreted as involving conflict between characters along the themes found to be salient discriminators of those characters in earlier studies of character representation. Thus there are a number of distinct ways in which viewers diverge from each other in their interpretation of television narrative. By interpreting the interpretations, as it were, we can discover some of the ways in which viewers come to different readings of the same text, drawing upon their sociocognitive knowledge of these particular characters, of people in general—their motivations and personalities, and of general social explanatory rhetoric.

Only in a few of the demonstrations of divergent interpretation could the interpretations be labelled either correct or incorrect. In other words, the text contains few single, unambiguous meanings, and thus the effects of such meanings cannot be straightforwardly anticipated from the researcher's own, often implicit, assessment of the meaning 'in' the text. The researcher must recognise her or his own role in interpreting, selecting, and, sometimes, disparaging the text. Most important, it is the viewers' interpretations (i.e. the product of an interaction between their social knowledge and the programme structure) which mediates television effects.

What Makes Viewers Diverge When Interpreting Narrative?
Although uses and gratifications research has pointed to the importance

of viewers' relationships with soap opera characters (Carveth and Alexander, 1985; Livingstone, 1988a; Rubin, 1985), the importance of these relationships in affecting interpretations has been little addressed. Yet television drama, and soap opera especially, inscribes multiple perspectives on pertinent issues into the text through the personification of perspectives in character portrayals. Interactions between characters thus enact conflicts and negotiations among different interpretations and perspectives on events.

Psychological factors

Various psychological factors could affect interpretive divergence (Eisenstock, 1984; Jose and Brewer, 1984; Noble, 1975; Potkay and Potkay, 1984) by influencing the viewers' experienced relationships with the characters. Potkay and Potkay (1984) show that viewers identify with cartoon characters according to their perceived similarity to the characters, and further that this identification is independent of character evaluation. Noble (1975) suggests that viewers need not identify with a character in order to adopt their perspective. Drawing upon the concept of 'parasocial interaction' (Horton and Wohl, 1956), Noble argues that viewers interpret narratives through a process of recognition, entering into the action by playing against a character who is similar to someone they know in real life.

Alternatively, it may be that, despite the findings of Potkay and Potkay (1984) for cartoon characters, character evaluation does play a role in soap opera in which viewers take the perspective of liked characters against disliked characters. Regular viewers of soap opera become more involved with the characters than do cartoon fans. Thus identification, recognition, and evaluation may all create divergence in interpretations of a multi-character narrative. If the same events are viewed from a variety of different perspectives, with varying evaluative stances and concerns, then different interpretations of the same narrative must result.

A study to investigate the nature and determinants of divergence

The remainder of this chapter will report on a study in which viewers' divergent interpretations of a television narrative were systematically studied in relation to the viewers' experienced relationships with the characters.

The narrative

A narrative was selected from *Coronation Street* which concerned a father opposing the marriage of his young daughter by his first marriage to a much older man on the grounds of the fiancé's previous adultery with the father's present wife. At least two readings were potentially available in this narrative: either love triumphs over prejudice, or naivety triumphs over wisdom. The themes of the narrative, however interpreted, reflect a mythic or romantic morality, supporting the idea that soap opera functions for viewers as contemporary mythology. The themes are carried by the central characters, so that the young daughter represents love/naivety and the father represents prejudice/wisdom, depending on the reading selected. The text provided various support for either of these readings. For example, the daughter's naivety was evidenced by initial ignorance of her fiancé's affairs, particularly with her stepmother, and by her faith in his new-found desire for stability. Yet this could be explained according to the 'love' reading, as she was new to the area and certainly her fiancé talked continually of wanting to settle down, seeing her as a golden opportunity to start a new life. The naivety/wisdom reading is more evidenced by the characters' pasts, such as the previous entanglements and the father's position of respect in the community, while the love/prejudice reading is amply supported by their present actions, such as the couple's happiness and the father's hostility.

Sociological factors

In terms of sociological or demographic factors which may affect divergence (Newcomb and Hirsch, 1984), one might ask whether the younger and female viewers will identify with the daughter while older and male viewers' take the father's part? It is increasingly argued that, in theory, women will interpret soap operas differently from men, as they participate in different discourses and because the 'gendered spectatorship' of the genre is a female one (Curti, 1988; Kuhn, 1984). Unfortunately, this position is typically supported by studies of female audiences alone, and still awaits empirical investigation which compares the interpretations of men and women. A second social variable to be studied here is that of age. As Hartley (1984) notes, generation membership indicates access to different discourses and interests and thus suggests possible differential interpretations according to viewers' ages. It seems reasonable to hypothesise that the two readings present in the narrative studied here would be adopted by groups of viewers differentiated by gender and age.

Implications for effects

Although we are not here directly concerned with 'effects', it should be noted that if the same narrative cues two quite different interpretations, then the effects of viewing should also be different, by increasing either romantic/optimistic or cynical/pessimistic thinking. In the context of the cultivation paradigm, this would lead to low correlations, often found in the literature (Hawkins and Pingree, 1983), if only one interpretation was tested. In relation to agenda-setting, McCombs and Weaver (1973) showed how psychological needs affected type of media use which in turn affected degree of media influence on cognitions. Implicitly, similar causal chains are proposed by the advocates of the interpretively active viewer, namely that knowledge, interests, and needs affect programme interpretation which in turn affects degree and type of media influence. Given the varied relationships which viewers experience with the characters in soap opera, effects mediated by identification, role modelling, and parasocial interation will surely depend upon programme interpretation.

Aims

The present research (see Livingstone, 1989b for further details) attempts to make some inroads into these issues by examining ordinary viewers' interpretations of a particular soap opera narrative, after they have watched it unfold over some time in natural viewing circumstances. The study aims to discover and describe the nature of any divergence, examining whether viewers fall into distinct interpretive positions. It will also investigate some psychological and sociological correlates of divergence, specifically whether the divergent groups are discriminable by age and/or gender of the viewers (Newcomb and Hirsch, 1984) and by psychological factors which may influence which perspective a viewer adopts on interpreting the narrative (identification, evaluation, and recognition).

Sample

The sixty-six viewers (forty-two female and twenty-four male) were obtained either through the Oxford Department of Experimental Psychology subject panel or in response to a national advertisement for soap opera viewers in SOAP magazine. They were of a wide range of ages (16 to 60) and occupations (mostly white collar workers such as secretaries and clerks, with some housewives, and a few students). All were regular viewers of *Coronation Street,* and they had watched the programme for an average of eleven years, watching on average three out of every four episodes). The average amount of the narrative selected for study which was actually viewed was 'most of it', and average amount remembered was 'most of it'.

Overview

In the narrative studied here, Susan Barlow, the 21-year-old daughter of Ken Barlow by his first marriage returns to the Street to live with her father and his new wife, Deirdre Barlow. Susan begins a romance with Mike Baldwin, a local factory owner some 20 years older than her. Two problems from the past complicate matters: Ken's guilt at neglecting Susan as a child, leaving her upbringing to his ex-wife; and Deirdre's adulterous affair with Mike a few years before, for which Ken has not forgiven them. Susan and Mike pursue their affair while Ken refuses to accept it. When

Susan announces her decision to marry Mike, Ken refuses to attend the wedding. Suppressing her guilty feelings, Deirdre tries to support both Ken and Susan. Ken and Mike come to blows, and the whole Street becomes involved. On the morning of the wedding, Susan's brother persuades Ken to attend, thereby atoning for his neglect of her childhood. He relents and gives away the bride. The story ends for the time being as the couple go on their honeymoon.

As we know from Chapter 5, the characters central to this narrative are perceived as follows. Ken: very moral (even staid) and weak, neither masculine nor feminine, fairly traditional (and not sexy) in his approach to life; Mike: very dominant and immoral (or roguish), very masculine, modern (and sexy) in his approach to life; Deirdre: very moral (and staid) and weak, fairly feminine (and mature and warm), somewhat modern (and sexy) in her approach to life. Unfortunately, this study was conducted before Susan had returned to live with the Barlows. Nonetheless, it is clear from this study that Ken and Mike are quite opposed characters who are bound to clash over moral/sexual issues, while Deirdre is in the middle, being similar to Ken in her moral position and relative weakness, while closer to Mike in her approach to life.

The story was selected because it typifies the personal, emotional, and moral concern of soap opera, it involves well-established characters, it was a typical but lengthy story (unfolding over several months), and it would clearly be 'read' in several distinct ways. Firstly, it can be seen as a traditional romance, with true love triumphing over adversity: Ken acts out his unreasonable and unforgiving prejudices and jealousies against the man chosen by his daughter. Alternatively, it can be seen as a failed attempt by wisdom and experience (the father) to rescue his naive and innocent daughter from the manipulative grasp of an older and immoral man.

Design

The questionnaire was administered to viewers just as the couple went on their honeymoon. It was divided into three parts. The first part requested demographic and viewing information. The second part indexed potential psychological correlates of interpretive divergence with five-point rating scales of identification ('How much are you at all like X'), recognition ('Think of the people you know, such as your family and friends. Do you know anybody at all like X? Who?'), evaluation ('How much do you like X'), and perspective-taking ('Do you sympathise with X's viewpoint') for each of the four main characters in the narrative (Mike, Deirdre, Ken, and Susan). The third part contained thirty statements of narrative interpretation (see Table 1), each with a five-point rating scale (strongly disagree—strongly agree). The statements were based on pilot testing in which a small sample of regular viewers completed an open-ended questionnaire about their interpretations of the narrative.

Analysis

In order to discover the emergent groupings among the viewers corresponding to divergent interpretations of the narrative, the data on viewers' agreement with the thirty interpretation statements were entered into a cluster analysis in order to cluster the viewers (see Livingstone, 1989b for details of these and all subsequent analyses), producing four clusters. These were compared in their endorsement of the interpretation statements using descriptive analyses of variance (the means for each cluster are shown in Table 1).

TABLE 1. *Thirty statements concerning narrative interpretation, showing mean agreement(a) for each cluster of viewers*

	R n=20	NR n=25	NC n=9	C(b) n=12	
01 Susan was right to disappoint her father for Mike's sake	4.40	3.88	3.67	2.75	*(c)
02 Ken acted reasonably, doing what he thought best for Susan	1.90	2.20	3.33	4.50	*
03 Susan's behaviour throughout was mature	3.50	2.84	3.67	2.92	
04 Ken put his feelings for Mike before his feelings for Susan	4.65	4.44	3.78	3.58	*
05 Until he met Susan, Mike had had no desire to marry and settle down	3.00	2.52	2.22	3.58	
06 When Ken finally gave Susan away, he still thought he had been right to oppose the marriage	4.15	4.32	4.33	4.75	
07 Susan and Mike's marriage will last	3.25	2.88	2.89	1.75	*
08 Ken was right to oppose the marriage	1.90	2.12	3.22	4.83	*
09 Deirdre was more supportive of Ken than of Mike and Susan	2.45	2.84	2.78	3.17	
10 Susan sees Mike more as a father-figure than as a husband	2.15	3.40	2.11	3.67	*
11 Ken's feelings for Susan stem more from his guilt about her childhood than from love	3.15	3.36	3.22	3.25	
12 Mike and Susan are right for each other	2.00	2.84	2.78	4.00	*
13 Deirdre told Ken she would support Susan for Tracy's sake, but this was just an excuse to do what she wanted	2.80	3.08	2.89	3.17	
14 Mike's feeling for Susan stems partly from revenge, to get back at Deirdre	1.50	2.28	1.56	2.33	
15 Susan's youth is important to Mike: he would not love her if she were older	2.15	2.72	1.89	3.00	
16 Susan does not truly love Mike, she only thinks she does	1.65	2.88	2.33	3.25	*
17 The marriage will have problems because of the age difference	2.40	3.16	2.44	3.75	*
18 Mike thinks Susan is a better person than she really is	2.00	3.04	2.22	3.58	*
19 After the honeymoon, Susan will not work and will have a baby	2.55	3.28	2.89	2.42	
20 Susan and Mike can overcome any problems they encounter	3.85	2.88	3.00	2.08	*
21 Susan determined to marry Mike to show Ken she is an adult	2.80	3.48	2.22	3.83	*
22 Ken acted unreasonably: he was vindictive and possessive	4.20	4.40	2.78	2.50	*

Continued overleaf

TABLE 1.   *Thirty statements concerning narrative interpretation, showing mean agreement(a) for each cluster of viewers (continued)*

23 Deirdre was jealous of Susan marrying Mike	1.70	2.68	2.33	2.67
24 Until she met Mike, Susan had had no desire to marry and settle down	3.35	3.56	3.44	3.92
25 Mike sees Susan more as a mistress than as a wife	1.90	2.56	2.00	2.92
26 Mike's money and success are important to Susan: she would not love him without them	2.00	2.84	1.56	3.08 *
27 The marriage will have problems as Mike won't like being tied down	2.50	3.24	2.67	3.67
28 Susan thinks that Mike is a better person than he really is	2.35	3.64	2.78	4.25 *
29 Mike does not truly love Susan, he only thinks he does	1.65	2.76	2.22	3.75 *
30 Deirdre's behaviour was weak and she could not decide what to do or who to support	2.45	3.28	2.00	2.92

(a) Agreement ratings on a five-point scale (5=strongly agree)
(b) R   = romantic
    NR = negotiated romantic
    NC = negotiated cynic
    C   = cynic
(c) * = analysis of variance significant at $p0.001$

The four clusters of viewers can be ranked in terms of their relative allegiance to either Ken or to Mike and Susan. One cluster of viewers are most strongly on Ken's side and against the couple, another is less on Ken's side, but more so than either of the other two clusters. A third cluster is the most against Ken and most on the side of the couple, Mike and Susan, and the final cluster again supports the couple, but rather less strongly. Hence, viewers occupy a range of interpretive positions between the pro-Ken and the pro-Mike and Susan textual positions. Bearing in mind that the narrative essentially concerns the perceived authenticity of a relationship, the pro-Ken cluster of viewers will be labelled 'cynics'($n=12$), the pro-couple cluster will be labelled 'romantics'($n=20$), and the intermediate positions will be labelled the 'negotiated cynics' ($n=9$) and 'negotiated romantics' ($n=25$).

The cynics

These viewers' interpretations of the narrative centre on their perception of Ken as having acted reasonably and they consider that he was right to oppose the marriage. They believe that Susan and Mike do not really love each other and that they both believe each other to be better people than they really are. These viewers are especially critical of Susan, who they perceive as wanting Mike for his money and success and as fulfilling her need for a father-figure.

The Romantics

By contrast, these viewers interpreted Ken's actions as unreasonable, vindictive, and possessive. They consider that Ken put his feelings for Mike before those for Susan and that Susan was right to disappoint her father for Mike's sake. They believe that Susan and Mike are right for each other, that the couple can overcome any problems that they encounter, and that the marriage will last.

The negotiated cynics

These viewers essentially agree with the cynics, but adopt a more moderate position by doubting whether Ken was right to oppose the marriage so wholeheartedly, whether Susan and Mike are deluded about each other, and whether Mike does not really love Susan. They also show more reservations in imputing unpleasant motivations to Susan, believing rather less than the cynics that Susan wants a father-figure, wants to prove herself an adult, or wants Mike's money and success. As this group of viewers is almost entirely female (eight out of nine), it may be that their identification with Susan as a woman mitigates against their basically cynical reading of the narrative, thereby producing a more balanced interpretation.

The negotiated romantics

This group of viewers basically agrees with the romantics, but also believes to some extent that the couple's perceptions of each other are idealised and that their love may not be 'true'. They give some credence to the 'father-figure' explanation, and anticipate some problems for the couple. Possibly they represent a 'realistic' reading.

Viewers' relationships with characters

The groups of viewers were, finally, compared in terms of their experienced relationships with the main characters. This revealed that there are more males among the cynics (seven out of twelve) than would be expected by chance, and the negotiated cynics are almost wholly female (eight out of nine). It showed that viewers across different clusters do not differ in terms of which characters they recognize as being like somebody they know in real life. However, there is once more a tendency for the two cynical clusters to differ from each other and from the others: the negotiated cynics know almost nobody like Susan or Mike (only one and two respectively) and the cynics are proportionately more likely to know someone like both Susan and Mike (eight and eight respectively). The age of the viewers was found to be constant across clusters, as was the length and frequency of viewing. Regarding the variables of identification with (or perception of self as similar to) the main characters, there was an effect for Mike in which the negotiated viewers judged themselves as slightly more similar to Mike than did the others. The strongest effect, however, was for identification with Ken, where the cynics saw themselves as more like Ken than did the romantic viewers. On character evaluation, the results again concern Ken. The cynics like Ken more than do either of the romantic clusters, and in fact they are the only viewers to like Ken at all (mean exceeds the scale midpoint). On the question of whether different clusters view events more or less from the perspective of different characters, only Deirdre was unimportant here. The romantic clusters sympathised with Mike and Susan more than did the cynical cluster. Further, sympathy with Susan also discriminated between the two cynical clusters and between the two romantic clusters. In contrast, the cynics, and to a lesser extent, the negotiated cynics, sympathised with Ken (the cynics sympathised more with Ken than did either of the romantic clusters, and the negotiated cynics more than the romantics. One might have expected the negotiated cynics to sympathise more with Ken than with Susan. Yet, possibly because they are mainly women, they could also see Susan's point of view, even though they did not agree with it as much as did the romantic clusters.

The picture is as follows. The cynics comprise a relatively large number of male viewers, and appear more likely to identify with Ken, evaluate Ken positively, and perceive the narrative sympathetically from Ken's viewpoint. The two romantic clusters consider themselves highly unlike Ken, although not particularly like any other character either. They also dislike Ken as a character. These viewers see events from the viewpoint of Mike and Susan, and cannot sympathise with Ken's position. The negotiated cynics are in an interesting position, for while their interpretation of events is closest to that of the cynics and they too dislike Susan and Mike, they nonetheless sympathise with Susan, and are less critical of her in their inferences about her thoughts and motives.

The relationships experienced with the characters proved important in determining the perspective taken on interpreting the narrative, with identification, evaluation, and to a lesser extent, recognition, all influencing interpretation. Recognition of Susan and Mike related to the differences between the interpretations of the two cynical clusters, but was otherwise relatively unimportant, which is surprising in view of Noble's (1975) evidence that recognition should be especially operative for television rather than for film and for female rather than male viewers. Identification proved an important factor, discriminating clusters along the pro-Ken to anti-Ken continuum, as a function of perceived similarity to Ken. This was clearly related to character evaluation, rather than independent of it as suggested by Potkay and Potkay (1984). The perspective-taking or sympathy variables were highly significant with respect to three of the four main characters and the means are consistent with the identification and evaluation judgements for the four clusters of viewers. Given viewers' often considerable involvement in soap opera, it certainly seems plausible that character evaluation, identification, and perspective-taking should become interrelated over time. The strongest results centred on Ken, showing that response to just one major character can significantly affect one's perspective on the narrative as a whole. Although causality can only be inferred here, not demonstrated, the durability of identification, evaluation and recognition relative to the perspective taken on a single narrative suggests that the former, the viewers' relationships with the characters, plays some causal role in influencing interpretation. To the extent that viewers' gender was associated with a specific interpretation, this did not occur in a predictable fashion, and age was quite unrelated to interpretive position. The narrative opposed young/female (Susan) against old/male (Ken). Yet women did not especially side with Susan. The female cluster (negotiated cynics) merely sided less strongly with Ken than did the viewers with whom they are otherwise closest (cynics).

Discussion

The viewers in the present study fell into four natural clusters in their interpretations of the same soap opera narrative. The four clusters are distinguishable according to two general considerations: firstly, an assessment of the rights and wrongs of Ken's opposition to the marriage, according to which the four readings may be ranked between an endorsement of Ken's actions to an endorsement of Susan and Mike's; and secondly, the nature of the inferences made by viewers about characters' motives and thoughts.

The evaluative differences allow viewers to become involved emotionally and take sides during the unfolding of the narrative. The inferences serve to 'fill out' the narrative, increasing coherence and interest through beliefs about the motives and thoughts which lie behind the characters' actions. The range of responses includes both sides of the narrative debate, as anticipated by consideration of the text itself, plus two intermediate but distinct positions.

The results support Newcomb and Hirsch's (1984) argument that television provides a 'cultural forum', showing the '*range* of response, the directly contradictory readings of the medium, that cue us to its multiple meanings' (p. 68). The determinants of this range were found to be not simply sociological (age and gender) but also psychological (identification, evaluation, recognition). Thus one cannot make straightforward assumptions about interpretations from a knowledge of the viewers' socio-structural position but one must also know how viewers relate to the characters. This is expecially true for soap opera, where regular viewers build up substantial relationships with the characters over years.

Areas of consensus

The four interpretative positions are not wholly divergent: the viewers agree on some of the thirty narrative statements. Interestingly, they do not disagree on any of the statements involving one of the characters, Deirdre (statements 9, 13, 23, 30). Yet textually, Deirdre plays a central role, personifying the conflict through her explicit links to both Ken (her husband) and Mike (her former lover). Just as in Radway's research (1985) the romance readers 'filtered out' the structural role of the secondary foil characters and focused on the hero and heroine alone, and similarly, in Liebes' (1984) and research on *Dallas* and that presented in Chapter 5, viewers simplified moral ambiguity into clearly oppositional 'good' and 'bad', so here viewers underplay the role of a centrally ambiguous character, simplifying the narrative to one in which there are two clearly opposed sides.

Two further patterns are evident in the distribution of differentiating and non-differentiating statements. Five statements involved imputing hidden motivations to characters to explain their actions, such as guilt, revenge, desire, and jealousy (statements 5, 11, 14, 23, and 24). None of these significantly differentiate the clusters, suggesting that viewers are reluctant to seek deeper psychological motivations as the 'glue' to connect their interpretations. Secondly, of the seven statements concerning Mike's role, only two discriminated the clusters, wheareas of the eight involving Susan, only two did not discriminate them. This suggests that the divergence in interpretations centres on Susan, again despite the fact that it is Mike's character which is structurally more interesting, for he is making the transition from 'baddie' (playboy, adulterer) to 'goodie' (reformed character, devoted fiancé). The narrative appears to be read not as a conflict between two men so much as a female/male conflict concerning the daughter's freedom to choose.

Futher issues in analysing interpretative divergence

The present research has adopted a quantitative approach to issues often studied ethnographically. While the use of a variety of approaches is always desirable, the present approach offers certain advantages: the complete data set can be economically reported; the four interpretative positions selected for discussion are representative of natural clusterings among viewers; the relative popularity of each position is calculable; and the results can be understood in relation to the hypothetical alternatives which might have been found (see below).

Several further empirical issues can be raised. The para-social relationships which viewers experience with characters appear to generate divergence, possibly more so than the viewers' socio-structural position. How general is this finding and does it depend upon the genre studied?

This raises the further question of whether the interpretative clusterings found here represent permanent or temporary divergences. For example, do some viewers consistently adopt a romantic view of events in all drama or even in all of their lives, while others are consistently cynical? If so, does this distinction map on to the viewers' own experiences of personal relationships? If not, how freely do viewers fluctuate, adopting different interpretive positions on different occasions?

The present discussion concerning the ways in which viewers' interpretations of television narrative diverge from both the text (or analysts' readings of the text) and from each other argues strongly for the concept of the active viewer, for the heterogeneous audience, for the mediating role of interpretations (and hence of social knowledge and context) in television's effects on viewers' social reality beliefs, and for the inappropriateness of talking of *the* message or the meanings *in* a programme. However, more theoretical work is required if, as proposed by Fry and Fry (1986), among others, research is to move towards:

> an orientation that places total power neither in the media text (as has been implicit in some semiotic textual analyses) nor in the interpretive capacities of the audience member (a position that has been often implicit in the uses and gratifications approach). Thus a semiotic model must address the question of the relative power of both the text and audience in determining the meaning of media texts (Fry and Fry, 1986, p. 444).

Specifically, several issues are raised by the present research which demand attention. These concern primarily the types of interpretative divergence which may exist and the relationship between the interpretations and the text. The following discussion uses the interpretations revealed in this study to illustrate some of the conceptual problems and issues facing research on the role of the viewer in determining the meanings of programmes.

The nature of divergence

What kinds of divergence are to be expected? While all would agree that Ken opposed the marriage of Susan and Mike, viewers clearly disagreed over the connotative issues of whether one side was in the right and why the characters acted as they did, and presumably they would also disagree over the deeper ideological themes of, for example, whether the programme is saying that young women should not marry much older men or that fathers always oppose their daughter's fiancé or that the patriarchal fabric of modern society is disintegrating. In relation to both connotation and ideology, the concept of the role of the reader/viewer comes into its own. The present research found that viewers diverge in their interpretations in relation to perspective taken, evaluative judgements of characters' actions, inferred cognitions which lie behind the actions, and predictions about future events, but not about inferred motives or the relative importance of two of the characters (Ken and

Susan) over the other two (Deirdre and Mike). Is this a general phenomenon, are there additional areas of textual interpretation, and how might different theories of textual analysis predict the loci of divergence? Although it often seems easier to assess the amount rather than types of divergence in interpretations, the question of the relative power of viewer and text to determine meanings requires a structural account of the role of the viewer (e.g. inferential strategies, attributional reasoning) in relation to the structure of the text (e.g. areas of openness, mechanisms of closure).

Dominant and oppositional readings

How should the four interpretative positions be understood in relation to the programme: is one the dominant or preferred reading (Hall, 1980) and one the oppositional reading? This issue bears on that of the relative power of text and viewer, for if one interpretation corresponds to the preferred reading and one is oppositional, it would seem that for the first, the text has more power in constructing meanings whereas the second group of viewers critically distance themselves from the text. Before addressing this issue, let us consider what alternative results could have been obtained.

At least four alternatives exist: no clear cluster structure, as either each viewer makes a different interpretation or all viewers agree with each other; a heavy majority for one reading (maybe the cynical one); a polarised division between romantics and cynics with few or no negotiated readings; interpretations determined by age and/or gender of viewers; and so forth. Yet four clusters emerged, ranging from cynical to romantic, with two distinct negotiated positions.

Two-thirds of the viewers adopted one of the romantic interpretations, believing the couple to be truly in love and that the marriage will overcome any problems and last forever. Yet content analysis has repeatedly demonstrated that soap opera marriages frequently end in divorce and that 'true love' is often illusory, deceitful, and temporary (Cantor and Pingree, 1983; Cassata and Skill, 1983). People's apparent faith in romance despite the evidence fits with their description of romance novels as 'a man and a woman meeting, the problems they encounter, whether the relationship will gel or not' (Radway, 1985, p. 344). As in this genre, in contrast with the soap opera, relationships always 'gel' without exception, the perception of uncertainty must be a construction of the reader. Allen (1985) suggests that the involvement of viewers lies not in predicting *what* will happen but in seeing *how* it happens (a concern with the paradigmatic, not the syntagmatic). The present study suggests that viewers may not in fact perceive the predictability in narrative that researchers identify, or alternatively that they suspend this knowledge and enter into the certainty or uncertainty of the characters themselves.

It is arguable that, given the nature of soap opera as a genre, the dominant reading inscribed in the text studied here is the cynical reading, with its emphasis on the naivity of young love and the fragility of relationships. It would then seem that the majority of viewers persist in the romantic, oppositional reading. This supports Alexander's (1985) explanation (see earlier) for her absence of a cultivation effect in relation to soap opera viewers' beliefs about relational fragility. This fits with the present results, which suggest that most viewers interpret narratives romantically. They would thus become further encultured into a romantic perspective (rather than one of relational fragility, as Alexander tested) by seeing this 'romance' played out. Further, when combined with the third of viewers making the contrasting interpretation, no clear effect on social reality beliefs would emerge from a cultivation study which did not differentiate among viewers according to their interpretations of the programme.

The present research illustrates a problem in relating interpretations to textual structure, for this involves specifying the nature of the text. How far is one reading favoured, another precluded, and a third made difficult by textual organisation? There are problems in assigning the viewer clusters to these categories of dominant, oppositional and negotiated (Hall, 1980; Morley, 1980; Morley, 1981) despite the existence of opposed, internally coherent interpretations. Further, while the romantics clearly endorse a dominant romantic ideology, idealising love and predicting a 'happy ever after' end for the characters, the cynics do not fit the oppositional category. Although they represent a rejection of and distance from one dominant ideological reading, they endorse another concerning notions of the patriarchal father, of daughters as property, the alignment of age and wisdom, and the corrupting influence of an adulterous older man. Neither reading appears critical in the political sense of oppositional, challenging the authority of the text, intended by Morley, and both groups viewed the programme referentially (Liebes and Katz, 1986). The two intermediate positions can be more straightforwardly seen to make negotiated readings. Yet the meaning of a negotiated reading depends on one's conception of the extreme readings between which it falls. Need the negotiation be between a dominant and an oppositional reading, or can it be applied also to a compromise between two dominant but contradictory discourses? In this sense, the negotiated readings expose the existence of incompatible yet dominant discourses centering on the same phenomenon and possibly they represent an attempt to reconcile the two.

The preferred reading

A further problem revealed by the present research is that the concept of a preferred reading confounds the idea of a majority reading by the audience with the idea of an ideologically normative reading. The narrative studied here suggests that a text may contain two normative, although opposed, readings, or even that the majority (here, the romantics) may make an alternative interpretation from the preferred reading (here, arguably the cynical position). This suggests a view of the text is required in which a number of normative alternatives are encoded, so that different viewers may select different readings and yet remain within a dominant framework. It also suggests the need for a view of divergence which is not simply a function of critical distance from the text, for the text is open to a number of referential readings. Thus, the opposed readings epitomised by the romantics and cynics each draw upon traditional, dominant rhetoric about gender relations, responsibilities and morality. More generally, despite interest in subversive or feminist interpretations of soap opera (Ang, 1985; Seiter, 1981), it seems that much interpretative divergence will reflect conventional rather than radical positions.

8
Audiences and Interpretations

Television and Everyday Understanding

Understanding how people in everyday life make sense of their social world can be furthered by considering how people are seen to make sense of television in recent research. And understanding how people routinely make sense of television programmes can also be furthered by these recent research developments (borrowing from literary theory, studying the activities of actual audiences, reconceiving the nature of programmes as open and yet structured and the roles of viewers as active and informed).

If we regard television programmes as texts rather than stimuli, we can accommodate their complexity more readily, expecting them to be multilayered, subject to conventional and generic constraints, open and incomplete in their meanings, and providing multiple yet bounded paths for the reader. Such complexity need not be regarded as noise or nuisance, to be eliminated by content analysis, avoided by artificial construction of empirical materials or presumed by implicit appeals to the commonsense of the academic reader. If we do not expect single, given meanings, then we need not be disturbed by our problems in finding them. Rather we will be prepared for the structural complexity and indeterminacy of actual programmes, as of course the viewers have to be.

Fact and fiction

On challenging the fact/fantasy or television/real life dichotomy, the interrelations between fact and fiction become apparent. For example, the fictional, conventionalised nature of real life scripts and narratives, the perceived reality of television programmes, the lost origins (whether mediated or direct knowledge) of many social 'facts' and the carryover of television experiences into everyday life and vice versa. Other distinctions can be introduced, for example, that between mindlessness and mindfulness or passivity and activity, which cut across that of television/life. This instead focuses attention on the mode of people's interaction with their world, mediated or not, and the nature of the interpretative responses which they make. The distinction between fact and fantasy programming which pervades the mass communication literature also loses much of its force. People may learn facts from soap opera (e.g. how to deal with family crises, how to open a bank account or the loneliness of the homeless at Christmas) and learn mythic narratives from the news or current affairs programmes (e.g. who are the goodies and baddies in the world, how the unjust are undone or that the meek do not inherit the earth). People may engage imaginatively with the news ('let's not go there for our holidays') and they may critique a drama ('that's not how to deal with your stubborn father'). Indeed, the distinction between approaching a text referentially— as if it reflected a true picture of the world, or critically—commenting on its constructed and conventional nature as a representation, is a further distinction which cuts across fact and fantasy or television and life, with applications beyond the domain (namely drama television; Katz and Liebes, 1986) in which the idea itself originated.

Applying the text-reader metaphor

The text-reader metaphor may be applied to more than television. It becomes an interesting question as to how far it can be applied to social actors in everyday life. Certainly, it represents an improvement on the stimulus-response model (or its communications equivalent, the speaker-message-hearer model), with its absolute distinction between the stimulus (or message) as repository of single and given meanings, and response (or the hearer) as the independent actions of the actor (again, single and clear in their significance). Texts, on the other hand, are constructed in anticipation of experienced and informed readers, and readers approach texts as structures awaiting their appropriate contribution. Indeed, the ecological approach to social perception, with its concepts of affordance and effectivity to replace those of stimulus and response, provides a closer psychological parallel to the text-reader approach (Gibson, 1950). There are many implications for social psychology of conceiving of situations and their rules as analogous to media/literary genres and their conventions, of people as characters with not only histories and person-alities but also narrative roles and oppositional interrelations, of events as narrative with developmental paths and choice points, and of social texts in general as multilayered, open, dynamic, conventional, and inviting interpretation. It seems that the analogy with texts as conceived by semiotics and cultural studies suggests more fruitful theoretical constructs than those currently being introduced into social psychology by discourse analysts (Brown and Fish, 1983; Potter and Wetherall, 1987; Trew, 1979). More like van Dijk's approach (1987), although richer, semiotics focuses on both macro- and microstructures in texts. It also locates them in a sociocultural context, whether of interpretative communities (Fish, 1980; Radway, 1984), hegemonic processes (Hall *et al.*, 1980), or mythic codes and conventions (Barthes, 1973). Another, related approach argues that:

> the narrative paradigm sees people as storytellers—authors and co-authors who creatively read and evaluate the texts of life and literature. It envisions existing institutions as providing 'plots' that are always in the process of re-creation rather than as scripts; it stresses that people are full participants in the making of messages, whether they are agents (authors) or audience members (co-authors) (Fisher, 1985, p. 86).

The Role of the Reader Revisited

In general, the concept of the person as reader is useful for both media studies and social psychology, as both programmes and everyday situations can be analysed as texts. The reader is skilled, knowledgeable, motivated, receptive. A reader cannot be completely passive, for the words will remain a blur of black and white marks, and so too the viewer or the social actor cannot be completely passive, for the programme, the world, will remain meaningless. Hence theories of powerful effects, with their hypodermic imagery, or notions of inevitable and unavoidable social representations, require rethinking. But neither can readers be wilful, turning *Alice through the Looking Glass* into a statistics textbook or a social realist novel (though they may see it as a funny children's book, a philosophical exercise, or even advice on playing chess). The 'toolkit' model cannot be applied to the reader, for readers are constrained by the structure of the text. So too are viewers constrained in their interpretations of programmes, so that certain readings are aberrant; one cannot create any meanings at will. Nor can a person, say, enter a school and enact the restaurant script (Schank and Abelson, 1977) without being considered to have misunderstood the situation (though she or he can act in a restaurant lightheartedly or seriously, accepting or critically, with or without an awareness of class and gender discrimination).

On this view, much that is currently dismissed as error in people's accounts can be reconceived as meaningful but divergent interpretations: people may validly do different things with texts from those anticipated by the researcher. Indeed, the range of things people do with texts is exactly our interest—the sense which people actually create of their circumstances and the ways in which they differ from each other, actively fitting their world to their own knowledge and past experiences.

The active viewer

The term 'activity' is the source of many confusions, for an active viewer need not be alert, attentive and original. Activity may refer to creative reading—making new meanings of the text, but it may also refer to the more mindless process of fitting the text into familiar frameworks or habits. Here the person is active in the sense of changing the context for and associations of the text ('doing' something with it) but not creative in the sense of doing something original or novel with the text. The notion of active, creative readings may be further divided, into readings invited by the text (as a function of openness) or those made despite the text (which we would term aberrant if they deny denotational aspects of the text or oppositional if they oppose ideological aspects of the text). As a term, 'active' has become fashionable and hence it has been used in many, often contradictory, ways which need to be clarified on use. To reject the tool-kit, do-what-you-will-with-the-text, model is not necessarily to reject a vigilant, attentive and creative reader or viewer, but nor is it to reject a habitual, schematic, unimaginative one. Rather, the point is that viewers must inevitably 'do' something with the text, but that they are likely to draw upon their formidable resource of knowledge and experience to do so, and creativity or habitual response will be a function of the relationships between the structures of the text, the social knowledge of the viewer and the mode of interaction between them (critical or referential, mindless or mindful, motivated or apathetic).

The relation between social psychology and media studies

We need, then, to examine the social knowledge of the reader, to conceive of readers in relation to texts and texts in relation to readers and to study the activities of actual readers, with all the methodological problems that this brings with it. As I have argued throughout the book, the first and last of these tasks represent a challenge to social psychology in developing media theory—providing a theory of viewers' everyday social knowledge and a range of methods for investigating their application in daily sense-making activities. We can then ask how people relate their knowledge of the world to the world of television, how the interpretations they make of programmes fit or challenge their prior experiences and the role of their knowledge in directing divergence in interpretations. We can further ask about the cognitive processes whereby interpretations are constructed and the impact on these processes of the mode of person-media interaction (McQuail *et al.*, 1972). Finally, we have access to a repertoire not only of methods to study this but also of problems, refinements and developments emergent from the use of these methods within social psychology. The second task, that of drawing on the text-reader metaphor and of conceiving of texts and readers (or situations and actors) as mutually constructed and integrated, conversely represents the contribution of media studies to social psychology. This allows psychology to overcome problems resulting from its restricting conception of meaning as information (which reduces much of sense-making activity to error and nonsense), of its limiting dichotomies of active versus passive or of receptive *tabula rasa* versus wilful constructivist (where the truth lies somewhere in between and is itself a function of the demands of the text as well as the orientation of the reader) and of the notion of meaning as fixed and unique, independent of interpretation or interpreter. As we learn more of the structure of texts, so too do we discover about readers; while similarly, as we learn more of the activities of readers, so too do we discover about texts. Our models of the text/programme frame our models of the reader/viewer, and vice versa.

Table 1 summarises some parallels between theories of texts and readers and theories of social actors and social situations, now that both sets of theories are turning towards an emphasis on the person as actively constructive, informed and socially located. There are many parallels between these apparently diverse theories, parallels often not apparent because the two domains are typically studied by different researchers in different disciplines. In some cases, the parallels are strong (e.g. in the use of representational concepts which depend on the spatial metaphor by both social cognition and cultural studies) and sometimes they are weak.

The vertical dimension of organisation distinguishes between the following categories of factors: background circumstances, representational or knowledge structures, interpretative processes which work towards both openness and closure, and outcomes. Interpretation here means the product of the processes operating on the representations in the context of the background circumstances and the interaction between viewer and text. Despite the apparent linearity of this framework, there are many feedback connections: for example, audience ratings affect future programme production; cognitive effects alter the representational resources used in future interpretation; and so on. Certain theoretical problems with these parallels or categories remain for future clarification. For example, can story grammar research be extended to complex narrative structures, can openness be distinguished in practice from indeterminacy, and how separable are specific representations (whether of television characters or of one's family) from abstract representations of people in general?

Future research is also needed to answer the question of a balance of power between the different factors in order to identify the power of the person to create, set against the power of the text to direct, the resultant meanings. For example, when do constructive processes reconstrue text structure, when are mechanisms of closure successful in directing interpretation, how do interpretations mediate effects, and so forth? Behind many of the factors lie general and unfortunately vague notions of cultural conventions, resources and meanings. In cultural studies, researchers with anthropological backgrounds attempt to specify the role of culture, but more specificity is needed to disentangle the relative power of viewer and text. In social psychology, the concept of social representation (Farr and Moscovici, 1984) has recently raised the issue of cultural meaning, but again theory is insufficiently advanced.

TABLE 1. *A taxonomy of factors influencing interpretation, showing conceptual parallels between theories of readers and of texts*

READER/VIEWER	*TEXT*
Background factors	
LIFE SITUATION	PRODUCTION CONTEXT
gender, age, class etc.	economic constraints
socialisation experiences	professional practices
expectations of media	beliefs about viewers
cultural resources	cultural resources
domestic viewing context	media institution
labour market position	production ideology
Representational factors	
SOCIAL KNOWLEDGE	TEXT STRUCTURE (VIRTUAL)
story grammar	narrative structure
genre knowledge	genre conventions
cultural conventions	cultural conventions
stereotypes and prejudices	ideological motivations
Implicit Personality Theory	opposition/transformation
biases and heuristics	preferred reading(s)
stories and folk tales	latent, mythic meanings
person prototypes	characterisation
Interpretation factors	
CONSTRUAL	READING
Closure: need for consistency	favour preferred reading
	mystify production aims
need for parsimony and clarity	deny contradictions
belief in objective media	realism undermines
	critical distance
self-fulfilling prophecies	illusory choice
confirmation of expectancies	repeat conventional views
	specific model reader
resolve ambiguity	favour one perspective
	offer clear conclusions
	undermine opposition
Openness: pleasure in novelty	
need for critical distance	challenge stereotypes
clash between text and	pose contradictions
own culture	multiple perspectives
	absence of hero figure
	indeterminate boundaries
	interweaving plots
	invite viewer's opinions
ignore/modify schema	
incorporate textual features	expect viewers' knowledge
alter expectancies	
challenge assumptions	omit cultural assumptions

TABLE 1—*continued*

READER/VIEWER	TEXT
Outcome factors	
EFFECTS	FEEDBACK IMPLICATIONS
reinforce/challenge ideas	
introduce/validate new ideas	
alter salience of ideas	
enhance identification	
selection of role models	
set an agenda	
alter behaviours/lifestyle	
	programme/channel loyalty
	audience ratings
	public criticism
	establish conventions
	and professional practices

Comprehension and Interpretation

Reading and information processing

The concept of the reader encourages the notion of multiple readers and of types of reader (and types of readings). This contrasts with the concept of the information-processor, which implies consensual responses, for the 'information' being processed is unitary and given, while 'processing' implies a single, linear set of automatic transformations by which the information is comprehended. As discussed earlier in the book, these two ways of conceptualising the person derive from different discourses and carry different implications. For example, the information-processing approach of traditional psychology and mass communications, throwing its emphasis on processing and leaving the information as given, tends to treat communication as information transfer. This raises questions of miscommunication or inaccurate transfer, in contrast to the questions of divergence among interpretations which result from the constructivist account of the reader and text. If in most instances of communication, it were easy to specify a correct and unique message, and if people generally agreed on this message, and if, further, we had a semantic theory which avoided intuitive identification of meanings, then the information processing approach might serve us well. Unfortunately, we lack a theory to identify the 'correct' meaning of a message, falling back on an implicit consensus among researchers (sometimes operationalised in the problematic procedures of content analysis). Moreover, people commonly and routinely disagree both between themselves and with researchers about the meanings of messages. Thus an approach which anticipates and theorises divergence, which sees texts as multiple rather than singular in meaning, and which conceives of texts and readers as related rather than independent is preferred—for both media research and for social psychology.

Interpretation and closure

Interpretation, or reading, is then an essentially variable process (not an automatic function of the nature of the 'information'), yet one which is constrained by the structure of the text. Further, it is a process which is socially located insofar as the experience and knowledge of the reader plays a central role. This is not to say, however, that texts do not contain information (on the news, we are told how many died in the train crash; in the crime drama, we discover 'who really did it'), nor that questions of accuracy or miscommunication are irrelevant (the viewers who hear forty people instead of fourteen, or the child who thinks the detective committed the crime, because she or he sees the detective re-enact the crime to establish the means, are clearly wrong or have missed the point).

Interestingly, much of the literature on sense-making, both in social psychology and in traditional mass communications, has confined itself to dealing with those aspects of texts which can be assessed in terms of correct and mistaken understandings. This is partly due to studying the under-standing of very simplified or artificial texts, partly due to focusing on children's acquisition of schemata (say, for identifying character roles or organising narrative sequence) and partly due to studying the application of models of social knowledge which are themselves at an early stage of theoretical development. Thus researchers focus mainly on texts on the level of denotation, for this is open to relatively less divergence than connotation or ideology. They consider texts mainly insofar as they are closed, discouraging and invalidating divergent or creative interpretations. One wonders whether, having begun with a focus on the denotational and closed, the theories can be developed later to encompass the connotational and open.

Let us distinguish between comprehension and interpretation. Compre-hension, deriving from the information-processing approach, can be seen to have a role in understanding complex texts: to some extent texts do convey information, certain meanings are fairly judged incorrect, and to some degree, a common or consensual meaning is received. Interpretation, then, concerns understanding texts insofar as they do not convey information but rather they implicate mythic or ideological meanings, involve narrative or conventional frames, or create cultural connections and resonances. Interpretations depend on the contribution of the reader in relation to the structure of the text and hence are not to be judged correct or mistaken but rather should be seen as a product of the reader's experience which generated them, or as more or less plausible given normative assumptions, or as more or less creative, critical or interesting. As interpretations are invited by textual openness, they are most likely to diverge one from another.

Interpretative modes

Katz *et al.* (1988) suggest a typology of interpretative modes deriving from basic distinctions between referential and critical modes and hot and cool modes. Thus, viewers may generate moral readings (from referential, hot viewing), ideological readings (critical, hot), ludic or playful readings (referential, cool) or aesthetic readings (critical, cool). Alternatively, we may distinguish between readings which diverge on the level of denotation (as studied by the information-processing and developmental psychology of Collins *et al.*, 1986 or Pingree *et al.*, 1984), on the level of connotation (focusing on the different horizons of expectation of reception theory, social knowledge structures or Piagetian schemata), on the level of ideology (accepting or opposing preferred readings, making opposition, dominant or negotiated readings, exploiting the 'semiotic democracy' of Fiske, 1987), or on the level of contextual relevance (with reference to different interpretative communities and social uses; Ang, 1985; Modleski, 1982; Radway, 1984). Doubtless there are yet further ways of subdividing varieties of readings.

The relation between interpretation and comprehension

Much confusion is generated by advocating that viewers are concerned only with comprehension or only with interpretation, and researchers can easily talk at cross-purposes by referring ambiguously to understanding or sense-making without distinguishing between these two processes. Let us say that traditionally, psychologists have found comprehension more interesting, for it reveals basic knowledge structures in viewers, while critical media researchers have found interpretation more interesting for it reveals cultural and contextual factors which differentiate among viewers. Each approach has addressed itself to a different aspect of the text. Yet clearly both comprehension and interpretation occur when making sense of television.

The questions for research must concern the relation between comprehension and interpretation, the relation between different aspects of texts, the development of increasingly sophisticated social knowledge structures (taking the child from comprehension to interpretation), the importance of divergence and consensus (for some divergence is trivial, other divergence is critically functional), and so forth.

In analysing issues of interpretation, the ultimate questions of power and effects can be easily forgotten. Maybe this is appropriate, one cannot always have one's eye on the end goal, and problems of theorising and studying actual interpretative activities are sufficiently complex and interesting in their own right. However, just as in social psychology the analysis of discourse is ultimately concerned with the persuasive power of rhetoric in social interaction, so too in media studies is the analysis of programmes and their audiences ultimately concerned with the power of the media to influence and the power of the audience to resist or enhance that influence. Just as interpretative processes mediate any effect which may result, so too do different modes of relationship between audience and programme mediate different types of effect: critical readings offer resistance to influence; passive, comprehension-oriented or referential readings encourage reinforcement or consolidation of past effects; active, interpretative readings allow for the introduction of new ideas or validation of uncertain associations; mindless viewing may enhance mainstreaming effects (Gerbner *et al.*, 1982); and so forth. Maybe active viewing (or in Petty *et al.*'s 1981 terms, central route processing) is more typical of relatively open texts, where divergence is meaningful, for active processing of closed texts may simply lead to aberrant readings. Certainly, consideration of both the nature and mode of audience interpretation will no longer permit us to talk of 'effects', 'viewing', 'a programme' or 'the audience' without differentiating among different types of each of these hitherto highly general constructs.

Bibliography

Abelson, R. P. (1981). The psychological status of the script concept. *American Psychologist,* **36,** 715–729.

Azjen, I., and Fishbein, M. (1980). *Understanding attitudes and predicting social behaviour.* Englewood Cliffs, N.J.: Prentice-Hall.

Allen, R. C. (1985). *Speaking of soap operas.* Chapel Hill: University of North Carolina Press.

Allen, R. C. (1987). (Ed.). *Channels of discourse.* Chapel Hill: University of North Carolina Press.

Alexander, A. (1985). Adolescents' soap opera viewing and relational perceptions. *Journal of Broadcasting and Electronic Media,* **29(3),** 295–308.

Ang, I. (1985). *Watching DALLAS: Soap opera and the melodramatic imagination.* New York: Methuen.

Antaki, C. (1988). (Ed.). *The analysis of everyday explanations.* London: Sage.

Argyle, J. M., Furnham, A., and Graham, J. A. (1981). *Social situations.* Cambridge: Cambridge University Press.

Arlen, M. (1981). Smooth pebbles at Southfork. In R. P. Adler (Ed.), *Understanding television: Essays on television as a social and cultural force,* 173–181. New York: Praeger.

Ashmore, R. D., and Del Boca, F. K. (1979). Sex stereotypes and implicit personality theory: Toward a cognitive-social psychological conceptualisation. *Sex Roles,* **5(2),** 219–247.

Ashmore, R. D., and Del Boca, F. K. (1986). *The social psychology of female-male relations: A critical analysis of central concepts.* Orlando, Florida: Academic Press.

Ashmore, R. D., Del boca, F. K., and Wohlers, A. J. (1986). Gender stereotypes. In R. D. Ashmore and F. K. Del Boca, *The social psychology of female-male relations: A critical analysis of central concepts.* Orlando, Florida: Academic Press.

Ashmore, R. D., and Tumia, M. L. (1980). Sex stereotypes and implicit personality theory. I. A personality description approach to the assessment of sex stereotypes. *Sex Roles,* **6(4),** 501–518.

Atkinson, J. M., and Heritage, J. (1984). *Structures of social action: studies in conversation analysis.* Cambridge: Cambridge University Press.

Bandura, A., and Walters, R. H. (1964). *Social learning and personality development.* New York: Holt, Rinehart and Winston.

Banister, D., and Fransella, F. (1971). *Inquiring man.* Harmondsworth: Penguin.

Barthes, R. (1973). *Mythologies.* London: Paladin.

Barthes, R. (1977). An introduction to the structural analysis of narratives. In T. Bennett, G. Martin, C. Mercer, and J. Woollacott (Eds.), *Culture, ideology and social process: A reader.* London: The Open University.

Bartlett, F. C. (1932). *Remembering: A study in experimental and social psychology.* Cambridge: Cambridge University Press.

Beaugrande, R., and Dressler, W. (1980). *Introduction to text linguistics.* London: Longman.

Bem, S. L. (1974). The measurement of psychological androgyny. *Journal of Consulting and Clinical Psychology,* **42(2),** 155–162.

Bem, S. L. (1981). Gender Schema Theory: A cognitive account of sextyping. *Psychological Review,* **88(4),** 354–364.

Bem, S. L. (1984). Androgyny and gender schema theory: A conceptual and empirical investigation. In *Nebraska Symposium on Motivation,* **32,** 179–226. Lincoln: University of Nebraska.

Berelson, B. (1952). *Content analysis in communication research*. Glencoe, Ill.: Free Press.
Berger, A. A. (1981). Semiotics and TV. In R. P. Adler (Ed.), *Understanding television: Essays on television as a social and cultural force*, 91–114. New York: Praeger.
Berger, P., and Luckmann, T. (1967). *The social construction of reality*. Harmondsworth: Penguin.
Berkowitz, L. (1978). (Ed.). *Cognitive theories in social psychology*. New York: Academic Press.
Berkowitz, L., and Rogers, K. H. (1986). A priming effect analysis of media influences. In J. Bryant and D. Zillman (Eds.), *Perspectives on media effects*. Hillsdale, N.J.: Erlbaum.
Bigsby, C. W. E. (1976). (Ed.). *Approaches to popular culture*. London: Edward Arnold.
Billig, M. (1982). *Ideology and social psychology*. Oxford: Basil Blackwell.
Billig, M. (1987). *Arguing and thinking: A rhetorical approach to social psychology*. Cambridge: Cambridge University Press.
Bisanz, G. L., LaPorte, R. E., Vesonder, G. T., and Voss, J. F. (1978). On the representation of prose: New dimensions. *Journal of Verbal Learning and Verbal Behavior*, **17**, 337–357.
Blumler, J. G., Gurevitch, M., and Katz, E. (1985). REACHING OUT: A future for gratifications research. In K. E. Rosengren, L. A. Wenner, and P. Palmgreen (Eds.), *Media gratifications research: Current perspectives*. Beverly Hills, Cal.: Sage.
Blumler, J. G., and Katz, E. (Eds.) (1974). *The uses of mass communications: Current perspectives on gratifications research*. Beverly Hills, Cal.: Sage.
Bobrow, D. G., and Norman, D. A. (1975). Some principles of memory schemata. In D. G. Bobrow and A. Collins (Eds.), *Representation and understanding: Studies in cognitive science*. New York: Academic Press.
Booth, J. (1980). Watching the family. In H. Baehr, (Ed.), *Women and media*. Oxford: Pergamon.
Bower, G. H. (1976). Experiments on story understanding and recall. *Quarterly Journal of Experimental Psychology*, **28**, 511–534.
Broadbent, D. E. (1958). *Perception and communication*. London: Pergamon.
Broverman, I., Vogel, S., Broverman, D., Clarkson, F., and Rosenkrantz, P. (1972). Sex-role stereotypes: A current appraisal. *Journal of Social Issues*, **28(2)**, 59–78.
Brown, R. (1986). *Social psychology: The second edition*. New York: The Free Press.
Brown, R., and Fish, D. (1983). The psychological causality implicit in language. *Cognition*, **14**, 237–273.
Bruner, J. S., Goodnow, J., and Austen, G. (1956, *A study of thinking*. New York: Wiley.
Bruner, J. S., and Tagiuri, R. (1954). The perception of people. In G. Lindzey (Ed.), *Handbook of social psychology*, **2**. Cambridge, Mass.: Addison-Wesley.
Brunsdon, C., and Morley, D. (1978). *Everyday television: 'Nationwide'*. British Film Institute Television Monograph no. 10. London: British Film Institute.
Bryant, J., and Zillman, D. (Eds.), (1986). *Perspectives on media effects*. Hillsdale, N.J.: Erlbaum.
Buckingham, D. (1987). *Public secrets: EastEnders and its audience*. London: British Film Institute.
Buckman, P. (1984). *All for love: A study in soap opera*. London: Secker and Warburg.
Burgelin, O. (1972). Structural analysis of mass communication. In D. McQuail, (Ed.), *Sociology of mass communications*. Harmondsworth: Penguin.
Burke, K. (1970). *The rhetoric of religion: Studies in logology*. Berkeley, Cal.: University of California Press.
Burnett, R. (1987). Reflection in personal relationships. In R. Burnett, P. McGhee, and D. D. Clarke, (Eds.), *Accounting for relationships: Explanation, representation and knowledge*. London: Methuen.
Cantor, J., Ziemke, D., and Sparks, G. G. (1984). Effect of forewarning on emotional responses to a horror film. *Journal of Broadcasting*, **28(1)**, 21–31.
Cantor, M., and Pingree, S. (1983). *The soap opera*. Beverly Hills, Cal.: Sage.
Carey, J. W. (1985). Overcoming resistance to Cultural Studies. In M. Gurevitch, and M. R. Levy, (Eds.), *Mass Communication Review Yearbook*, **5**. Beverly Hills, Cal.: Sage.
Carveth, R., and Alexander, A. (1985). Soap opera viewing motivations and the cultivation process. *Journal of Broadcasting and Electronic Media*, **29(3)**, 259–273.

Cassata, M., and Skill, T. (1983). *Life on daytime television: Tuning-in American serial drama*. Norwood, N.J.: Ablex.

Chang, J. J., and Carroll, J. D. (1968). How to use PROFIT, a computer program for property fitting by optimising nonlinear or linear correlation. Bell Laboratories, Murray Hill, New Jersey 07974.

Collins, R., Curran, J., Garnham, N., Scannell, P., Schlesinger, P., and Sparks, C. (1986). (Eds.). *Media, culture and society: A critical reader*. London: Sage.

Collins, W. A. (1983). Interpretation and inference in children's television viewing. In J. Bryant and D. A. Anderson (Eds.), *Children's understanding of television*. New York: Academic Press.

Collins, W. A., and Getz, S. K. (1976). Children's social responses following modeled reactions to provocation: prosocial effects of televised drama. *Journal of Personality*, **44**, 488–500.

Collins, W. A., and Wellman, H. M. (1982). Social scripts and developmental patterns in comprehension of televised narratives. *Communication Research*, **9(3)**, 380–398.

Coward, R. (1984). *Female desire*. London: Paladin.

Crocker, J., Fiske, S. T., and Taylor, S. E. (1984). Schematic bases of belief change. In R. Eiser, (Ed.), *Attitudinal judgment*. New York: Springer-Verlag.

Coulthard, M., and Montgomery, M. (1981). (Eds.) *Studies in discourse analysis*. London: Routledge and Kegan Paul.

Culler, J. (1981). *The pursuit of signs*. London: Routledge and Kegan Paul.

Curran, J. (1976). Content and structuralist analysis of mass communication (project 2). Open University course paper for D305.

Curran, J., Gurevitch, M., and Woollacott, J. (1977). (Eds.). *Mass communication and society*. London: Edward Arnold.

Curran, J., Gurevitch, M., and Woollacott, J. (1982). The study of the media: Theoretical approaches. In M. Gurevitch, T. Bennett, J. Curran, and J. Woollacott (Eds.), *Culture, society and the media*. London: Methuen.

Curti, L. (1988). Genre and gender. *Cultural Studies*, **12(2)**, 152–167.

Davidson, E. S., Yasuna, A., and Tower, A. (1979). The effects of television cartoons on sex-role stereotyping in young girls. *Child Development*, **50**, 597–600.

van Dijk, T. A. (1987). *Communicating racism: Ethnic prejudice in thought and talk*. Newbury Park, Cal.: Sage.

Doise, W. (1987). *Levels of explanation in social psychology*. Cambridge: Cambridge University Press.

Dorr, A. (1983), No shortcuts to judging reality. In J. Bryant and D. Anderson (Eds.), *Children's understanding of television: research on attention and comprehension*. New York: Academic Press.

Drabman, R. S., Robertson, S. J., Patterson, J. N., Jarvie, G. J., Hammer, D., and Cordua, G. (1981). Children's perception of media-portrayed sex roles. *Sex Roles*, **7**, 379–389.

Drabman, R. S., and Thomas, M. H. (1975). Does TV violence breed indifference? *Journal of Communication*, **25(4)**, 86–89.

Durkin, K. (1985a). Television and sex-role acquisition 1: Content. *British Journal of Social Psychology*, **24**, 101–113.

Durkin, K. (1985b). Television and sex-role acquisition. 2: Effects. *British Journal of Social Psychology*, **24**, 191–210.

Dyer, R. (1981). Introduction. In R. Dyer, C. Geraghty, M. Jordan, T. Lovell, R. Paterson, and J. Stewart, (1981). *Coronation Street*. British Film Institute Television Monograph no. 13. London: British Film Institute.

Dyer, R., Geraghty, C., Jordan, M., Lovell, T., Paterson, R., and Stewart, J. (1981). *Coronation Street*. British Film Institute Television Monograph no. 13. London: British Film Institute.

Eagleton, T. (1983). *Literary theory: An introduction*. Oxford: Blackwell.

Eco, U. (1979a). Introduction: The role of the reader. *The role of the reader: Explorations in the semiotics of texts*. Bloomington: Indiana University Press.

Eco, U. (1979b). Narrative structures in Fleming. *The role of the reader: Explorations in the semiotics of texts*. Bloomington: Indiana University Press.

Eisenstock, B. (1984). Sex-role differences in children's identification with counterstereo-typical televised portrayals. *Sex Roles*, **10(5/6)**, 417–430.

Eiser, J. R. (1986). *Social psychology: Attitudes, cognition and social behavior*. Cambridge: Cambridge University Press.

Farr, R. (1981). The social origins of the human mind: a historical note. In J. P. Forgas, (Ed.). *Social cognition: Perspectives on everyday understanding*. London: Academic Press.

Farr, R. (1987). Social representations: A French tradition of research. *Journal for the Theory of Social Behaviour*, **17(4)**, 343–369.

Farr, R. M., and Moscovici, S. (1984). (Eds.). *Social Representations*. Cambridge: Cambridge University Press.

Fejes, F. (1984). Critical mass communications research and media effects: The problem of the disappearing audience. *Media, Culture and Society*, **6(3)**, 219–232.

Feuer, J. (1984). Melodrama, serial form and television today. *Screen*, **25(1)**, 4–17.

Fish, S. (1980). *Is there a text in this class? The authority of interpretive communities*. Cambridge, Mass.: Harvard University Press.

Fisher, W. R. (1985). The narrative paradigm: In the beginning. *Journal of Communication*, **35**, 74–89.

Fiske, J. (1982). *Introduction to communication studies*. London: Methuen.

Fiske, J. (1984). Popularity and ideology: A structuralist reading of DR. WHO. In W. D. Rowland and B. Watkins (Eds.), *Interpreting television: Current research perspectives*, 58–73. Beverly Hills, Cal.: Sage.

Fiske, J. (1987). *Television culture*. London: Methuen.

Fiske, J., and Hartley, J. (1978). *Reading television*. London: Methuen.

Fiske, S. T., and Taylor, S. E. (1984). *Social cognition*. New York: Random House.

Forgas, J. P. (1979). Multidimensional scaling: A discovery method in social psychology. In G. P. Ginsberg (Ed.), *Emerging strategies in social psychological research*. New York: Wiley.

Forgas, J. P. (Ed.) (1981). *Social cognition: Perspectives on everyday understanding*. London: Academic Press.

Forgas, J. P. (1983). What is social about social cognition? *British Journal of Social Psychology*, **22**, 129–144.

Forgas, J. P. (1985). Person prototypes and cultural salience: The role of cognitive and cultural factors in impression formation. *British Journal of Social Psychology*, **24**, 3–17.

Fowler, R. (1981). *Literature as social discourse*. London: Batsford.

Fry, D. L., and Fry, V. H. (1986). A semiotic model for the study of mass communication. In M. L. McLaughlin (Ed.), *Communication Yearbook*, **9**, 463–479. Beverly Hills, Cal.: Sage.

Garfinkel, H. (1967). *Studies in ethnomethodology*. Englewood Cliffs, N.J.: Prentice-Hall.

Gerbner, G., and Gross, L. (1976). Living with television: The violence profile. *Journal of Communication*, **26(2)**, 173–199.

Gerbner, G., Gross, L., Morgan, M., and Signorielli, N. (1982). Charting the mainstream: Television's contributions to political orientations. *Journal of Communication*, **32(2)**, 100–127.

Gerbner, G., Gross, L., Morgan, M., and Signorielli, N. (1986). Living with television: The dynamics of the cultivation process. In J. Bryant and D. Zillman (Eds.), *Perspectives on media effects*. Hillsdale, N.J.: Erlbaum.

Gergen, K. J. (1973). Social psychology as history. *Journal of Personality and Social Psychology*, **26(2)**, 309–320.

Gergen, K. J., and Gergen, M. M. (1986). Narrative form and the construction of psychological theory. In T. Sarbin (Ed.), *The narrative perspective in psychology*. New York: Praeger.

Gibson, J. J. (1950). *Perception of the visual world*. Boston: Houghton Mifflin.

Gilligan, C. (1982). *In a different voice: Psychological theory and women's development*. Cambridge, Mass.: Harvard University Press.

Gilmour, R., and Duck, S. (1980). *The development of social psychology*. London: Academic Press.

Gitlin, T. (1978). Media sociology: The dominant paradigm. *Theory and Society*, **6**, 205–253.

Gliner, G., Goldman, S. R., and Hubert, L. J. (1983). A methodological study on the evaluation of learning from story narratives. *Multivariate Behavioral Research*, **18**, 9–36.

Goffman, E. (1971). *Relations in public*. New York: Basic Books.

Goffman, E. (1974). *Frame analysis*. Harmondsworth: Penguin.

Goffman, E. (1981). *Forms of Talk*. Oxford: Blackwell.

Gouldner, A. W. (1976). *The dialectic of ideology and technology*. New York: Seabury Press.

Grant, D. (1970). *Realism*. London: Methuen.

Hall, S. (1980). Encoding/Decoding. In S. Hall, D. Hobson, A. Lowe, and P. Willis (Eds.), *Culture, Media, Language*. London: Hutchinson.

Hall, S., Hobson, D., Lowe, A., and Willis, P. (Eds.), (1980). *Culture, Media, Language*. London: Hutchinson.

Halliday, M. A. K. (1978). *Language as social semiotic*. London: Edward Arnold.

Halloran, J. D. (1970). The social effects of television. In J. D. Halloran (Ed.), *The effects of television*. London: Panther Books.

Hamilton, D. L. (1981). *Cognitive processes in stereotyping and intergroup behavior*. Hillsdale, N.J.: Erlbaum.

Harre, R. (1984). Some reflections of the concept of 'Social Representation'. *Social Research*, **51(4)**, 927–938.

Harre, R., and Secord, P. (1972). *The explanation of social behaviour*. Oxford: Blackwell.

Hartley, J. (1984). Encouraging signs: Television and the power of dirt, speech and scandalous categories. In W. D. Rowland and B. Watkins, (Eds.), *Interpreting television: current research perspectives*. Beverly Hills, Cal.: Sage.

Hawkes, T. (1977). *Structuralism and semiotics*. London: Methuen.

Hawkins, R. P. (1977). The dimensional structure of children's perceptions of television reality. *Communication Research*, **4(3)**, 299–320.

Hawkins, R. P., and Pingree, S. (1983). Television's influence on social reality. In E. Wartella, and D. C. Whitney (Eds.), *Mass Communication Review Yearbook*, **4**, 53–76. London: Sage.

Heider, F. (1958). *The psychology of interpersonal relations*. New York: Wiley.

Heider, F. (1979). On balance and attribution. In P. W. Holland, and S. Leinhardt (Eds.), *Perspectives on social network research*. New York: Academic Press.

Henley, N. M. (1969). A psychological study of the semantics of animal terms, *Journal of Verbal Learning and Verbal Behavior*, **8**, 176–184.

Herzog, H. (1986). Decoding 'Dallas'. *Society*.

Himmelweit, H. T., Swift, B., and Jaeger, M. E. (1980). The audience as critic: A conceptual analysis of television entertainment. In P. H. Tannenbaum, (Ed.) *The entertainment functions of television*. Hillsdale, NJ.: Erlbaum.

Hirsch, P. M. (1980). The 'scary world' of the nonviewer and other anomalies: A reanalysis of Gerber *et al.* findings on cultivation analysis, Part I. *Communication Research*, **7(4)**, 403–456.

Hobson, D. (1982). *Crossroads: The drama of a soap opera*. London: Methuen.

Hodge, R., and Tripp, D. (1986). *Children and television: A semiotic approach*. Cambridge: Polity.

Hodge, R., and Kress, G. (1988). *Social semiotics*. Cambridge: Polity.

Hoggart, R. (1957). *The uses of literacy*. London: Chatto and Windus.

Hohendahl, P. U. (1974). Introduction to reception aesthetics. *New German Critique*, **3(Fall)**, 29–63.

Holub, R. C. (1984). *Reception theory: A critical introduction*. London: Methuen.

Holland, N. (1975). *5 readers reading*. Yale University Press.

Horton, D., and Wohl, R. R. (1956). Mass communication and para-social interaction. *Psychiatry*, **19**, 215–229.

Hovland, C. I., Lumsdaine, A. A., and Sheffield, F. D. (1949). *Experiments on mass communications*. Princeton: Princeton University Press.

Howitt, D. (1982). *Mass media and social problems*. Oxford: Pergamon.

Ingarden, R. (1973). *The cognition of the literary work of art*. Evanston, Ill.: Northwestern University Press.

Intintoli, M. J. (1984). *Taking soaps seriously: The world of GUIDING LIGHT*. New York: Praeger.

Iser, W. (1980). The reading process: A phenomenological approach. In J. P. Tompkins, (Ed.). *Reader-response criticism: from formalism to post-structuralism*. Baltimore: Johns Hopkins University Press.

James, W. (1890). *Principles of psychology*. New York: Holt, Rinehard and Winston.

Jauss, H. R. (1982). *Towards an aesthetic of reception*. Minneapolis: University of Minnesota Press.

Johnson-Laird, P. N. (1983). *Mental models: Towards a cognitive science of language, inference and consciousness*. Cambridge: Cambridge University Press.

Jones, L. E. (1983). Multidimensional models of social perception, cognition and behavior. *Applied Psychological Measurement*, **7(4)**, 451–472.

Jordan, M. (1981). Realism and convention. In R. Dyer, C. Geraghty, M. Jordan, T. Lovell, R. Paterson, and J. Stewart, (1981). *Coronation Street*. British Film Institute Television Monograph no. 13. London: British Film Institute.

Jose, P. E., and Brewer, W. F. (1984). Development of story liking: character identification, suspense and outcome resolution. *Developmental Psychology*, **20(5)**, 911–924.

Kahneman, D., Slovic, P., and Tversky, A. (Eds.), (1982). *Judgment under uncertainty: Heuristics and biases*. New York: Cambridge University Press.

Katz, E. (1977). *Social research on broadcasting: Proposals for further development*. A report to the British Broadcasting Corporation. London: British Broadcasting Corporation.

Katz, E. (1978). Of mutual interest. *Journal of Communication*, **28(2)**, 133–141.

Katz, E. (1980). On conceptualising media effects. *Studies in Communication*, **1**, 119–141.

Katz, E. (1987). Communications research since Lazarsfeld. *Public Opinion Quarterly*, **51**, S25–S45.

Katz, E., and Lazarsfeld, P. F. (1955). *Personal influence*. Glencoe, Ill.: The Free Press.

Katz, E., and Liebes, T. (1986). Mutual aid in the decoding of *Dallas:* Preliminary notes from a cross-cultural study. In P. Drummond and R. Paterson (Eds.), *Television in transition*. London: British Film Institute.

Katz, E., Iwao, S., and Liebes, T. (1988). On the limits of diffusion of American television: a study of the critical abilities of Japanese, Israeli and American viewers. A report to the Hoso Bunka Foundation, Tokyo.

Kelley, H. H. (1972). Attribution in social interaction. In E. E. Jones, D. E. Kanouse, H. H. Kelley, R. E. Nisbett, S. Valins, and B. Weiner, (Eds.), *Attribution: Perceiving the causes of behaviour*. Morristown, N.J.: General Learning Press.

Kelly, G. A. (1955). *The psychology of personal constructs*. Vol. 1. *A theory of personality*. New York: Norton.

Kershaw, H. V. (1981). *The Street Where I Live*. Manchester: Granada.

Kim, M. P., and Rosenberg, S. (1980). Comparison of two structural models in Implicit Personality Theory. *Journal of Personality and Social Psychology*, **38(3)**, 375–389.

Kintsch, W. (1977). *Memory and cognition*. New York: Wiley.

Kohlberg, L. (1964). Development of moral character and ideology. *Review of Child Development Research*. Vol. 1. New York: Russell Sage Foundation.

Kohler, W. (1930). *Gestalt psychology*. London: Bell and Sons.

Kreizenbeck, A. (1983). Soaps: promiscuity, adultery and new improved cheer. *Journal of Popular Culture*, **17(2)**, 175–181.

Kress, G. (1983). Linguistic and ideological transformations in news reporting. In H. Davis and P. Walton (Eds.), *Language, image, media*. Oxford: Blackwell.

Krippendorf, K. (1982). *Content analysis*. Beverly Hills, Cal.: Sage.

Kruskal, J. B., and Wish, M. (1978). *Multidimensional Scaling*. Sage University Paper series on Quantitative Applications in the Social Sciences, series no. 07–001. Beverly Hills, Cal.: Sage.

Kuhn, A. (1984). Women's genres. *Screen*, **25(1)**, 18–29.

Lang, K. and Lang, G. E. (1985). Method as master or mastery over method. In M. Gurevitch, and M. R. Levy (Eds.), *Mass Communication Review Yearbook*, **5**, Beverly Hills, Cal.: Sage.

Langer, E. J., Blank, A., and Chanowitz, B. (1978). The mindlessness of ostensibly thoughtful action: the role of 'placebic' information in interpersonal interactions. *Journal of Personality and Social Psychology*, **36**, 635–642.

Lazarsfeld, P. F. (1941). Remarks on administrative and critical communications research. *Studies in Philosophy and Science*, **9**, 3–16.

LaPorte, R. E., and Voss, J. F. (1979). Prose representation: A multidimensional scaling approach. *Multivariate Behavioral Research*, **14**, 39–56.

Lerman, C. (1983). Dominant discourse: The institutional voice and control of topic. In H. Davis and P. Walton (Eds.), *Language, image, media*. Oxford: Blackwell.

Lerner, M. J. (1980). *Belief in a just world: a fundamental delusion*. New York: Plenum.

Levi-Strauss, C. (1972). *Structural anthropology*. Harmondsworth: Penguin.

Levy, M. R., and Windahl, S. (1985). The concept of audience activity. In K. E. Rosengren, L. A. Wenner, and P. Palmgreen (Eds.), *Media gratifications research*. Beverly Hills, Cal.: Sage.

Lewis, J. (1987). The framework of political television. In Hawthorn, J. (Ed.), *Propaganda, persuasion and polemic*. London: Edward Arnold.

Liebert, R. M., Sprafkin, J. N., and Davidson, E. S. (1982). *The early window: Effects of television on children and youth*. New York: Pergamon.

Liebes, T. (1984). Ethnocriticism: Israelis of Moroccan ethnicity negotiate the meaning of 'Dallas'. *Studies in Visual Communication*, **10**(3), 46–72.

Liebes, T. (1986a). On the convergence of theories of mass communication and literature regarding the role of the 'reader'. Paper presented at the Conference on Culture and Communication, Philadelphia, October, 1986.

Liebes, T. (1986b). Cultural differences in the retelling of television fiction. Paper presented at the International Communications Association Annual Conference, Chicago, May, 1986.

Liebes, T., and Katz, E. (1986). Patterns of involvement in television fiction: A comparative analysis. *European Journal of Communication*, **1**, 151–171.

Liebes, T., and Katz, E. (1988). DALLAS and Genesis: primordiality and seriality in popular culture.

Liebes, T., and Livingstone, S. M. (1989). Mothers and lovers: British and American soap operas cope with the women's dilemma. Paper presented to the International Communications Association Annual Conference, San Francisco, May.

Linz, D., Donnerstein, E., and Penrod, S. (1984). The effects of multiple exposures to filmed violence against women. *Journal of Communication*, **34**(3), 130–147.

Liss, M., Reinhardt, L. C., and Fredriksen, S. (1983). TV heroes: The impact of rhetoric and deeds. *Journal of Applied Developmental Psychology*, **4**, 175–187.

Litton, I., and Potter, J. (1985). Social representations in the ordinary explanation of a 'riot'. *European Journal of Social Psychology*, **15**, 371–388.

Livingstone, S. M. (1987a). *Social knowledge and programme structure in representations of television characters*. Doctoral dissertation, University of Oxford.

Livingstone, S. M. (1987b). The Implicit Representation of Characters in *Dallas:* A multidimensional scaling approach. *Human Communication Research*, **13**(3), 399–420.

Livingstone, S. M. (1987c). The representation of personal relationships in television drama: realism, convention and morality. In R. Burnett, P. McGhee, and D. D. Clarke (Eds.), *Accounting for relationships: explanation, representation and knowledge*. London: Methuen.

Livingstone, S. M. (1988a). Why people watch soap opera: An analysis of the explanations of British viewers. *European Journal of Communication*, **3**, 55–80.

Livingstone, S. M. (1988b). Viewers' interpretations of soap opera: the role of gender, power and morality. In P. Drummond, and R. Paterson, (Eds.), *Television and its audience: international research perspectives*. London: British Film Institute.

Livingstone, S. M. (1988c). The text-reader metaphor: from TV drama to TV news. Paper presented to the Conference on Television News: Content, Cognition and Control, The Hebrew University of Jerusalem, June.

Livingstone, S. M. (1988d). Talk about technology: domesticity, gender and control. Paper presented to the BPS Social Section Conference, University of Kent, September.

Livingstone, S. M. (1989a). Interpretive viewers and structured programs: the implicit representation of soap opera characters. *Communication Research*, **16**(1), 25–57.

Livingstone, S. M. (1989b). Interpreting a television narrative: how different viewers see a story. *Journal of Communication*, in press.

Livingstone, S. M. (1989c). The reception of television narrative: a study in constructive remembering. Unpublished manuscript.

Lovell, T. (1981). Ideology and "Coronation Street". In Dyer, R., Geraghty, C., Jordan, M., Lovell, T., Paterson, R., Stewart, J. (1981). *Coronation Street*. British Film Institute Television Monograph no. 13. London: British Film Institute.

Lucaites, J. L., and Condit, C. M. (1985). Re-constructing narrative theory: a functional perspective. *Journal of Communication*,

Lull, J. (1988). (Ed.). *World families watch television.* Newbury Park, Cal.: Sage.

Lunt, P. K. (1987). *Perceived causal structure and attributional reasoning.* Doctoral dissertation, University of Oxford.

Lunt, P. K. (1988). The perceived causal structure of examination failure. *British Journal of Social Psychology,* **27,** 171–179.

Lunt, P. K. (in press). The perceived causal structure of unemployment. In K. Grunert, and F. Olander, (Eds.), *Understanding economic behaviour.*

Lunt, P. K., and Livingstone, S. M. (1989). Psychology and statistics: on testing the opposite of the idea you first thought of. *The Psychologist,* in press.

McCombs, M., and Gilbert, S. (1986). News influence on our pictures of the world. In J. Bryant and D. Zillman (Eds.), *Perspectives on media effects.* Hillsdale, N.J.: Erlbaum.

McCombs, M. E., and Shaw, D. (1972). The agenda-setting function of the mass media. *Public Opinion Quarterly,* **36,** 176–187.

McCombs, M. E., and Weaver, D. (1973). Voters' need for orientation and use of mass media. Paper presented to the International Communication Association Annual Conference, Montreal, May.

McCombs, M. E., and Weaver, D. (1985). Towards a merger of gratifications and agenda-setting research. In K. E. Rosengren, L. A. Wenner, and Palmgreen, P. (Eds.), *Media gratifications research: current perspectives.* Beverly Hills, Cal.: Sage.

McQuail, D., Blumler, J. G., and Brown, J. R. (1972). The television audience: A revised perspective. In D. McQuail (Ed.), *Sociology of mass communications: Selected readings.* Harmondsworth, Middx.: Penguin.

McRobbie, A. (1983). JACKIE: An ideology of adolescent femininity. In E. Wartella, D. C. Whitney, and Windahl, S. (Eds.), *Mass Communication Review Yearbook,* **4,** Beverly Hills, Cal.: Sage.

Mander, M. S. (1983). 'Dallas': The mythology of crime and the moral occult. *Journal of Popular Culture,* **17(2),** 44–50.

Mandler, J. M. (1984). *Stories, scripts, and scenes: Aspects of schema theory.* Hillsdale, N.J.: Erlbaum.

Masterman, L. (Ed.) (1984). *Television mythologies: Stars, shows, and signs.* London: Comedia/MK Media Press.

Miell, D. (1987). Remembering relationship development: constructing a context for interactions. In R. Burnett, P. McGhee, and D. D. Clarke, (Eds.), *Accounting for relationships: explanation, representation and knowledge.* London: Methuen.

Modleski, T. (1982). *Loving with a vengeance: mass-produced fantasies for women.* New York: Methuen.

Morgan, D. L. (1988). *Focus groups as qualitative research.* Newbury Park, Cal.: Sage.

Morley, D. (1980). *The Nationwide audience: Structure and decoding.* British Film Institute Television Monograph no. 11. London: British Film Institute.

Morley, D. (1981). The Nationwide audience: A critical postscript. *Screen Education,* **39,** 3–14.

Morley, D. (1986). *Family television: cultural power and domestic leisure.* London: Comedia.

Moscovici, S. (1973). Preface to C. Herzlich, *Health and illness: a social psychological analysis.* London: Academic Press.

Moscovici, S. (1976). *Social influence and social change.* London: Academic Press.

Moscovici, S. (1981). On social representation. In J. P. Forgas, (Ed.), *Social cognition: perspectives on everyday understanding.* London: Academic Press.

Moscovici, S. (1984). The phenomenon of social representations. In R. M. Farr and S. Moscovici (Eds.), *Social Representations.* Cambridge: Cambridge University Press.

Murray, J. P. and Kippax, S. (1979). From the early window to the late night show: International trends in the study of television's impact on children and adults. In L. Berkowitz (Ed.), *Advances in Experimental Social Psychology,* **12.**

Murray, K. (1985). Life as fiction. *Journal for the Theory of Social Behaviour,* **15(2),** 173–188.

Neisser, U. (1976). *Cognition and reality.* New York: Freeman.

Newcomb, H. (Ed.), (1982). *Television: The critical view.* Oxford: Oxford University Press.

Newcomb, H. M. (1988). One night of prime time: an analysis of television's multiple voices. In J. W. Carey, (Ed.), *Media, Myths and Narratives: Television and the press.* Newbury Park: Sage.

Newcomb, H. M., and Hirsch, P. M. (1984). Television as a cultural forum: Implications for research. In W. D. Rowland and B. Watkins (Eds.), *Interpreting television: Current research perspectives*, 58–73. Beverly Hills, Cal.: Sage.

Noble, G. (1975). *Children in front of the small screen.* London: Sage.

Noelle-Neumann, E. (1974). *The spiral of silence: a theory of public opinion. Journal of Communication*, **24(2)**, 43–52.

Osgood, C. E., Suci, G. J., and Tannenbaum, P. H. (1957). *The measurement of meaning.* Urbana: University of Illinois Press.

Owens, J., Bower, G. H., and Black, J. B. (1979). The 'soap opera' effect in story recall. *Memory and Cognition*, **7(3)**, 185–191.

Palmerino, M., Langer, E., and McGillis, D. (1984). Attitudes and attitude change: mindlessness-mindfulness perspective. In J. R. Eiser, (Ed.), *Attitudinal judgment.* New York: Springer-Verlag.

Paterson, R., and Stewart, J. (1981). *Street* life. In R. Dyer, C. Geraghty, M. Jordan, T. Lovell, R. Paterson, and J. Stewart, (1981). *Coronation Street.* British Film Institute Television Monograph no. 13. London: British Film Institute.

Patte, D. (1975). Structural network in narrative: the Good Samaritan. In S. Wittig (Ed.), *Structuralism: An interdisciplinary study.* Pittsburgh, P.A.: Pickwick.

Petty, R. E., Ostrom, T. M., and Brock, T. C. (1981). *Cognitive responses in persuasive communications: a text in attitude change.* Hillsdale, N.J.: Erlbaum.

Phillips, D. A. (1986). Natural experiments on the effects of mass media. In L. Berkowitz, (Ed.), *Advances in Experimental Social Psychology*, **19.** New York: Academic Press.

Piaget, J. (1968). *Structuralism.* London: Routledge and Kegan Paul.

Pingree, S. (1978). The effects of nonsexist television commercials and perceptions of reality on children's attitudes about women. *Psychology of Women Quarterly*, **2(3)**, 262–277.

Pingree, S., Hawkins, R. P., Rouner, D., Burns, J., Gikonyo, W., and Neuwirth, C. (1984). Another look at children's comprehension of television. *Communication Research*, **11(4)**, 477–496.

Pingree, S., Starrett, S., and Hawkins, R. (1979). Soap opera viewers and social reality. Unpublished paper cited in R. P. Hawkins, and S. Pingree (1983), Television's influence on social reality. In E. Wartella, and D. C. Whitney (Eds.), *Mass Communication Review Yearbook*, **4,** 53–76. London: Sage.

Potkay, C. R., and Potkay, C. E. (1984). Perceptions of female and male comic strip characters II: Favorability and identification are different dimensions. *Sex roles*, **10(1/2)**, 119–128.

Porter, D. (1982). Soap time: Thoughts on a commodity art form. In H. Newcomb (Ed.). *Television: The critical view.* Oxford: Oxford University Press.

Potter, J., and Wetherell, M. (1987). *Discourse analysis.* London: Sage.

Propp, V. (1968). *The morphology of the folktale.* Austin: University of Texas Press.

Radway, J. (1984). *Reading the romance: Women, patriarchy and popular literature.* Chapel Hill: University of North Carolina Press.

Radway, J. (1985). Interpretive communities and variable literacies: The functions of romance reading. In M. Gurevitch, and M. R. Levy (Eds.), *Mass Communication Review Yearbook*, **5,** Beverly Hills, Cal.: Sage.

Reeves, B., Chaffee, S. H., and Tims, A. (1982). Social cognition and mass communication research. In M. E. Roloff and C. R. Berger (Eds.), *Social cognition and communication.* London: Sage.

Reeves, B., and Greenberg, B. (1977). Children's perceptions of television characters. *Human Communication Research*, **3,** 113–127.

Reeves, B., and Lometti, G. (1978). The dimensional structure of children's perceptions of television characters: A replication. *Human Communication Research*, **5,** 247–256.

Rice, M., Huston, A., and Wright, J. (1987). The forms of television: effects on children's attention, comprehension and social behaviour. In O. Boyd-Barrett, and P. Braham, (Eds.), *Media, knowledge and power.* London: Croom-Helm.

Richardson, K., and Corner, J. (1986). Reading reception: mediation and transparency in viewers' accounts of a TV programme. *Media, Culture and Society*, **8(4)**, 485–508.

Roberts, D. F., and Bachen, C. M. (1981). Mass communication effects. *Annual Review of Psychology*, **32,** 307–356.

Rommetweit, R. (1984). The role of language in the creation and transmission of social representations. In R. Farr and S. Moscovici, (Eds.), *Social representations*. Cambridge: Cambridge University Press.

Rosch, E., and Lloyd, B. B. (1978). *Cognition and categorisation*. Hillsdale: Erlbaum.

Rosenberg, S. (1977). New approaches to the analysis of personal constructs in person perception. In J. K. Cole, and A. W. Landsfield (Eds.), *1976 Nebraska Symposium on Motivation*. Lincoln, Nebraska: University of Nebraska Press.

Rosenberg, S., and Sedlack, A. (1972). Structural representations of Implicit Personality Theory. In L. Berkowitz (Ed.), *Advances in Experimental Social Psychology*, **6**, 235–297. New York: Academic Press.

Rosengren, K. E., Wenner, L. A., and Palmgreen, P. (Eds.), (1985). *Media gratifications research: Current perspectives*. Beverly Hills, Cal.: Sage.

Roskam, E. E. (1981). *The MDS(X) Series of Multidimensional Scaling Programs*. Program Library Unit, University of Edinburgh.

Rowland, W. D., and Watkins, B. (1984). *Interpreting television: Current research perspectives*. Beverly Hills, Cal.: Sage.

Rubin, A. M. (1984). Ritualized and instrumental television viewing. *Journal of Communication*, **34(3)**, 67–77.

Rubin, A. M. (1985). Uses of daytime television soap operas by college students. *Journal of Broadcasting and Electronic Media*, **29(3)**, 241–258.

Sarbin, T. (1986). (Ed.), *The narrative perspective in psychology*. New York: Praeger.

Schank, R. C., and Abelson, R. P. (1977). *Scripts, plans, goals, and understanding: An inquiry into human knowledge structures*. Hillsdale, N.J.: Erlbaum.

Schiffman, S. S., Reynolds, M. L., and Young, F. W. (1981). *Introduction to multidimensional scaling: Theory, methods, applications*. New York: Academic Press.

Schneider, D. J., Hastorf, A. H., and Ellsworth, P. C. (1979). *Person perception*. Reading, Mass.: Addison-Wesley.

Schroder, K. C. (1987). Convergence of antagonistic traditions? The case of audience research. *European Journal of Communication*, **2**, 7–31.

Schroder, K. C. (1988). The pleasure of DYNASTY: The weekly reconstruction of self-confidence. In P. Drummond and R. Paterson, (Eds.). *Television and its audience: international research perspectives*. London: British Film Institute.

Seiter, E. (1981). The role of the woman reader: Eco's narrative theory and soap operas. *Tabloid*, **6.**

Seiter, E., Krentzer, G., Worth, E. M., and Borchers, H. (1987). Don't treat us like we're so stupid and naive: towards an ethnography of soap opera viewers. Paper presented at the Seminar of Rethinking the Audience, University of Tubingen, February, 1987.

Shoben, E. J. (1983). Applications of multidimensional scaling in cognitive psychology. *Applied Psychological Measurement*, **7(4)**, 473–490.

Sigman, S. J., and Fry, D. L. (1985). Differential ideology and language use: readers' reconstructions and descriptions of news events. *Critical Studies in Mass Communication*, **2**, 307–322.

Silj, A., *et al.* (1988). *East of Dallas: The European challenge to American television*. London: British Film Institute.

Silverstone, R., (1981). *The message of television: Myth and narrative in contemporary culture*. London: Heineman.

Silverstone, R. (1984). Television and the transsexual. *Semiotica*, **49**, 377–410

Silverstone, R., Morley, D., Dahlberg, A., and Livingstone, S. M. (1989). Condemned to the family: The household context of information and communication technologies. Working paper, Centre for Research into Innovation, Culture and Technology, Brunel University.

Smith, M. B. (1983). The shaping of American social psychology: a personal perspective from the periphery. *Personality and Social Psychology Bulletin*, **9(2)**, 165–180.

Snyder, M., and Uranowitz, S. W. (1978). Reconstructing the past: Some cognitive consequences of person perception. *Journal of Personality and Social Psychology*, **36**, 941–950.

Social Trends, (1989). Vol. 19. Government Statistical Service Publication.

Suleiman, S., and Crosman, I. (Eds.), (1980). *The reader in the text*. Princeton: Princeton University Press.

Sutherland, J. C., and Siniawsky, S. J. (1982). The treatment and resolution of moral violations on soap operas. *Journal of Communication, 32,* 67–74.

Tajfel, H. (1978). (Ed.). *Differentiation between social groups: studies in the social psychology of intergroup relations.* London: Academic Press.

Tan, A. S. (1979). TV beauty ads and role expectations of adolescent female viewers. *Journalism Quarterly, 56,* 283–288.

Taylor, L., and Mullan, B. (1986). *Uninvited guests: The intimate secrets of television and radio.* London: Chatto and Windus.

Tedesco, N. S. (1974). Patterns in prime time. *Journal of Communication, 24,* 119–123.

Tichenor, P. J., Donohue, G. A., and Olien, C. N. (1970). Mass media flow and differential growth of knowledge. *Public Opinion Quarterly, 34,* 159–170.

Tompkins, J. P. (1980). (Ed.). *Reader-response criticism: From formalism to post-structuralism.* Baltimore: Johns Hopkins University Press.

Trew, T. (1979). Theory and ideology at work. In R. Fowler, B. Hodge, G. Kress, and T. Trew, (Eds.), *Language and control.* London: Routledge and Kegan Paul.

Tuchman, G. (1979). Women's depiction in the mass media. *Signs, 4,* 528–542.

Turrow, J. (1974). Advising and ordering: daytime, prime time. *Journal of Communication, 24,* 138–141.

Weedon, C. (1987). *Feminist practice and poststructuralist theory.* Oxford: Blackwell.

Wilkinson, S. (1986). (Ed.). *Feminist social psychology: developing theory and practice.* Milton Keynes: Open University Press.

Williams, R. (1974). *Television: Technology and cultural form.* London: Fontana.

Wober, J. M. (1984). TV's menu: the viewers' order. Working paper, IBA Research Department, London.

Wright, W. (1975). *Six guns and society: A structural study of the Western.* Berkeley, Cal.: University of California Press.

Wyer, R. S., and Srull, T. K. (1980). The processing of social stimulus information: A conceptual integration. In R. Hastie *et al.,* (Eds.), *Person memory: The cognitive basis of social perception.* Hillsdale, N.J.: Erlbaum.

Author Index

Subject Index

Aberrant readings 41, 90, 198
Accommodation 100
Active viewer 2, 5, 15, 21, 23, 32, 36, 37, 49, 52, 101, 191, 198
Administrative mass communications research 10
Agenda-setting 17, 30, 49, 176
Assimilation 100
Attitude change 51
Attributions 5, 28, 76, 85, 88, 98, 173
Authorial intention 42

Behaviourism 8, 9, 21, 30, 49, 89
Bias 37, 62

Causal claims 12, 14, 16, 105, 156–8
Character representation 111–13, 143, 144, 150, 162, 166, 174
Child development 36, 52, 97
Communication technologies 103, 106
Complexity 1, 3, 25, 30, 64, 79, 171, 174, 189
Comprehension 64, 196–8
Connotation 15, 49, 74, 87, 196–7
Consensus 29, 166
Content analysis 11, 16, 23, 24, 34, 50, 57, 100, 157
Convergence of traditional and critical mass communications 32, 43, 44, 61, 111, 145
Coronation Street 38, 54, 55, 68, 109, 116, 117, 121–4, 131–3, 136–8, 159, 167, 175
Correspondence theory of meaning 62
Crisis in social psychology 7, 8, 11, 14
Critical distance 48, 172, 187, 190, 197
Critical mass communications 7–11, 16, 38
Crossroads 45, 56
Cultivation theory 14–17, 24, 25, 49, 176
Cultural forum 48, 75, 140, 183
Cultural imperialism 48
Cultural studies 7, 43, 157, 193

Dallas 45, 46, 48, 49, 54, 55, 115, 116, 120, 121, 128–30, 136–8
Demographic factors 101, 102, 176, 177, 183
Denotation 15, 74, 87, 196, 197
Discourse analysis 6, 11, 89, 90, 93, 107, 157, 190, 197
Divergent interpretations 39, 42, 49, 71, 77, 152, 165–74, 184–6, 195
Domain specificity 152–4
Dominant versus oppositional readings 46–8, 186, 187
Durability of representations 147
Dynasty 48, 54

Eastenders 20, 48, 54–6, 96, 118, 124, 133–8
Ecological approach 190
Effects research 9, 11–17, 21, 24, 30, 93, 176
Elaboration likelihood model 51
Emotional realism 46
Empirical reception research 43, 45–7, 101, 104, 111
Error in recall 171, 174, 191, 196
Ethnography 45, 97, 103, 184
Evaluation 141, 151, 169, 170, 175, 182
Everyday life 4, 5, 45, 60, 65
Experimental materials 1, 5, 13, 24, 63, 153, 158
Explanatory rhetoric 76, 97, 171, 188

Fact–fiction distinction 4, 5, 9, 20, 36, 189
False consciousness 34
Family 91, 103
Focus group discussions 107
Free trait descriptions 148, 149, 151
Fundamental attribution error 100

215

'Soap opera effect' 105
Social class 47, 102, 117, 142, 159–62
Social cognition 6, 7, 9, 13, 18, 23–9
Social construction of reality 27, 28, 37, 62
Social knowledge 1, 2, 22, 23, 30, 36, 52, 82, 96, 99, 102, 110, 112, 151, 167, 192
Social learning theory 13, 49
Social perception 6, 61, 91, 152
Social psychology 6–12, 61, 86, 97, 191, 192
Social realism 56, 59, 116, 117
Social representations 5, 6, 11, 88–93, 193
Social situations 3, 4
Spatial metaphor of meaning 108–10, 193
Spiral of silence 17, 49
Stimulus-response model 61, 62, 190
Story grammar 29, 67, 85, 86, 193
Suicide 14
Symbolic annihilation 15
Symbolic interactionism 26, 28, 31
Syntagm 54, 73, 113

Television audience 3, 4, 54, 55
Television characters 22, 113
Television news 87
Text-reader metaphor 2, 6, 7, 97, 190, 192
The Pattern of Marriage 91
'Toolkit' model 35, 191, 192
Top-down versus bottom-up processes 26, 29, 144, 156, 159
Traditional mass communication theory 8, 10, 24, 29, 195
Two-step flow model 8

Unitary meanings 21, 39, 62, 90, 189, 195
Uses and gratifications 8, 21, 35, 37, 50, 51, 174

Virtual and realised texts 39, 42, 90, 93

Wandering viewpoint 40, 98